GREAT BATTLES
OF THE
CIVIL WAR

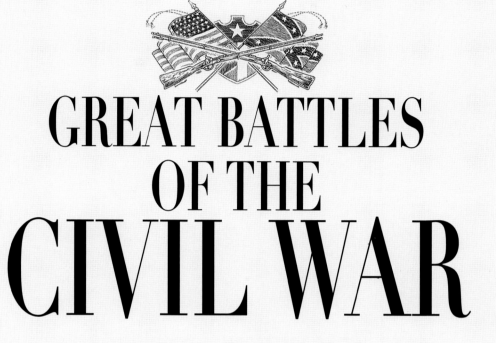

GREAT BATTLES
OF THE
CIVIL WAR

John Macdonald

Foreword by General John Keegan

CHARTWELL
BOOKS, INC.

This edition first published in 2003 by
Chartwell Books, Inc.
A Division of Book Sales, Inc.
114 Northfield Avenue
Edison, New Jersey 08837

Conceived, edited and designed by Marshall Editions
The Old Brewery
6 Blundell Street
London N7 9BH
UK
www.quarto.com

Copyright © 1988 Marshall Editions

ISBN–10: 0-7858-1758-1
ISBN–13: 978-0-7858-1758-1

Printed and bound in China by 1010 Printing Limited

10 9 8 7 6 5 4 3 2

Editor	**James Harpur**
Deputy Editor	**Louise Tucker**
Research	**Jazz Wilson**
Text Editors	**Anne Kilborn**
	Maggi McCormick
	Shelley Turner
Editorial Assistant	**Pat Hunter**
Managing Editor	**Ruth Binney**
Art Director	**David Goodman**
Picture Research	**Ann Usborne**
Library of Congress Research	**Linda Christenson**
Production	**Anna Pauletti**
Chief Illustrator	**Harry Clow**

Historical consultant
The publishers gratefully acknowledge the assistance of
Edwin C. Bearss, Chief Historian, National Park Service, and
the Division of Publications, N.P.S., Harpers Ferry, West Virginia

Picture captions

Page 2

(1) Stars and Stripes (35 Stars, 1863–4); **(2)** Faded "butternut" Confederate uniform jacket worn by Private Andrew J. Duncan, Company K, 21st Mississippi Infantry, and later of Company D, 27th Mississippi Cavalry; **(3)** Confederate kepi; **(4)** Coffee pot used by Captain P Babcock, Jr., US Signal Crps; **(5)** Union kepi; **(6)** Union officer's uniform with V Corps badge (MAltese cross), worn by Lieutenant Colonel Henry Curran, 146th New York Infantry, killed at the Battle of the Wilderness, May 1864; **(7)** Shaving mug, razor, and mess plate used by Captain H.A. Kelly, Company C, 20th Pennsylvania Cavalry; **(8)** US Model-1850 staff and field officer's sword carried by Lieutenant Daniel Sweeney, Company G, 69th New York Infantry, killed at Petersburg, August, 1864; **(9)** Confederate sword belt with Mississippi state buckle; **(10)** Confederate Battle Flag; **(11)** Union officer's sash and, resting on it, captain's shoulder straps worn by Captain Henry Bailey, 36th Massachusetts Infantry, killed at Spotsylvania, May, 1864.

Page 4

(12) Trumpet used by 4th New Hampshire Infantry; **(13)** Union kepi; **(14)** Northern sheet music in honor of Major General George B McClellan, USA.

Contents

Picture captions

Page 6
(15) US Hotchkiss shot from the Battle of Malvern Hill; **(16)** Confederate 12-pound shell from Petersburg, Virginia; **(17)** Confederate-used US 1798 cavalry sword, used at the Battle of Antietam, resting on Union officer's sash; **(18)** Relic Confederate Cook & Brother saber bayonet from campsite near Five Forks, Virginia, 1865; **(19)** Relic Whitney .44 revolver found by the owner of Talley's Farm after the Battle of Chancellorsville; **(20)** Fired US .58 rifle-musket bullets from site of a skirmish on Major General William T. Sherman's Atlanta campaign.

Foreword by John Keegan

The Civil War was about territory—which was to be slave and which free. But it was also about terrain, the word soldiers use to describe the ground over which they fight. Terrain is one of the most profound influences of all that bear upon war-making. It determines where battles can—and cannot—be fought. It forces armies into avenues of advance and retreat. It marks the lines where a defensive campaign may succeed and an offensive campaign probably will not. It sets the boundaries—river, mountain, forest, flood—which define a theater of operations.

Of no war is this more true than the Civil War, fought over a vast hinterland as yet barely opened for settlement. A comprehensive road network there was none. Long-range communication over land was exclusively by railroad and, though possession of the railroads was to be one of the war's principal strategic objects, their course too was determined by primary topographical features. The only other means of moving large armies and supplies in bulk was by river. Rivers were, from the outset of the war, the most important of all the geographical features along and across which the armies maneuvered.

It was the river system which determined the North's strategy from before the war began. General Winfield Scott's "Anaconda Plan" proposed that the Confederacy should be cut off from the outside world by a blockade of the Atlantic coast and the Gulf of Mexico, and then bisected by the seizure of the Mississippi River system. The early battles were fought in a blaze of publicity near the two capitals, Washington and Richmond. But the "campaign in the West", of which the victories of Ulysses S. Grant were the key events, was

meanwhile bringing the headwaters of the Mississippi under Union control, while its lower reaches and outfall to the sea were taken by amphibious forces. Grant's capture of Vicksburg in July, 1863, put the whole course of the river into the North's hands, after which the South's fate was effectively sealed.

But there was much fighting yet to do and on all of it the facts of geography bore heavily. In retrospect, it may be seen that the South had committed a cardinal strategic error by fixing its capital at Richmond in Virginia, only a hundred miles from Washington. It did so for good reasons. Richmond was an economic and communications center which the Confederacy believed it had to hold. But the effort to do so forced it to fight a series of offensive campaigns which it lacked the strength to sustain. Had it instead chosen Charleston, Montgomery, or another of the Deep South cities as its capital, the Southern generals would have been able to draw the armies of the North into the roadless and largely riverless tracts of the Carolinas and impose a protracted war upon the North which its population might eventually have lost the will to fight.

Even fighting where it did, however, the Confederacy was given considerable assistance from the geography. The country between Richmond and Washington is densely wooded and broken by many small rivers—such as Bull Run on which North and South twice clashed. The terrain greatly impeded the North's ability to develop an offensive, and the worst of it, like the Wilderness area, slowed the progress of Grant's advance on Richmond in 1864 to a snail's pace. At the same time the corridor of the Shenandoah Valley provided the South's most aggressive general,

Stonewall Jackson, with a covered approach toward Washington, which he used to keep the Northern capital under strategic menace at critical periods during 1862. The rich open farmland of Pennsylvania also offered Lee a field of easy maneuver, quite different from the close country that impeded the Northern armies near Richmond, when he made his great sally northward in the summer of 1863.

Great Battles of the Civil War has used the creative and interesting idea of applying the new technique of computer mapping to the strategic— and tactical—geography of the war. The result is successful and illuminating. The author has chosen seventeen of the most important battles and displayed their course with four different sorts of mapping. Large conventional maps put each battle in its strategic context. Smaller conventional maps relate the battlefield to its immediate surroundings. A computer-drawn map then combines the three dimensions of the topography with the troop movements of the two sides, showing how contour and elevation affected deployment and maneuver. Finally an artist's panoramic depiction of action at key moments conveys a brilliantly graphic impression of how the fighting would have appeared to an airborne observer.

All students of the American Civil War will find much that is novel and instructive in the result. The war, it is said, has been more written about than any other in history. It is, indeed, difficult to represent its nature or development in any original way. The author of this work seems nevertheless to have succeeded. His book will find a place in all comprehensive libraries of the Civil War.

John Keegan

JOHN KEEGAN was for twenty-five years a Senior Lecturer in Military History at the Royal Military Academy Sandhurst, UK. He is now the Defense Correspondent of the London *Daily Telegraph*. He is the author of many books, including *The Face of Battle*, *The Mask of Command*, which includes a study of Ulysses S. Grant, and *Zones of Conflict*, an atlas of world strategic geography.

The nation divided

"The political hostilities of a generation were now face to face
with weapons instead of words."

GENERAL PIERRE G.T. BEAUREGARD, CSA

THE UNITED STATES of America had been anything but united for some 40 years before the nation was torn by civil war in 1861. This young, fast-developing republic had, in effect, cultivated two societies in its midst, each with a different outlook, different values, different needs. It was a recipe for dissent, though few could have predicted that political squabbling over diverging interests would transform into a bitter four-year conflict costing more than 600,000 American lives.

Slavery, a vital prop to the economy of the Southern states, was at the root of the trouble. In this vast agricultural community, where life was slow, well-ordered, and rather old-fashioned, more than three-and-a-half million blacks were in bondage. Cotton was the principal crop, representing nearly 60 percent of US exports just before the war, and large numbers of slaves were employed to raise and harvest it. Less than six million whites, ranging from the rich, plantation-owning aristocracy to impoverished laborers, occupied this enormous area, which had relatively few cities of any size, and limited manufacturing capacity.

In contrast, the Northern states, where slavery had died out, had many large towns and cities, burgeoning industries, and a thriving farming system to feed its ever-growing population (estimated at 18 million in 1860). European immigrants were streaming in, eager to share in the North's prosperity and optimism. It was

commerce, not cotton, that was king in the free states.

The acquisition and settlement of huge new territories to the west fanned contention between the two factions: Southerners sought to extend slavery into these lands, while Northerners attempted to curb the spread of what they regarded as an outdated and undesirable practice.

Between 1820 and 1850, compromise followed uneasy compromise on this issue. Then, in 1854, when demands for the abolition of slavery were gaining widespread support in the North, Congress passed the Kansas-Nebraska Act. This ill-advised piece of legislation left it to "popular sovereignty" among the settlers to decide whether these two new territories should be slave or free, thereby opening the way for violent campaigning in which more than 200 people died.

The rift deepened in 1857. First, a financial depression hit the commercial North hard, but left the cotton states untouched and smug in the conviction that their slave-based economy was superior. Next, the Supreme Court handed down a judgment in a slave versus master case which rocked Northern sentiment: slaves had no rights under the Constitution and, as the law stood, slavery could not be banned in any territory.

Two years later it was the South's turn to be shaken. There were now more free states than slave states represented in both houses of Congress, tipping the power

balance in the North's favor. But more immediately frightening was the abolitionist John Brown's attempt to seize a Federal arsenal and armory at Harpers Ferry and distribute the weapons to slaves to use in an uprising. Here was a threat that could not be ignored, and many voices were raised in both camps for dissolution of the Union, so that North and South could go their separate ways.

Secession from the Union had long been on the lips of politicians in the South, where a state's rights were valued higher than Federal authority; but it was not until the winter of 1860 that a break finally was made. It came after the election of the Republican candidate, Abraham Lincoln, to the presidency of the United States. Lincoln, who was anti-slavery and a champion of Northern interests, was perceived by Southerners to herald the downfall of their way of life. South Carolina led the way out of the Union on December 20, promptly followed by Mississippi, Florida, Alabama, Georgia, and Louisiana.

In early February, 1861, at Montgomery, Alabama, representatives of the seceded states met to create a new nation, the Confederate States of America. The provisional constitution which it adopted was broadly similar to that of the United States, but of course it allowed for the keeping of slaves. The man elected to lead the Confederacy was Jefferson Davis, a former US Secretary of War. A month

ABRAHAM LINCOLN (1809–65)

JEFFERSON DAVIS (1808–89)

Lincoln, the President of the United States from 1861 to 1865, could arguably be ranked among the great statesmen of history. He was a man of wit and intelligence, integrity and vision, and had a strong sense of justice.

A native of Kentucky, Lincoln received almost no formal education, and, during his early years, tried his hand at various occupations, including rail splitting. In 1836, he began practicing as an attorney, but only came to political prominence 20 years later in the new Republican party. In May, 1860, he won his party's nomination for president, and, in November, was elected to that office.

During the Civil War, Lincoln grew in authority, and he was reelected president in 1864. However, his vision of Northern magnanimity toward the defeated Confederacy and a swift return to amicable union was terminated by an assassin's bullet on April 14, 1865.

Davis, an aristocratic Southerner with a distinguished military and political career, was elected as the President of the Confederate States at Montgomery, Alabama, in February, 1861.

Born in Kentucky, Davis graduated from West Point in 1828. In 1845, he was elected to the House of Representatives, but resigned a year later to fight in the Mexican War. He was again in public life in 1847 as a US senator from Mississippi; and, in 1853, he became Secretary of War under President Franklin Pierce. Four years later, he reentered the Senate and served in it until January, 1861, when he resigned.

Davis was an upright, moral man of noble bearing. He was highly intelligent and a gifted speaker. His major faults as president seem to have stemmed from his inability to get on with people, and his failure to delegate power effectively.

After the war, Davis was imprisoned by the Federals until his release in 1867.

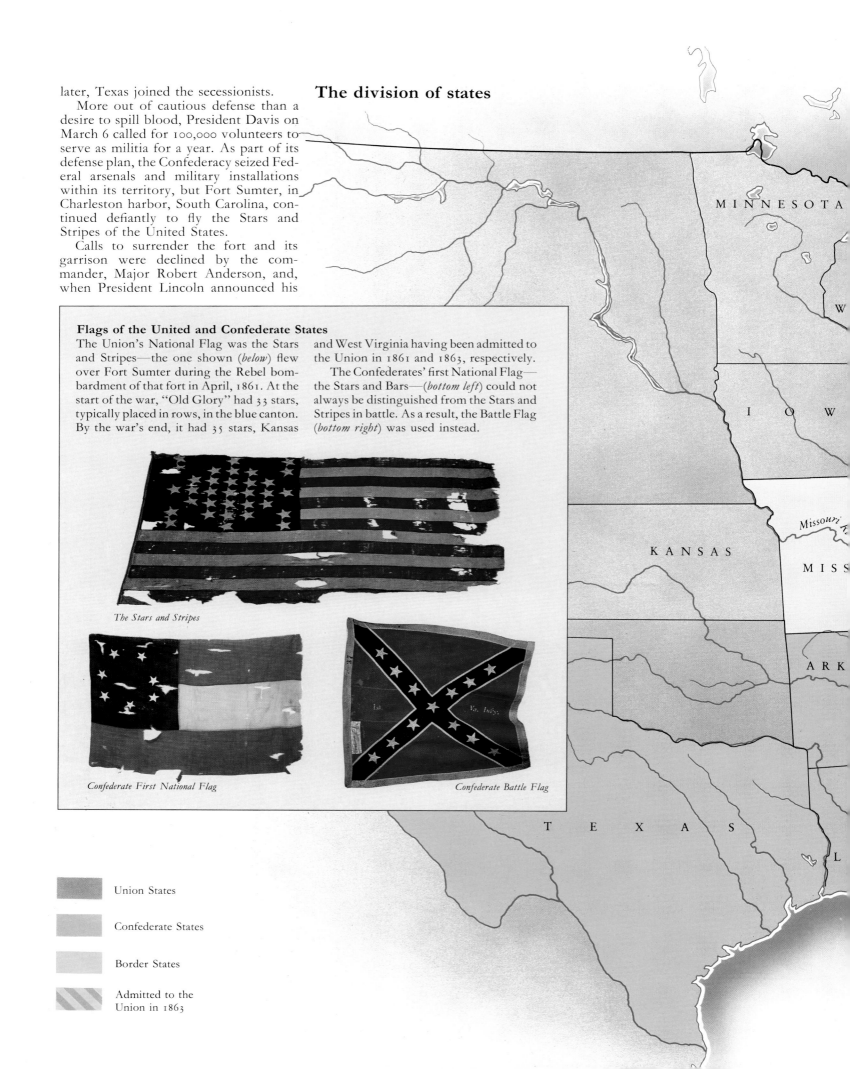

later, Texas joined the secessionists.

More out of cautious defense than a desire to spill blood, President Davis on March 6 called for 100,000 volunteers to serve as militia for a year. As part of its defense plan, the Confederacy seized Federal arsenals and military installations within its territory, but Fort Sumter, in Charleston harbor, South Carolina, continued defiantly to fly the Stars and Stripes of the United States.

Calls to surrender the fort and its garrison were declined by the commander, Major Robert Anderson, and, when President Lincoln announced his

The division of states

Flags of the United and Confederate States

The Union's National Flag was the Stars and Stripes—the one shown (*below*) flew over Fort Sumter during the Rebel bombardment of that fort in April, 1861. At the start of the war, "Old Glory" had 33 stars, typically placed in rows, in the blue canton. By the war's end, it had 35 stars, Kansas and West Virginia having been admitted to the Union in 1861 and 1863, respectively.

The Confederates' first National Flag—the Stars and Bars—(*bottom left*) could not always be distinguished from the Stars and Stripes in battle. As a result, the Battle Flag (*bottom right*) was used instead.

The Stars and Stripes

Confederate First National Flag

Confederate Battle Flag

MINNESOTA

W

I O W

Missouri R.

KANSAS

MISS

ARK

TEXAS

L

Union States

Confederate States

Border States

Admitted to the Union in 1863

intention to resupply Sumter, it became evident to the Confederates that they would have to use force to capture it.

At 4.30 a.m. on April 12, 1861, the first shot of the American Civil War was fired by a Southern cannon. The Confederacy, therefore, was the aggressor, just as Lincoln had wanted it to be. He could now, with justification, appeal to his nation to back him in putting down armed insurrection.

As soon as President Lincoln called for 75,000 volunteers to serve for three months in the interest of suppressing the rebellion, four so-far undecided slave states in the upper South—Virginia, North Carolina, Tennessee, and Arkansas—opted for the Confederacy. The other border slave states—Maryland, Kentucky, and Missouri—stayed with the Union, which enjoyed another bonus when the western area of Virginia broke away from its parent state, pledging loyalty to Washington. Eventually, it was admitted to the Union as the state of West Virginia.

Thus the battle lines were drawn: 23 Northern states against 11 Southern. War fever gripped both sides in the weeks after the fall of Fort Sumter, with a rush to muster, arm, and train troops in readiness for what had become an inevitable trial by combat. The South was committed to the defense of the Confederacy, the North was committed to the preservation of the Union, and only force would resolve whose will would prevail.

The map shows the alignment of the states at the start of, and during, the war. The western area of Virginia broke away from its parent state and was admitted, as West Virginia, to the Union on June 20, 1863.

The battles marked on both the map and the inset are those featured in this book.

First Bull Run

"There stands Jackson like a stone wall!
Rally behind the Virginians!"

BRIGADIER GENERAL BARNARD BEE, CSA

THERE WAS A HOLIDAY atmosphere abroad in Washington, D.C. on the afternoon of July 16, 1861. The excitement was brought on by the news that the main Union army was leaving its camps on Arlington Heights and around Alexandria, across the Potomac River from the Federal capital, to march against the Confederates.

"On to Richmond!" was the Northern battle cry, for the Rebel government, which had been transferred from Montgomery, Alabama, to Richmond, Virginia, in late May, was now less than 100 miles south of Washington. Almost since the Confederate capture of the Federal Fort Sumter in mid-April, there had been a popular notion that the sooner Richmond was taken, the quicker the rebellion would end.

This was certainly the view of the Lincoln administration, which had been acutely aware that those regiments hastily raised at the end of April for three months' service would soon be due for disbandment, without having struck a blow to preserve the Union.

The military hierarchy, however, did not believe that its recruits had received enough training to justify an early move on the enemy. Urging action on Brigadier General Irvin McDowell, who commanded the Union army south of the Potomac, President Abraham Lincoln brushed aside arguments about unreadiness with these words:

"You are green; the Rebels are green. You are all green alike."

And so it was that in mid-July, columns of Union infantry, artillery, and cavalry, numbering 35,000 men, found themselves heading down dusty roads and a turnpike in the direction of Manassas Junction, 30 miles away, where a Confederate army lay in wait.

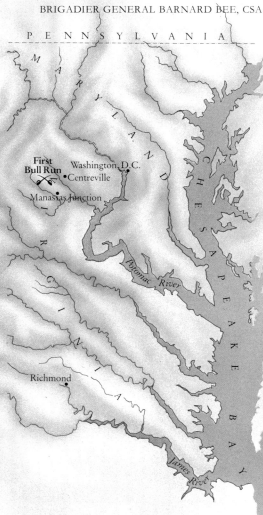

The Confederates, a force of 23,000 men led by Brigadier General Pierre G.T. Beauregard, were strung out behind a creek called Bull Run, blocking the main road and rail routes to Richmond. An efficient spy network had warned Beauregard of the direction of march and the strength of the Union army; as the latter now approached, he clamored for reinforcements to meet the Federals on something like equal terms.

It took the Federals until the morning of July 18 to reach Centreville, seven miles away from Manassas Junction, where they were to concentrate and await the arrival of supply wagons. Straggling and lack of discipline on the march were rife, as McDowell himself described:

"They [the troops] stopped every moment to pick blackberries or get water; they would not keep in the ranks, order as much as you pleased."

Military precision was further impeded by the presence of large numbers of civilians, who had followed the army to secure a good view of the coming battle.

While McDowell set off from Centreville to reconnoiter to his left, he ordered Brigadier General Daniel Tyler to send forward detachments from his First Division to give the impression of a continuing move toward Manassas Junction, but not to bring on a fight. However, at Blackburn's Ford across Bull Run, his men got into a sharp skirmish with the Confederates and broke under fire.

It was a bad start for the Union campaign. And it was made worse when two badly shaken units claimed their right to disband because their term of enlistment had expired. For many starry-eyed young men in fancy uniforms, it was the first hint that war might not be such a romantic adventure after all.

After this setback, McDowell, who had no detailed maps of the area and no trained scouts, continued a cautious reconnaissance of Beauregard's lines. He used his aides to study the lie of the land and, although their efforts were makeshift, he formed a plan of attack from their reports. It was a good plan, too, if he had had a well-trained army to execute it.

Leaving Colonel D.S. Miles's Fifth Division at Centreville, with instructions

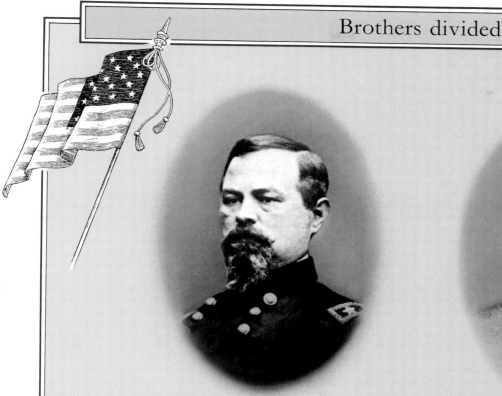

IRVIN McDOWELL (1818–85)

PIERRE GUSTAVE TOUTANT BEAUREGARD
(1819–93)

McDowell, who led the US Army at First Bull Run, was educated in France and went to West Point, the United States Military Academy, where he graduated 23rd in his class in 1838. Afterward, he joined the US Army as an artillery officer, took part in the Mexican War (1846–8), and rose steadily in rank.

When the Civil War broke out, McDowell, who had served with distinction on the staff of General Winfield Scott, the US commander in chief, was a major in Washington. He was in close contact with President Lincoln and government officials, and, as a senior regular officer with obvious planning and organizational abilities, he impressed them so much that he was promoted to brigadier general on May 14, 1861.

Shortly afterward, and with General Scott's blessing, McDowell was given command of the main US field army. Pushed into fighting the first big battle of the war before he was ready, McDowell was defeated at First Bull Run, and relegated to the command of a division under Major General George B. McClellan.

The following year, as a corps commander in Major General John Pope's army, he again found himself fighting at Bull Run, in the second battle of that name: it was another Union defeat. In the reshuffle which followed, McDowell, now a major general, was removed from field command, and in fact never returned to command troops in combat.

Proud of his French ancestry, and a keen student of Napoleon Bonaparte, Beauregard commanded the Confederate battle line at First Bull Run. He was a West Point graduate, coming second in his class in 1838. At the United States Military Academy, one of his instructors was Major Robert Anderson, whom he bombarded into surrender at Fort Sumter at the outbreak of the Civil War; and a fellow cadet was Irvin McDowell, whom he defeated at First Bull Run.

Beauregard was commissioned in the US Engineers, distinguished himself in the war with Mexico, and served for a short time as the superintendent of West Point, before resigning in 1861 to offer his services to the Confederacy. Upset because he was not offered command of Louisiana's forces, Beauregard signed on as an enlisted man in a New Orleans unit. He overcame his pique, however, when he was appointed the first brigadier general in the Confederate States Army.

After First Bull Run, Beauregard was made a general, and served as second-in-command of the Army of the Mississippi under General Albert Sidney Johnston, from whom he took over at the Battle of Shiloh after Johnston had been mortally wounded. In 1862–3, Beauregard conducted the defense of Charleston, South Carolina; he ended the war as commander of the Department of North Carolina and Southeastern Virginia.

Uniforms of the Union and Confederate armies

In early 1861, as men rushed to enlist all over the Union and the Confederacy, units were raised with dashing titles—Tigers, Hussars, Bucktails, Guards, Zouaves, and the like—and with equally dashing uniforms.

European armies, in particular that of France, influenced the Americans' choice of dress. Many outfits favored the French peaked forage cap, the kepi, with plain tunic and trousers.

Also popular was the colorful dress of French North African troops, the Zouaves. This usually comprised a short jacket and waistcoat, a broad sash, baggy pantaloons, gaiters, and a tassled fez. Particularly famous among Federal Zouave units were the 5th New York Volunteers, Duryée's Zouaves, who distinguished themselves in various battles for the Army of the Potomac. Other young men found themselves wearing the kilts or tartan trews of Scottish Highlanders, the plumed bowler hats of the Italian Bersaglieri, the peakless caps and elaborate trappings of German hussars, or the distinctive rifle green of Berdan's Sharpshooters. Berdan's men were used as snipers, and played an active part throughout the war including defending Malvern Hill against Rebel infantry, during the Battle of the Seven Days.

The majority of these uniforms were shortly discovered to be too fancy for rigorous duty—they caused confusion on the battlefield, and some were so flashy that they made easy targets. Soon most of the exotic-sounding units were absorbed into state regiments, and their fine plumage was replaced by more prosaic attire.

In the North, a loose dark blue flannel sack coat over light blue trousers, and a black-visored forage cap became regulation uniform. Cap badges indicated the unit, and colored facings the branch of service: blue, infantry; red, artillery; yellow, cavalry; green, medical. In the western armies, many soldiers, particularly in the cavalry, preferred the broad-brimmed felt hat to the forage cap.

As well as his rifle-musket, the Union infantryman was supposed to carry a cartridge-box, containing 40 rounds of ammunition, a percussion cap-pouch, a bayonet, a canteen of water, a haversack for his rations, a blanket, a rubber sheet or half of a shelter tent, a knapsack, containing 160 spare rounds of ammunition, and a change of clothing and personal belongings. Most veterans, however, contrived to lighten their load considerably.

Private, USA, in regulation dress

Private, Berdan's Sharpshooters

Private, 5th New York Volunteers, (Duryée's Zouaves)

Private, CSA, in butternut

Private, CSA, in regulation dress

Private, Louisiana Tigers

For their regulation uniform, the South opted for a gray tunic over light-blue trousers, and a gray forage cap with a pompom on the crown in the color of the appropriate branch of the service: light blue, infantry; red, artillery; yellow, cavalry; black, medical. This rather splendid uniform was never on general issue, and in many cases, the states themselves decided what their troops should wear.

The South, like the North, had their Zouave regiments from the start of the war. One of the most famous and colorful outfits was the Louisiana Tigers, made up mostly of Irishmen from New Orleans, who fought at First Bull Run.

The Confederacy did not possess suffi-cient clothing factories to supply its armies; so, when uniforms wore out, Rebel soldiers turned to their families for replace-ment garments, relied on captured cloth-ing (which often led to confusion in a fight), or just wore civilian dress.

By 1862, many Confederates were wear-ing home-made jackets and trousers in various hues of gray or butternut (a brownish dye) and broad-brimmed felt hats. Invariably scruffy, often without shoes, they traveled light. In addition to their weapons and ammunition, Rebel infantrymen carried their scant belongings rolled in a blanket, which was worn bandolier-fashion. A wooden or metal canteen completed their kit.

to threaten the Confederate center in the Blackburn's Ford area, McDowell in-tended his First Division to move west along the Warrenton Turnpike at 2.30 a.m. on the 21st; at dawn they were to begin a brisk demonstration against the Rebel left flank near Stone Bridge.

Meanwhile, his Second and Third Div-isions (commanded by Colonel David Hunter and Colonel Samuel P. Heintzel-man respectively) were to set off on a night march looping north and west, cross the stream at Sudley Ford, and be in position to take Beauregard in the left and rear by 7 a.m.

Not everything went according to plan, however. The route for the flanking force had not been properly reconnoi-tered. It was twelve miles long instead of six, there were frustrating delays on the march, and the flagging troops were not ready to do battle until nearly 10 a.m. By that time, of course, the Confederates had been alerted.

Moreover, Tyler's supposed "brisk demonstration" at Stone Bridge had amounted to little more than desultory firing, allowing Colonel N.G. Evans, commanding the far left of the Confede-rate line, to move the bulk of his force to meet the main attack.

Even so, all might not have been lost for McDowell had he managed to main-tain his overwhelming superiority of numbers over Beauregard. For that, he was dependent on Brigadier General Robert Patterson, a veteran of the War of 1812, who led a 16,000-strong Union army in the lower Shenandoah Valley, 50 miles northwest. Patterson's job was to stop Confederate General Joseph E. Johnston and his 11,000 men from leav-ing the valley to unite with Beauregard: he failed.

Johnston's spearhead brigade arrived by rail at Manassas on July 19, and by the 21st nearly 8,500 men from his command were there. In addition, Beauregard had been sent Brigadier General T.H. Holmes's brigade and Colonel Wade Hampton's Legion, raising his strength to 32,500. Johnston, who was the senior officer, formally assumed command of the combined Confederate armies, but he did not know the area and so seemed content to let Beauregard take control.

As it happened, Beauregard had formed a similar plan to that of McDowell: a powerful hook to turn the enemy's left flank. It would also have had the advantage of severing the Union army's line of retreat to Alexandria and Arlington Heights. But the Federals struck first.

A plan to squeeze the Confederacy

In the heady days of spring 1861, when 75,000 short-term Union volunteers were being raised, and a swift victory predicted, 75-year-old Lieutenant General Winfield Scott (*below*), commander in chief of the US Army, was alone in his view that it would take 300,000 men and two or three years to crush the rebellion. Yet he was nearer the truth than anyone else at that time. As it turned out, the war lasted four years, and more than two and a quarter million men enlisted in the Union army.

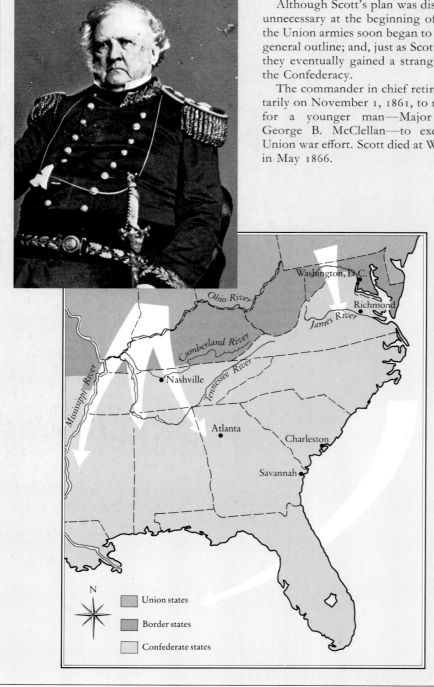

Scott had already formulated a strategy—nicknamed the Anaconda Plan—which would squeeze the Confederacy into submission (*see map below*): he advocated taking time to train the volunteers properly; blockading the Southern seaports; and then, with the Confederacy's inland borders also sealed off, advancing south in both the east and the west. In particular, he saw the four great western rivers, the Mississippi, the Ohio, the Tennessee, and the Cumberland, as the natural routes into the Rebel heartland.

Although Scott's plan was dismissed as unnecessary at the beginning of the war, the Union armies soon began to follow its general outline; and, just as Scott foresaw, they eventually gained a stranglehold on the Confederacy.

The commander in chief retired voluntarily on November 1, 1861, to make way for a younger man—Major General George B. McClellan—to execute the Union war effort. Scott died at West Point in May 1866.

It was a flimsy line that met their onslaught. Colonel Evans, who had moved a mile northwest to a position at a right angle to the main Confederate body to counter McDowell's turning march, had six companies of the 4th South Carolina Regiment, Major R. Chatham Wheat's battalion of Louisiana Tigers, and two 6-pounder guns.

Strung out on a low rise between the road from Sudley to Manassas and the Matthews House, in the direct path of the approaching enemy, Evans' line managed to hold off attacks for an hour before being reinforced. Nearest to Evans were the brigades of Brigadier General Barnard Bee and Colonel Francis S. Bartow, from the Army of the Shenandoah, having been sent by Johnston to strengthen the left when he first heard sustained firing from that direction.

Bee had chosen a strong position on the Henry House Hill plateau about half a mile away across the valley behind Evans' line. At first, he was reluctant to advance to what he regarded as a less favorable position; then he and Bartow (who were both killed later in the battle) relented when pressed by Evans.

Even with the help of two brigades and Captain John Imboden's Staunton Artillery, it soon became evident that the Confederate blocking force could not stem for long the steadily lengthening Federal line of battle, backed by three batteries of artillery.

About 11.30 a.m., they began to fall back in disorder toward Henry House Hill, where Brigadier General Thomas J. Jackson, who had also been ordered to the left with his Virginian Brigade, had taken post along a fringe of pines on its southeast slope. Sighting these steady ranks, Bee yelled to his retreating troops:

"There stands Jackson like a stone wall! Rally behind the Virginians!"

In doing so, he bestowed a nickname on a soldier who would become one of the South's greatest heroes: "Stonewall" Jackson.

Imboden's valiant battery was now badly shot up, and down to its last three rounds; but it did not withdraw until the Rockbridge, Washington, Leesburg, and Loudoun Artillery galloped up in support of Jackson.

Another Confederate unit to sustain heavy casualties at this time was the 650-strong Hampton Legion. From a position overlooking the Warrenton Turnpike on the right of the Henry House Hill line, it engaged Colonel Erasmus D. Keyes's brigade on its way to join McDowell's attack. The Legion, which lost 121 men,

McDowell's plan collapses

Federal Brigadier General Irvin McDowell planned to surprise the Confederates positioned behind the Bull Run stream by sending off his Second and Third Divisions on a flanking march at night to smash the Rebel left. Meanwhile the Federal First Division (3) would advance down the Warrenton Turnpike (6) to hold the attention of the Rebels at the Stone Bridge (4), which crossed Bull Run.

During the early hours of July 21, the leading brigades of the Federal flanking force (2) set off, and later crossed Bull Run at Sudley Ford (1). However, delays meant that instead of attacking at dawn, as had been intended, the Federals were not in a position to give battle to the Rebels until nearly 10 a.m.

By this time, the bulk of Colonel Evans' Confederate brigade (5) had managed to leave their position at the Stone Bridge to meet the danger to their flank. Evans, who was later reinforced, gained precious time for the Rebels by halting the momentum of the Union assault.

The critical moment of the battle came during mid-afternoon: the Rebel line (10), for so long held by Brigadier General Pierre G. T. Beauregard on Henry House Hill (11), drove the Federals off the plateau and past the Stone House (above), standing at the intersection of the Sudley Road (13) with the Warrenton Turnpike.

Federals to the west of the Sudley Road were then driven back by the Rebel far left (12), under Brigadier General E. Kirby Smith and Colonel Jubal Early. The exhausted Federals (14) were now in full flight: some headed toward Sudley Ford (7), while others (8) cut across country. Union troops (9) around the Stone Bridge joined the disorderly retreat toward Centreville and Washington.

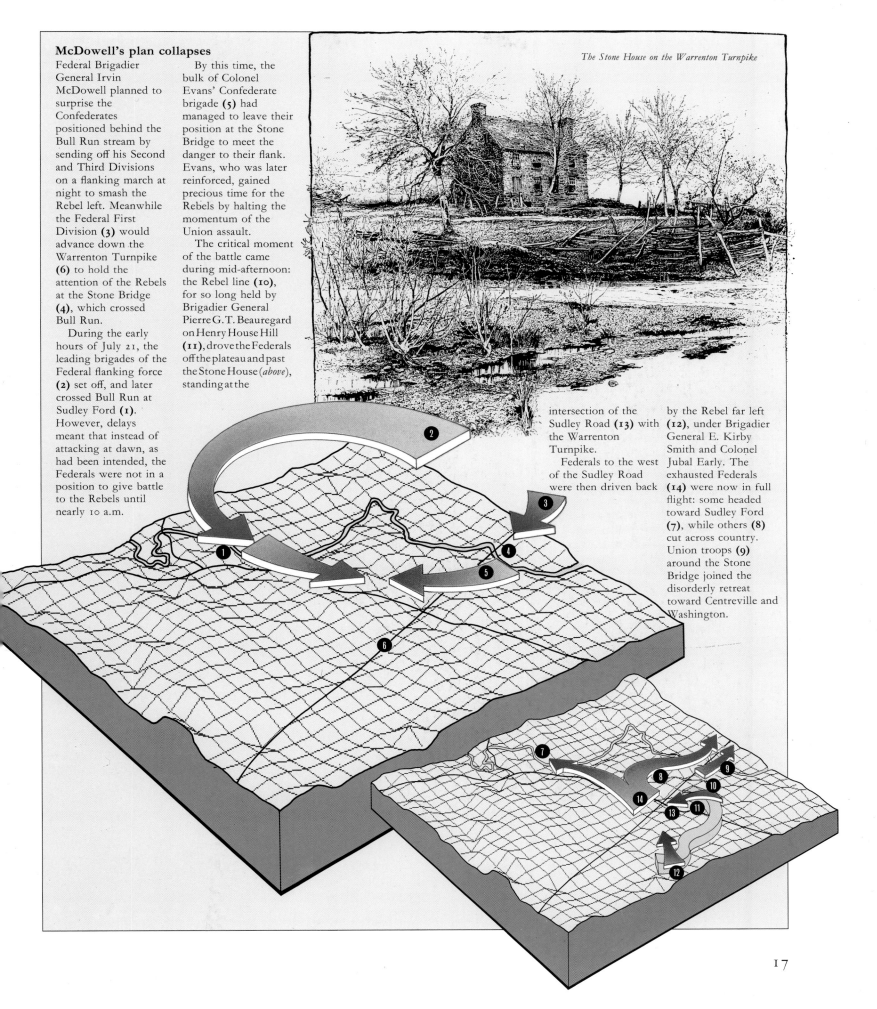

The Stone House on the Warrenton Turnpike

THE CLIMAX ON HENRY HOUSE HILL

The battlefield

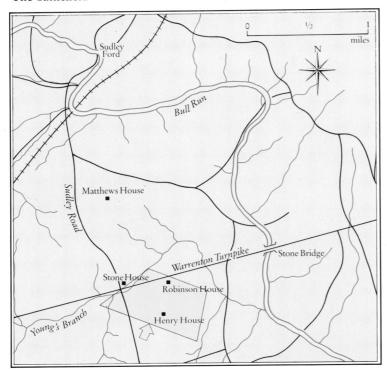

By midmorning on July 21, Brigadier General Irvin McDowell's plan to catch the Confederate left by surprise had been thwarted. The Federal flanking force had met stout resistance from Colonel N.G. Evans' brigade, supported by the brigades of Brigadier General Barnard Bee and Colonel Francis S. Bartow.

However, the increasing weight of Union numbers began to tell on this small Confederate blocking force. Soon the Rebels were compelled to retreat to the top of Henry House Hill. There, they rallied around Brigadier General Thomas J. Jackson's Virginians on the hill's southeastern side.

McDowell kept up the Union pressure by sending regiments up onto the plateau against the stiffening Rebel line. For about three hours, the fighting raged to and fro over this pocked terrain. Finally, about midafternoon, Brigadier General Pierre G.T. Beauregard ordered the entire Rebel line to charge.

The plateau of Henry House Hill (3), which dominated the surrounding area, was the scene of the heaviest fighting. From the morning to midafternoon, many charges and countercharges were made across it. The hill itself was named after a two-story, wooden structure (8)

belonging to a widow, Mrs Henry, who was mortally wounded during the battle. A free black farmer, named Robinson, owned the other house (2) on the northeast corner of the plateau.

Before Beauregard ordered the final decisive charge, Brigadier General Thomas J. Jackson's brigade, around which the Confederates had rallied, had taken a position just in front of a fringe of trees (4) on the southeast rim of the plateau. While General Joseph Johnston ordered forward Confederate troops to the hill, Beauregard placed them in line of battle.

Toward the center of the Confederate line, 26 guns (5) of mixed caliber were brought up, and proved a powerful presence.

At about midafternoon, the battle reached a climax when Beauregard sent his entire battle line (6) forward. He later stated that the charge "was made with such keeping . . . that the whole plateau was swept clear of the enemy who were driven down the slope."

Most Federals (9) fell back past the Stone House, at the junction of the Warrenton Turnpike (1) with the Sudley Road (10). In a state of confusion, they began to leave the field altogether after the collapse of their right flank a little later.

With the final Confederate advance, the Union guns (7), situated southwest of Henry House, fell into Rebel hands. These guns, comprising mostly Parrott rifles, belonged to Griffin's and Ricketts' batteries. In fact, the guns' vulnerable forward position meant that they changed hands five times during the battle.

The Federal gunners here took heavy casualties, including Captain James B. Ricketts. General Beauregard, who was an old acquaintance of Ricketts, in a gesture of magnanimity, sent his own surgeons to attend to the wounded Federal captain.

checked Keyes, who then moved off into the bottom of Young's Branch and took no further part in the battle.

All that morning Generals Johnston and Beauregard had stayed on their right, four miles to the south, hoping to mount an assault on the Union left. Uneasy about the firing coming from his own far left, Johnston had been trickling units in that direction; and it was just as well that he did. By 11.15, with the din of a full-scale battle rising from the area of the Warrenton Turnpike, the Confederate generals finally gave up all thought of an offensive, ordered reinforcements across to their threatened left, and dashed to the scene of the fighting. They arrived on Henry House Hill around noon, in time to help stem the retreat, bring up more troops, and form a cohesive line of battle based on Jackson's excellent reverse-slope position, which hid the Confederates from enemy view and helped to protect them from artillery fire.

There were still not enough Southern regiments on the field, however, so Johnston somewhat reluctantly consented to go to the rear to speed up and direct reinforcements, while Beauregard took charge of the battle.

Meanwhile, in the fields on the north side of the Warrenton Turnpike, which cut through the valley in front of Henry House Hill, McDowell was preparing to capitalize on his morning's success. He knew he had to occupy the high ground, so he regrouped his weary forces, added more troops, and got ready to advance up the slopes in concert with a flanking thrust along the Sudley Road, which skirted the western edge of the hill.

McDowell had intended for Tyler to bring his "diversionary" First Division over to the west bank of Bull Run, but Tyler was slow to respond. The first of his brigades to cross, led by Colonel William T. Sherman (who was later in the war to gain great fame), was directed into the thick of the fighting and took the heaviest casualties among Union forces at Bull Run. When Keyes's brigade eventually made a move, it was intercepted by Hampton's Legion, and Brigadier General Robert Schenck's brigade stayed where it was until it was too late.

McDowell realized that a great chance had been missed. If Tyler had driven forward with the combined weight of Keyes's and Schenck's commands, they would have rolled up the lightly held Confederate right.

Before the battle resumed in earnest, the Union commander did the Confederates a favor by moving Ricketts' and

Mathew Brady: photographing the war

Among the host of civilians accompanying General McDowell's army to Bull Run was a small bespectacled man with a goatee beard. He wore a long white duster coat and a straw hat, and drove a strange-looking hard-topped wagon.

He was Mathew B. Brady, the famous photographer and owner of two fashionable galleries in New York and Washington. To the consternation of his family and friends, he had decided to go in search of war pictures. "A spirit in my feet said go, and I went," he later explained.

Action photographs were impossible because the exposure of up to ten seconds required by the wet plate process of the day blurred all movement. Brady, however, took a number of static views around Bull Run, and in doing so found himself accused of contributing to the panic during the Union retreat. A newspaper reported that some of the raw Union troops, on seeing the huge brass-barreled lens of his

camera, mistook it for the South's rumored rapid-firing steam cannon and fled.

Thereafter, Brady was to be seen in battle areas throughout the war, along with his specially-built darkroom wagon, which the soldiers nicknamed the "Whatisit." He provided many memorable scenes of the conflict, but his views of dead and wounded did not meet with public approval when he exhibited them.

The war pictures of Mathew Brady and other photographers, such as Alexander Gardner and Timothy O'Sullivan, could not be reproduced in the newspapers of the 1860s because the necessary technology did not then exist, but many were used as the basis for line engravings in illustrated publications.

This photographer's portable darkroom was converted from Mathew Brady's own buggy. A rather strange-looking wagon, it was dubbed the "Whatisit" by the soldiers.

Mathew B. Brady (*top*), photographed here the day after the first battle of Bull Run, was the most famous of the photographers who recorded the war.

Among the photographs exhibited by Mathew Brady at his New York gallery in October, 1862 were these two. In fact, they were taken by Brady's employee Alexander Gardner, and they show some of the Confederate dead after the Battle of Antietam, in September of that year.

For the general public, the stark reality of the pictures destroyed, at a stroke, romantic notions of the Civil War.

Griffin's excellent regular batteries forward to the western edge of the Henry House Hill plateau, a position from which their fire passed harmlessly over the Confederates' heads. About this time, too, McDowell daringly went forward to the Henry House to reconnoiter, and made the disconcerting discovery that a properly formed, resolute Rebel line of battle was beyond the crest of the hill.

In stifling heat and rolling smoke, Union regiments moved haphazardly up onto the clear ground of the plateau, which became the scene of a three-hour struggle for supremacy. McDowell's first attack, which culminated in noisy, close-quarter combat, was dispersed by a spirited charge ordered by Beauregard.

A second Federal assault was quickly organized and, again, delivered piecemeal. Nevertheless, it carried them to the top of the hill which, according to Beauregard, was the key to victory.

Placing the time between 2.30 and 3 p.m., the Confederate commander felt that if he could hold on to the hill until the arrival of strong reinforcements, the day would be his. So, once more, he ordered forward his entire line in a charge which swept the Union troops right off the hill.

Those Federal regiments to the west of the Sudley Road which had remained unscathed by the Rebel charge were soon assailed by a steadily increasing number of units sent up on the double by General Johnston. The appearance of Brigadier General E. Kirby Smith's brigade (lately arrived by train from the Shenandoah Valley) caused consternation in the Union lines, and when Colonel Jubal Early's brigade further extended the Confederate left, they finally broke.

Long marches, exhausting heat, and five hours of battle made the Federals decide that enough was enough. They had generally acquitted themselves well, but they had no more fight left in them. Their hurried departure was protected by Major George Sykes's battalion.

The Confederates, diverted by the false alarm of an impending attack on their supply depot near Manassas Junction, did not follow up their victory. Parting shots from their artillery, however, helped to spread panic among the melee of retreating Union troops and civilian spectators. Streams of defeated, dejected soldiers, many of whom discarded their equipment, continued on walking in the rain and darkness until they got back within the Washington defenses. Apprehension gripped the population in the Federal capital; but Confederate patrols, who had followed the retreat, kept their distance.

The strategic importance of the railroads

When General Johnston rapidly transferred more than 8,000 men by train from the Shenandoah Valley to reinforce the Confederate Army at Bull Run, he gave the world its first demonstration of the strategic importance of railroads in wartime.

In 1861, America had just over 30,000 miles of track, shown on the map (right). Nearly three-quarters of it lay in Union territory in the north and west.

The Federal railroads, which linked the Atlantic seaboard with the Mississippi Valley, were used to the full throughout the war for the movement of troops and supplies. Also, the network was constantly being developed: tracks were laid and locomotives and rolling stock were built, including specially designed hospital cars.

The South, whose railroad system was less developed and extensive, had always relied on Northern industry to supply and repair its locomotives and cars. Thus, although the Confederacy worked its network as hard as it could, it had an uphill fight against deteriorating equipment. To underline the Richmond government's lack of resources, no new rails were made during the war: any new line laid to service troops was built at the expense of an equivalent length of track somewhere else.

Because the railroads played such an important part in the war effort of the North and South, they inevitably became military targets. As well as locomotives and rolling stock, bridges and tracks were destroyed in raids. Rails were often torn up, heated on fires made from the ties, beaten out of shape (above right), and twisted around trees in order to render them unusable.

Federals of Colonel Oliver O. Howard's brigade advance up Henry House Hill toward the end of the battle.

The aftermath

The First Battle of Bull Run, or Manassas, as the South called it, was neither big nor decisive. The Union had an army of 35,000, the Confederacy 32,500; yet only 18,572 Federals and 18,053 Confederates were actually engaged in the fighting. The casualty lists, which seemed horrifying enough at the time, were, in fact, light. McDowell lost a total of 2,896 men, and Beauregard 1,982.

This first battle of the Civil War, which so many on both sides had hoped would settle the North–South dispute, proved to be no more than a dress rehearsal for a long, bitter, and bloody war. However, the Union defeat did galvanize the government into action: McDowell was removed from his command, and replaced by Major General George B. McClellan, who would soon raise Union morale and create the new 150,000-strong Army of the Potomac.

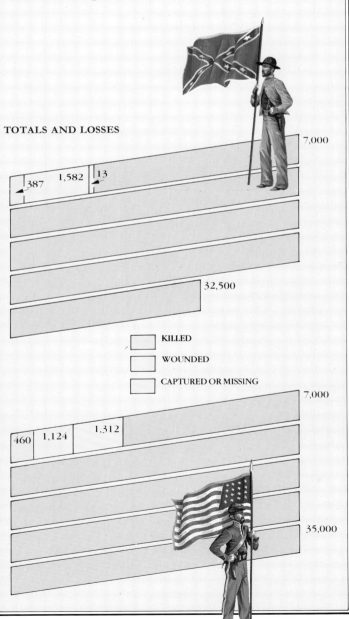

TOTALS AND LOSSES

387   1,582   13   7,000

32,500

☐ KILLED

☐ WOUNDED

☐ CAPTURED OR MISSING

460   1,124   1,312   7,000

35,000

Shiloh

APRIL 6–7, 1862

"There will be no fighting at Pittsburg Landing; we will have to go to Corinth. . . ."

BRIGADIER GENERAL ULYSSES S. GRANT, USA

THE YEAR 1862 BEGAN badly for the Confederates in the western theater. General Albert Sydney Johnston was having to defend a 400-mile line stretching across Kentucky from the Mississippi River at Columbus, up through Bowling Green, then down to the Cumberland Gap, at the Tennessee border. But the line was starting to crumble.

The Confederates' right flank was exposed after they were routed at Mill Springs, eastern Kentucky, on January 19. Soon after, Union forces under Brigadier General Ulysses S. Grant took Forts Henry and Donelson, which commanded the Tennessee and Cumberland Rivers respectively.

Johnston was forced to withdraw and concentrate his scattered troops at Corinth, Mississippi, where the Mobile & Ohio Railroad crossed the Memphis & Charleston. The latter was particularly vital to the Confederacy, being its only east-west cross-country link.

By March, nearly 45,000 Confederate troops had gathered at Corinth under Johnston and his second-in-command General Pierre G. T. Beauregard, who had fought at Bull Run. Their best chance was to strike at Grant's Army of the Tennessee before it was reinforced by Major General Don Carlos Buell's Army of the Ohio, then on the march from Nashville.

Grant, who on March 17 had been given overall command of Union operations in the area, had 33,000 largely raw troops encamped at Pittsburg Landing on the west bank of the Tennessee River, just 22 miles northeast of Corinth. Five miles downriver, at Crump's Landing, was Brigadier General Lew Wallace (later the author of *Ben Hur*) and another 5,000 men. Four miles farther on, at Savannah on the east bank, was Grant's headquarters. When Buell and his army of 25,000

arrived here from Nashville, Grant planned to move all his forces to Pittsburg and Hamburg Landings, ready to strike at Johnston.

The principal Union campsite at Pittsburg Landing was idyllic: it was also undefended. Set amid some nine square miles of woods and small fields on a plateau rising 100 feet above the landing, the camp had its back to the Tennessee, its front toward Corinth, its right flank anchored on Owl Creek and the larger Snake Creek into which it ran, and its left on Lick Creek.

Nearest the landing was Brigadier General W.H.L. Wallace's Second Division, and to its left, was Brigadier General Stephen A. Hurlbut's Fourth Division, then the camp of Colonel David Stuart's Second Brigade of Sherman's Fifth Division, close to Lick Creek. A mile in front

of Wallace and Hurlbut lay Major General John McClernand's First Division. But in the vanguard were the greenest troops of all, the majority of Sherman's division and Brigadier General Benjamin Prentiss's Sixth Division.

As March turned to April, the days in the Federal camps were spent instilling drill and discipline in the recruits. There were no far-ranging cavalry patrols out, and the infantry pickets were posted just beyond the landward perimeter of the position. Grant himself stated on April 5:
"There will be no fighting at Pittsburg Landing; we will have to go to Corinth. . . ."

Meanwhile, on April 3, General Johnston ordered forward from Corinth some 40,000 men to attack Grant, supposedly at 3 a.m. on April 5. However, delayed orders, bad roads, and storms meant that the attack was postponed for 24 hours. Also, on the evening of April 5, the encamped army, about two miles from the Union lines, was not arrayed as Johnston had planned. He had intended to advance with three corps formed in column. Major General Leonidas Polk's I Corps was to be on the left, Major General Braxton Bragg's II Corps in the center, and Major General William Hardee's III Corps on the right. A Reserve Corps under Brigadier General John Breckinridge would support them.

But Beauregard issued written battle orders that materially changed the style of attack. By the time Johnston read them on April 4, the march was under way and it was too late to do anything about it. The Confederates would now advance in three lines: Hardee followed by Bragg and Polk, with Breckinridge in reserve. In fact, Beauregard wanted to call off the assault because of the delays.

However, Johnston was adamant. At a

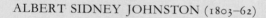

ALBERT SIDNEY JOHNSTON (1803–62)

An imposing six-footer, with great presence and dynamism, General Johnston, who was mortally wounded at Shiloh, was the highest-ranking officer of either the South or the North to be killed in the Civil War.

Johnston was born in Kentucky and went to West Point, from which he graduated in 1826. Six years later, he saw active service in the Black Hawk Indian War (1832). Johnston resigned his commission in 1834, but two years later he was in uniform again with the army of the new republic of Texas, which he rose to command. He fought two battles against the United States Indians on the River Neches, and served in the Mexican War with Major General Zachary Taylor, who was impressed by his conduct.

When Taylor became president, he made Johnston a paymaster in the US Army, a post which Johnston held until 1855. Then he became, successively, colonel of the 2nd Cavalry, a brevet brigadier general in command of the Utah military district; and, in early 1861, commander of the Pacific Coast.

At the outbreak of the Civil War, Johnston declined the Union's offer of "the most important command," and followed the fortunes of his adopted state, Texas, and the South.

In September 1861, he was given overall command of Confederate forces in the western theater. However, he was castigated for the losses of Fort Henry and Fort Donelson, and the abandonment of Nashville, Tennessee; all the same, he retained the confidence of President Davis, who remarked: "If Sidney Johnston is not a general, I have none."

In early 1862, Johnston decided to strike Grant at Pittsburg Landing, Tennessee, before the Federals could be reinforced by the Army of the Ohio. The result was the Battle of Shiloh, and Johnston's death from a bullet wound. In fact, his life might have been saved at the time if his surgeon had been available: Dr D.W. Yandell had been ordered by Johnston to attend to a large number of wounded men, including many Federals. Johnston apparently said to Yandell: "These men were our enemies a moment ago; they are our prisoners now. Take care of them." Meanwhile, Johnston bled to death. President Davis summed up this tragedy for the Confederacy with the words: "Our loss is irreparable. . . ."

THE FEDERAL STAND AT THE HORNET'S NEST

During the morning of April 6, the thrust of the initial Confederate attack had pushed the Federal positions back toward the Tennessee. Brigadier General Benjamin Prentiss, whose camp the Rebels had overrun early on, was forced back a mile to a strong position along a sunken road.

Prentiss's line, which included the greenest of the Union troops, was extended to his right by brigades of Brigadier General W.H.L. Wallace, and, to his left, by regiments of Brigadier General Stephen Hurlbut's division. For several hours, the Federals, standing or crouching behind the natural bank of the road, fought off a dozen determined Rebel attacks on their position which was dubbed by the Rebels the "Hornet's Nest," because of the intensity of fire stirred up every time an assault was mounted on it.

By the end of the fighting in this area, there were so many dead Rebels in the field in front of the sunken road that, so General Grant related, it was possible to walk across it "stepping on dead bodies without a foot touching the ground."

In the early afternoon of April 6, Prentiss's Federals (1), were entrenched in a sunken farm road, screened in front by dense thickets (7). There, they fought off the last of four attacks made by Colonel Randal L. Gibson's brigade of Major General Braxton Bragg's division.

Colonel Gibson's Confederates comprised the 19th Louisiana Volunteers (2), the 1st Arkansas (3), and the 13th and 4th Louisiana Volunteers (4,5). The Confederates had to advance across an open field (6) exposed to Union artillery. As they neared the thicket, rifle fire poured into their ranks.

At about 5 p.m., Prentiss was finally outflanked: he surrendered with 2,200 men. However, their brave stand had forestalled the Rebel advance and inflicted heavy casualties.

In fact, the Union surrender served to break the momentum of the Rebel attack; the push in this sector was halted while the transfer of prisoners was organized. By the time the Rebels resumed their offensive, Grant had formed another defensive line, which held off the Rebels until nightfall.

26

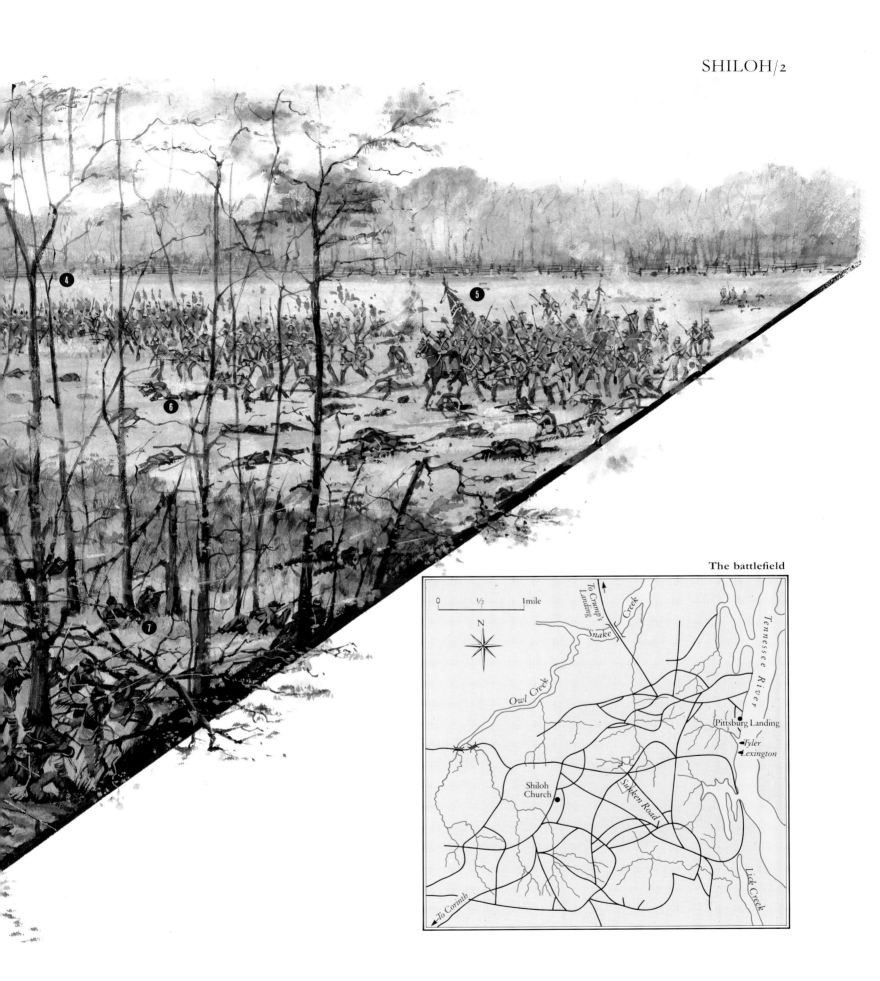

The battlefield

As the Civil War gathered momentum, great battles involving more than 100,000 men were fought on fields swept by high-velocity weapons. Consequently, the task of identifying soldiers' remains grew increasingly difficult for burial parties, such as the one photographed here, collecting the skeletons of unknown soldiers at Cold Harbor, Virginia, in 1865.

Some soldiers, fearful that their families might never find their corpses should they be killed, wore around their necks little wooden labels with their name and unit inscribed on them. Also, some firms offered other means of identity, including silver badges such as the one advertised (*above*) by Drowne & Moore. Not many soldiers could have bought them, for it is a sad fact that unknown warriors lie in more than 55 percent of the graves in the 80 National Civil War Cemeteries.

council of war on the Saturday evening, he dismissed any thought of returning to Corinth, telling his generals:

"Gentlemen, we shall attack at daylight tomorrow."

Later, he said to a member of his staff:

"I would fight them if they were a million. They can present no greater front between these two creeks than we can, and the more men they crowd in there, the worse we can make it for them."

Over in the Federals' camps, nothing much had changed. Only Prentiss, made uneasy by the appearance of Rebel scouts on his front, bothered to strengthen and advance his pickets.

And so, at 5.14 precisely on a beautiful Sunday morning, the first shot of the Battle of Shiloh, named after a country church around which some of the Federals were camped, rang out. The Confederate lines moved forward, driving in the pickets and frightening masses of wild birds and animals which fled into the drowsy Union camps. General Bragg described the scene:

"The enemy was found utterly unprepared, many being surprised and captured in their tents, and others, though on the outside, in costumes

better fitted to the bedchamber than to the battlefield."

Beauregard grudgingly conceded that it was "the most surprising surprise."

Before long, thousands of frightened Federals had run away to take shelter under the bluffs along the Tennessee River. But thousands more did stay to fight. Equally, thousands of Rebels turned tail or went looting through the abandoned camps, but thousands more pushed on with the attack.

While Prentiss and Sherman were bearing the brunt of the initial Confederate attack and McClernand, W.H.L. Wallace and Hurlbut were rushing to get their commands under arms and into line, Grant was on his way to the scene. He had heard the cannonade while breakfasting at Savannah and immediately boarded a steamer for Pittsburg Landing. Arriving around 8 a.m., Grant, who was on crutches after a riding accident, went off to encourage his division commanders.

During the next hour, the Union forces were hard pressed. Prentiss was pushed nearly a mile back to a strong position along a farm road fringed with woods on one side and a field on the other. On his left was Hurlbut and Stuart's brigade; to the right were Wallace, McClernand,

Federal retreat and counterattack

Contrary to the original plans of Confederate General A.S. Johnston, the Rebel advance at dawn on April 6 on the Union positions in front of Pittsburg Landing and around Shiloh Church (6) was in four parallel lines. Major General Hardee's corps (4) led the assault, followed by the corps of Major Generals Bragg and Polk (3,2). Brigadier General Breckinridge's Reserve Corps (1) took up the rear.

To face this powerful Rebel force, the Federals had the divisions of Brigadier Generals Hurlbut, Prentiss, Sherman, and Major General McClernand (10,8,5,7, respectively). The fierce Confederate thrust soon pushed the bulk of the Federals back toward the Tennessee (11). However, troops, principally under Prentiss, frustrated Confederate assaults for about eight hours around the Hornet's Nest (9).

The initial Rebel charge on Prentiss's camp is captured in this sketch by A.C. Redwood. Prentiss's men fell back and re-formed at a sunken farm road.

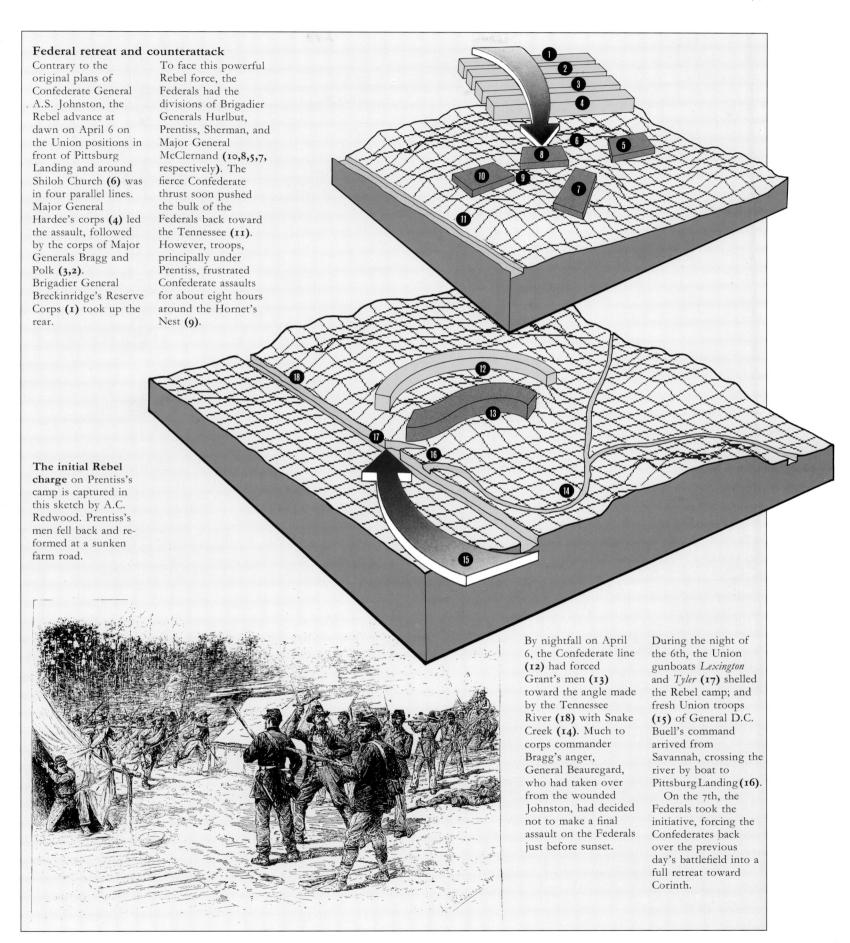

By nightfall on April 6, the Confederate line (12) had forced Grant's men (13) toward the angle made by the Tennessee River (18) with Snake Creek (14). Much to corps commander Bragg's anger, General Beauregard, who had taken over from the wounded Johnston, had decided not to make a final assault on the Federals just before sunset.

During the night of the 6th, the Union gunboats *Lexington* and *Tyler* (17) shelled the Rebel camp; and fresh Union troops (15) of General D.C. Buell's command arrived from Savannah, crossing the river by boat to Pittsburg Landing (16).

On the 7th, the Federals took the initiative, forcing the Confederates back over the previous day's battlefield into a full retreat toward Corinth.

and Sherman, whose command had been badly mauled. Johnston, who wanted to force Grant into an untenable position with his back to Owl and Snake Creeks, concentrated on Wallace, Prentiss, and Hurlbut.

Throughout the day no fewer than 12 Rebel assaults were made on the line held by Prentiss and Wallace, and seven on Hurlbut. The casualties, especially in front of Prentiss and Wallace, a position which the Confederates called the "Hornet's Nest," were enormous. While directing operations against Hurlbut, Johnston had an artery in his leg severed by a minié ball: by 2.30 p.m. he was dead through loss of blood, and Beauregard assumed command.

Grant, who had watched his lines bending under Confederate pressure, had sent for Lew Wallace's division at Crump's Landing and hurried up the vanguard of General Buell's approaching army. As his left and right flanks fell back farther, he knew the center had to hold while a new line was organized, so he told Prentiss to hang on at all costs.

By late afternoon, after an epic eight-hour struggle for the Hornet's Nest, Confederate numbers began to tell. Wallace was fatally wounded as he sought to extricate his shattered division, Hurlbut was retiring, and the Rebels were edging around Prentiss's flanks in force. Shortly after 5 p.m., surrounded, the gallant Prentiss surrendered with 2,200 men.

Because many Rebels stopped to gaze at the captured Federals, and an escort for them had to be organized, the Confederate advance was disrupted. By the time the push got going again, the Federals had formed a new line extending two miles from Pittsburg Landing on the left to Snake Creek on the right.

Bragg's men, who had been in battle for nearly 11 hours and were almost out of ammunition, made attempts on Grant's left, now protected by a line of artillery and the supporting fire of two gunboats, *Lexington* and *Tyler*. About 6 p.m., as firing was dying away all along the line, the leading brigade of Buell's advance guard arrived on the Union left. At about the same time, Beauregard, who was ill with an infection, issued an order to withdraw and regroup. Bragg was furious, for he was confident that a night attack would deliver total victory.

Throughout the evening Grant's bloody and battered army received the reinforcements it vitally needed. Two of Buell's divisions, along with Lew Wallace's, which had been delayed on the march, gave him about 18,000 fresh

Union gunboats in the western theater

Federal advances into Tennessee and down the Mississippi Valley in the first half of 1862 owed much to the Western Flotilla. On February 6, the flotilla's gunboats moved against the Rebel Fort Henry, commanding the Tennessee River, and bombarded the fort (*right*) into submission. Eight days later, they were on the Cumberland River, helping to wreck Fort Donelson.

In March and April, the flotilla was on the Mississippi, contributing to the fall of the Rebel strongpoints of Island No. 10, south of Columbus, and New Madrid, a little farther downriver. In May, the Federals resisted an attack by the Confederate River Defense Fleet near Fort Pillow, 80 river miles above Memphis, Tennessee. The Rebels then retired to Memphis. On June 6, the Battle of Memphis (*above*) took place: the Rebel fleet was destroyed.

troops with which to confront the enemy on Monday morning.

Torrential rain made Sunday night wretched for the soldiers, and the Rebels' miseries were compounded by 8-inch shells from the gunboats, which crashed into their lines every ten minutes throughout the night. At first light the battle-weary Confederates were attacked by fresh Federal troops. In a way, it was

April 6 in reverse. Despite the immense courage of his men, Beauregard decided that the odds were too great. He ordered a withdrawal which began at 2.30 p.m. without haste and in good order.

The Federals, who were glad to see the backs of the Rebels, remained in possession of the field and claimed victory. But the price of their narrowly won success had been high.

The aftermath

The Battle of Shiloh proved to be one of the bloodiest fought in the western theater, and produced enormous numbers of casualties.

Grant had approximately 51,000 troops over the two days, including the 18,000 men he received from Buell and Lew Wallace for the second day of the battle. He lost a total of 13,047 men. The Confederates had about 40,000 men and their total losses were 10,694.

Southern hopes of recovering west and middle Tennessee were dashed forever at Shiloh. The battle turned out to be just another obstacle in the path of the Union's inexorable conquest of the Mississippi Valley, which, when it was completed in 1863, split the Confederacy and assured its eventual downfall.

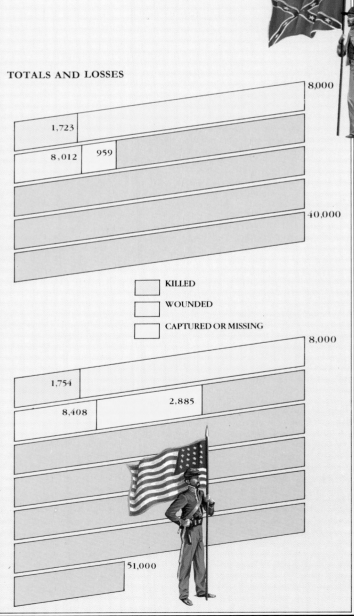

TOTALS AND LOSSES

8,000

1,723

8,012 | 959

40,000

☐ **KILLED**

☐ **WOUNDED**

☐ **CAPTURED OR MISSING**

8,000

1,754

8,408 | 2,885

51,000

Seven Pines

MAY 31–JUNE 1, 1862

"I am convinced that the stubborn and desperate resistance of my division saved the army on the right bank of the Chickahominy. . . ."

BRIGADIER GENERAL SILAS CASEY, USA, after the battle

SIX DAYS AFTER the disaster at Bull Run in July 1861, General Irvin McDowell was removed from the command of the principal Union army in the east and replaced by Major General George B. McClellan. "Little Mac," as the diminutive general was known, was a born organizer who transformed the burgeoning ranks of raw volunteers into the 150,000-strong Army of the Potomac. He imbued his men with military pride—and they loved him for it.

However, an impatient government and public felt that he had taken too long about it. The war, they believed, could be won quickly only by fighting, and not by drilling.

In March, 1862, McClellan was at last persuaded to move against the Rebels, who had lately abandoned their winter lines covering Manassas Junction. Anticipating a powerful Federal flanking attack on Richmond, General Joseph E. Johnston repositioned his Confederate forces near Culpeper, Virginia, half-way between the two capitals. From there, he could intercept the Union army, whichever way it advanced.

McClellan chose to move his army by water to the tip of the Virginia Peninsula, then march on Richmond, 75 miles inland, with his flanks protected by the York and James Rivers. A hastily assembled fleet of 400 assorted ships and boats carried out this huge operation in two weeks, without a hitch.

Then things began to go wrong. President Lincoln, nervous that the Washington defenses had been left undermanned, withheld one of McClellan's corps, under General McDowell, to protect the capital. And the weather became very wet, turning the already swampy peninsula into a quagmire.

Hindered by mud, and under the erroneous impression that he was outnum-

bered, McClellan began a cautious advance that stopped dead before Confederate earthworks. These, stretching south from Yorktown and blocking the peninsula, were at first held by only 11,000 men under Major General John B. Magruder. Although reinforcements came from the main Rebel army at Culpeper, Johnston decided that the Yorktown line could not be defended against the heavy Federal siege guns then being brought up.

The day before McClellan was finally ready to begin his bombardment, Johnston withdrew. The Federals followed and met the Rebel rearguard at Williamsburg on May 5, where a sharp battle ensued. Johnston continued his retreat and McClellan pushed on up the peninsula, moving the bulk of his army along the north bank of the Chickahominy River, a tributary of the James.

Toward the end of May, the Confederates were alarmed to learn that McDowell's corps was now moving south to unite with the right wing of the Army of the Potomac. Johnston, therefore, resolved to strike the main Union force north of the Chickahominy on May 29, before it could be reinforced. However, Johnston then learned that McDowell was retiring, and so he called off the assault on McClellan's main army. Instead, he turned his attention to two Union corps lying south of the Chickahominy.

If he moved quickly, he could neutralize them before help could arrive from across the river. May 31 was set as the date for the attack. The night before, Johnston received help from drenching rain that swelled the Chickahominy: bridges were flooded, and the two Union corps were effectively isolated. It was a rare chance to disable two-fifths of McClellan's army.

The Federal positions south of the river were scattered. Brigadier General Erasmus D. Keyes's IV Corps was in the van, his picket line just six miles from Richmond, extending northward from the White Oak Swamp to the Chickahominy. Half a mile behind his skirmishers, on the main road from Richmond to Williamsburg, lay Brigadier General Silas Casey's division, its rifle-pits and artillery emplacement protected by an abatis, a defensive tangle of felled trees. Another half-mile behind Casey was Brigadier

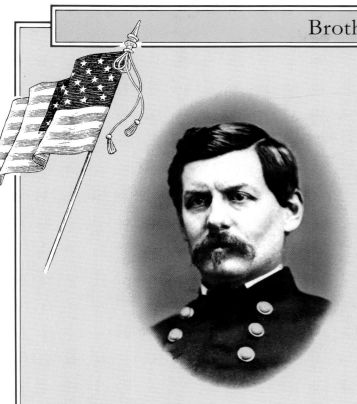

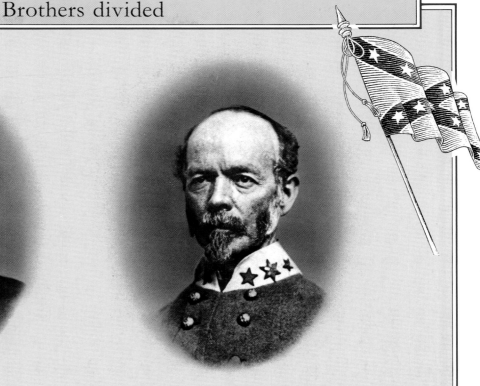

GEORGE BRINTON McCLELLAN (1826–85)

Supremely confident and a brilliant organizer, "Little Mac," who led the Army of the Potomac at Seven Pines, was born in Philadelphia. After graduating from West Point at the top of his class, he served with distinction in the Mexican War, and went to the Crimean War (1853–6) to study European methods of warfare. Soon afterward, he left the army and became a railroad engineer, with great success. When the Civil War broke out, he led the Ohio volunteers for the Union.

After the Union defeat at First Bull Run, McClellan's modest success against the Confederates in western Virginia led to his being called to Washington. There, he did a superb job in organizing and equipping the Army of the Potomac. Upon Winfield Scott's retirement in November 1861, McClellan was named general in chief of all US armies, a position that he held until March, 1862.

Frequently criticized for the slowness of his operations, McClellan was recalled to Washington when his Peninsula Campaign in Virginia collapsed in 1862. By September of that year, however, he again found himself in command of the Army of the Potomac, and, in that month, he turned back General Lee's first invasion of the North at Antietam. But, because McClellan failed to capitalize on his success, Lincoln relieved him of his command.

Two years later, in 1864, as a Democratic politician, McClellan ran against Lincoln for the presidency and lost.

JOSEPH EGGLESTON JOHNSTON (1807–91)

One of the war's best defensive strategists, Johnston was the Confederate commander at Seven Pines. A native of Virginia, he graduated from West Point in 1829, and saw active service in the Mexican War and against the plains Indians. At the start of the Civil War, Johnston offered his services to the Confederacy, and was first given command of the Army of the Shenandoah. He then assumed overall control of Confederate forces at First Bull Run.

In spring 1862, Johnston was seriously wounded at the Battle of Seven Pines, and was out of action until the following November. Then, he was given the difficult appointment of overseeing far-flung Rebel forces in the western theater.

A string of disasters followed for the South in the western theater in 1863, nevertheless, President Davis, who disliked Johnston, reluctantly agreed to give him field command of the Army of Tennessee. Johnston revitalized this army, and, throughout May and June 1864, conducted a masterly withdrawal in the face of Major General William T. Sherman's advance into northwest Georgia.

President Davis, however, removed Johnston from command on July 17, citing his lack of success, and Johnston went into retirement. The following February, he agreed to command what was left of the Army of Tennessee and other Rebel units opposing Sherman's march northward from Savannah. Johnston fought well against overwhelming odds until compelled to surrender on April 26, 1865.

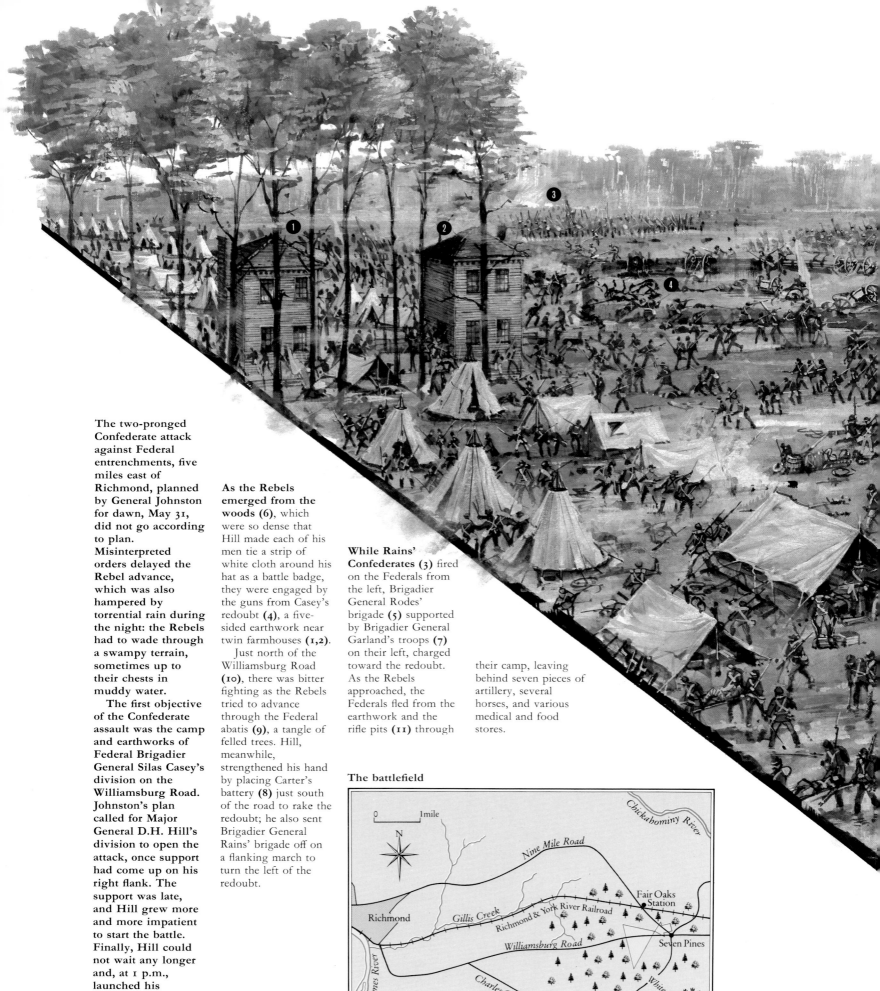

The two-pronged Confederate attack against Federal entrenchments, five miles east of Richmond, planned by General Johnston for dawn, May 31, did not go according to plan. Misinterpreted orders delayed the Rebel advance, which was also hampered by torrential rain during the night: the Rebels had to wade through a swampy terrain, sometimes up to their chests in muddy water.

The first objective of the Confederate assault was the camp and earthworks of Federal Brigadier General Silas Casey's division on the Williamsburg Road. Johnston's plan called for Major General D.H. Hill's division to open the attack, once support had come up on his right flank. The support was late, and Hill grew more and more impatient to start the battle. Finally, Hill could not wait any longer and, at 1 p.m., launched his division against Casey's men.

As the Rebels emerged from the woods (6), which were so dense that Hill made each of his men tie a strip of white cloth around his hat as a battle badge, they were engaged by the guns from Casey's redoubt (4), a five-sided earthwork near twin farmhouses (1,2).

Just north of the Williamsburg Road (10), there was bitter fighting as the Rebels tried to advance through the Federal abatis (9), a tangle of felled trees. Hill, meanwhile, strengthened his hand by placing Carter's battery (8) just south of the road to rake the redoubt; he also sent Brigadier General Rains' brigade off on a flanking march to turn the left of the redoubt.

While Rains' Confederates (3) fired on the Federals from the left, Brigadier General Rodes' brigade (5) supported by Brigadier General Garland's troops (7) on their left, charged toward the redoubt. As the Rebels approached, the Federals fled from the earthwork and the rifle pits (11) through their camp, leaving behind seven pieces of artillery, several horses, and various medical and food stores.

The battlefield

By middle to late afternoon, the Confederates had overrun the first Union defense line at Casey's redoubt, and occupied the Union camp. Soon, they were half a mile on down the Williamsburg Road, assaulting the second Federal line at Seven Pines. Here, the Federals, with most of Brigadier General Keyes's corps and part of Brigadier General Heintzelman's, fought off Hill's men, who were supported by only one brigade— out of a possible nine—from Major General Longstreet.

The Confederates were unable to exploit their success against the Federal left during the first day's fighting. Had the Rebel attack been delivered in concert with the planned hammer blow against the Federals' exposed right flank, north of Seven Pines, the Confederates might well have won a resounding victory. As it was, Union reinforcements were able to cross the flooded Chickahominy River late on the first day, and bolster the Union right.

On the next day, June 1, there was no concerted effort on either side to attain an advantage: the battle ended in stalemate, with both armies back to more or less their original positions.

General Darius Couch's division, occupying an entrenched position at Seven Pines, the intersection of the Williamsburg Road with Nine Mile Road.

The Union left was protected by White Oak Swamp; but its right was exposed. Four regiments and some artillery were grouped around Fair Oaks Station on the Richmond & York River Railroad, a mile north of Seven Pines on the Nine Mile Road. But there was nothing between them and the Chickahominy two miles farther on. Two miles behind the Seven Pines earthworks was an incomplete and unmanned third line of defense, and three miles beyond that was the III Corps of Brigadier General Samuel Heintzelman.

Johnston, it seems, intended to launch a two-pronged attack early on May 31 under the direction of Major General James Longstreet. In essence, Major General D.H. Hill's division was to advance along the Williamsburg Road, supported on his right by Brigadier General Benjamin Huger's division marching by the Charles City Road, which branched off the Williamsburg Road.

Longstreet's division was to move on the Nine Mile Road, followed by Brigadier General W.H.C. Whiting's division, and give support to Hill's left flank. Hill was to open the attack when Huger arrived on his right, and Longstreet was to join in as soon as he heard their firing. It was a logical plan that should have succeeded, but a "misunderstanding" about its execution developed between Johnston and Longstreet on the eve of battle, and the Confederate effort dissolved into a fiasco.

Longstreet got off to a slow start on May 31. He did not advance along the Nine Mile Road, but inexplicably moved his division across country to follow D.H. Hill on the Williamsburg Road. On the way, he had to bridge and cross flooded Gillis Creek; and, in so doing, he got in front of, and delayed for several hours, Huger, upon whose arrival on Hill's right the start of the assault depended.

Earlier, Whiting's division had been ready to move by the Nine Mile Road but found its way blocked by some of Longstreet's regiments. Whiting asked headquarters to have the road cleared so that he could get into position, but Johnston told him to stay where he was for the time being because Longstreet was to take precedence on the Nine Mile Road! For much of the rest of that confusing day, Johnston remained ignorant of the exact whereabouts and intentions of the man on whom he was relying for the successful execution of his plan.

By midday, General Hill, unaware of the confusion, was seething with impatience at Huger's delay in supporting his right. At 1 p.m., Hill decided to open the assault alone. He drove in the Federal pickets and, in a brisk fight, pushed Casey out of his entrenchments and back to Couch's second line at Seven Pines, where the battle escalated around mid-afternoon.

Although there were now another nine Confederate brigades crowding in behind the narrow front at Seven Pines, only one, from Longstreet's division, joined in Hill's brave struggle against most of Keyes's corps and part of Heintzelman's.

Meanwhile, Longstreet issued a stream of conflicting orders for an assault by half of his division, together with that of Huger, on the Federal left, which never came to anything. He then turned his attention to his left where a half brigade under Colonel Micah Jenkins had made a dashing sweep through the Union lines.

At 4 p.m., Longstreet sent a message to Johnston urgently requesting Whiting's command to be sent from the Nine Mile Road to his left to assist him in "driving" the Federals. This note, showing plainly that his plans had gone astray, prompted Johnston into action at last.

Johnston had only himself to blame. He had not kept in contact with Longstreet, and had no idea of how the battle was progressing. For the first time that day, Johnston took the field himself, leaving at his headquarters President Jef-

Union soldiers perform the grim task of burning dead horses after the Battle of Seven Pines. In the background can be seen the distinctive twin farmhouses which lay behind the five-sided redoubt that was occupied by men of Federal Brigadier General Silas Casey's division.

A "barbarous" act of war

When the Confederates abandoned Yorktown and withdrew up the peninsula through Williamsburg, Rebel Brigadier General Gabriel J. Rains arranged for primed mortar shells to be buried in roads, and near watering places and likely rest areas; others he had wired up to door handles. That these devices worked is evident from the number of mentions of them in Federal reports.

Union commander McClellan described the practice as "barbarous," and Confederate General James Longstreet wrote to Rains, then in command of the rear guard leaving Williamsburg, saying: "It is the desire of the major general commanding that you put no shells or torpedoes behind you, as he does not recognize it as a proper or effective method of war."

Rains, however, was simply ahead of his time. Commanders in future conflicts would use with devastating effect what are now called booby-trap bombs and antipersonnel mines.

Sumner saves the day

On the morning of May 31, Major General D.H. Hill's Rebel division (1) advanced up the Williamsburg Road and through the dense woodland bordering it. At 1 p.m., Hill sent his men charging into the clearing where Brigadier General Silas Casey's Federal division (8) was entrenched. After an hour or so of fierce fighting, the Federals were driven back to a second defensive line at Seven Pines crossroads (7). There, they held off Rebel assaults until, under threat of being flanked on their right, they withdrew eastward.

Meanwhile, north of the action around Seven Pines, just before 5 p.m., Confederate General Johnston led Brigadier General W.H.C. Whiting's troops (2) along the Nine Mile Road to attack the Federals he believed to be at Fair Oaks Station (6). The Rebels, however, came under fire from elements of Brigadier General Darius Couch's division (5) around the Adams House, who, cut off from the bulk of their division, had been heading north toward the Chickahominy River (3). As the Confederates turned and attacked Couch's men, Federal reinforcements (4) from Brigadier General Edwin Sumner's II Corps began to arrive. These men had been forced to negotiate a rickety bridge over the flooded Chickahominy River. When told that the bridge would be impossible to cross, the indomitable Sumner is reported to have thundered in reply: "Sir, I tell you I *can* cross. I am ordered."

Fresh Union troops continued to strengthen and extend Couch's line to the west. As darkness brought an end to the day's fighting, successive Rebel assaults had failed to dislodge the Federals. Sumner's determination had thwarted Johnston's men.

Federal troops from Brigadier General Edwin Sumner's corps cross the rain-swollen Chickahominy River to reinforce the precarious Union position near Fair Oaks Station.

ferson Davis and his military adviser, General Robert E. Lee.

Although he did not know where Longstreet's left was, Johnston sent Brigadier General John B. Hood's brigade of Whiting's division off through the woods toward Seven Pines while he led two other brigades down the Nine Mile Road to Fair Oaks Station. Nearby they met a small Federal force under Brigadier General John J. Abercrombie. These Union troops were attempting to make their way toward the safety of the north bank of the Chickahominy River.

Johnston directed several piecemeal jabs against Abercrombie and was repulsed each time. Then, to his surprise, he was enfiladed by the lead elements of Brigadier General Edwin V. Sumner's II Corps, which had managed to negotiate a narrow, swaying wooden bridge over the flooded river to help Keyes and Heintzelman. Although two more brigades

reinforced Johnston, the Confederate commander was fighting a losing battle against Union infantry increasing in numbers and supported by artillery.

When dusk fell, firing began to fade away at both Seven Pines and Fair Oaks. At that moment Johnston rode forward a little and was hit in the shoulder by a minié ball and in the chest by a shell splinter. He was carried from the field, severely wounded. Overall control then devolved temporarily on Major General Gustavus W. Smith, who was in poor health and had been given no active assignment in the battle.

The next morning, Smith decided not to renew the unequal fight at Fair Oaks, and Longstreet did not carry out his orders to push hard at Seven Pines. There was some heavy fighting on the Confederate right, but these outbreaks had subsided by 1 p.m.

By June 2, the divisions of Longstreet

and Hill were on their way back to their camps around Richmond, though Whiting remained facing the Federals on the Nine Mile Road, and Huger's command lay across the Williamsburg Road. Everything was much as it had been before May 31. The Confederates had been able to achieve nothing.

Union posters advertise for recruits with appeals to avoid the draft and offers of bounty. In March, 1863, the Lincoln administration bolstered its volunteer system with a draft law.

Spying by balloon

The first reconnaissance of enemy troop movements from a manned balloon was made during the Civil War. This novel means of observation was mainly pioneered for the Union army by Professor T.S.C. Lowe.

Lowe's trio of balloons—the large *Intrepid*, which was 38 feet wide and 45 feet high, and the smaller *Washington* and *Constitution*—were frequently used during McClellan's Peninsula Campaign in 1862. As soon as Lowe went aloft, his craft invariably attracted heavy fire from the Confederates.

The professor's balloon unit had portable hydrogen gas-making equipment, which allowed it to move freely to obtain the best vantage point. And the innovative Lowe, photographed (*below*) prodding the *Intrepid* as it is being filled with gas, did not wait to be hauled down before making his report: he took a telegraph up with him.

The Confederates possessed only one balloon, which flew briefly in the spring of 1862. It was a multi-hued affair, manufactured from silk dresses donated by Southern ladies. Because the only gas supply was in Richmond, the Rebel balloon had to be inflated there and then towed along, tethered either to a train or a boat.

The need for conscription

When the war began, volunteers for the Confederate States Army were enlisted to serve for one year. Thus, in the spring of 1862, there was the prospect of widespread disbandments, a potential disaster prevented by a conscription act, which came into force on April 14 that year. With certain exceptions, every able-bodied man aged between 18 and 35 was drafted into military service for three years, or the duration of the war. It was not a popular move, but it guaranteed manpower for the Rebel armed forces.

The Union introduced conscription to bolster its volunteer system only in March, 1863. Even so, the Federal draft law was not so positive as that of the Confederacy and, indeed, led to corruption. From then until the end of the war, a quota was levied against each state in the Union every time that Washington wanted to raise more manpower. This quota was, in turn, divided among the Congressional districts in each state. The idea was that if a district or state could reach its target with volunteers, there would be no need to resort to conscription.

In order to avoid the draft, states, districts, and towns raised funds to induce volunteers to enlist on promise of a generous bounty. However, this practice gave birth to the bounty-jumpers—unscrupulous men who signed on, took the money, then promptly deserted to start the get-rich-quick process all over again under another name.

Each time a draft was imposed, rich young men could buy themselves out on payment of $300, or could claim immunity for the rest of the war by supplying a substitute to fight on their behalf.

The aftermath

The Battle of Seven Pines, or Fair Oaks, as the North called it, ended indecisively with both sides claiming victory. Only small proportions from both the Confederate and Union armies—about 26,000 men in each case—fought during the two days. Johnston's army, which engaged in the fighting practically without artillery support, had a total of 6,134 casualties. The Union forces, who rallied well and were ably served by their batteries, lost a total of 5,031 men.

For the Confederacy, Johnston and Longstreet had bungled—and they knew it.

However, the wounding of Johnston resulted in the appointment of a new commander of the principal Southern force in the eastern theater: Robert E. Lee, who would shortly lead his famous Army of Northern Virginia to a series of memorable victories.

TOTALS AND LOSSES

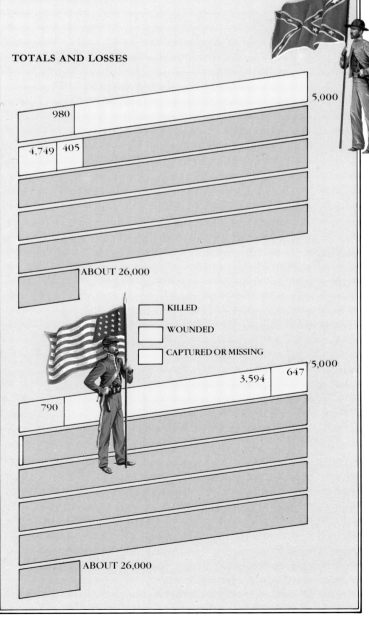

980

4,749 | 405

5,000

ABOUT 26,000

KILLED

WOUNDED

CAPTURED OR MISSING

3,594 | 647

5,000

790

ABOUT 26,000

The Seven Days

"It was not war — it was murder."

MAJOR GENERAL D.H. HILL, CSA

A DIFFICULT, POTENTIALLY dangerous situation confronted General Robert E. Lee when he succeeded the wounded General Joseph E. Johnston on June 1, 1862, as commander of the Confederate forces in the eastern theater. A large, well-equipped Union army under Major General George B. McClellan lay within a couple of miles of Richmond. The Confederate capital was poorly fortified, and defended by an outnumbered, badly coordinated collection of somewhat demoralized troops.

Lee responded to the crisis by taking an immediate and far-reaching grip on his troops, whom he named the Army of Northern Virginia. In three short weeks, Lee strengthened defense lines near Richmond and brought up reinforcements. He improved the organization and equipment of his soldiers, made himself known to all units and—above all—formulated a plan to drive off the Federals from the vicinity of Richmond.

During this time, the bulk of McClellan's 125,000-strong Union army was concentrated south of the Chickahominy River, a tributary of the James River. Only Brigadier General Fitz-John Porter's V Corps was stationed on the north side, largely to guard the approach to the main Federal supply base at White House on the Pamunkey River.

In the fighting that occurred around Richmond between June 25 and July 1, which became known as the Seven Days, Lee at once showed the audacity and strategic genius which would distinguish him as one of the world's great generals. His cunning—and daring—plan was to smash Porter's isolated corps, and then cut off McClellan's main army from its supply base. Lee decided to leave 22,000 men under Major General John B. Magruder in Richmond's eastern defenses to face 75,000 Federals. Meanwhile, he proposed to push 32,000 troops across the Chickahominy north of the city to join Major General Thomas J. "Stonewall" Jackson's force, which was en route from the Shenandoah Valley, and overwhelm Porter's corps of 25,000 Union troops near Mechanicsville before it could be reinforced.

June 26 was the date set for the Confederate attack. Unknown to Lee, McClellan had also intended to begin an offensive that day. But then McClellan learned of the approach of Jackson. Under the erroneous impression that he would be confronted by an enormous Rebel force of 200,000, McClellan canceled his assault.

Lee, meanwhile, ordered the divisions of Major Generals Ambrose Powell Hill, James Longstreet, and Daniel Harvey Hill to move up to the Chickahominy to be ready to cross when Jackson arrived. At the same time, Magruder began a demonstration to convince the Federals that the Richmond defenses were still strongly manned.

Battle was expected to open around 7 a.m., but hour after hour dragged by without any sign of Jackson. By 3 p.m., A.P. Hill decided to cross the Chickahominy on his own initiative. Lee deduced from A.P. Hill's advance that Jackson was in position, so he ordered D.H. Hill and Longstreet to follow.

A.P. Hill's division ran into Porter's corps which was strongly entrenched on a high bank behind Beaver Dam Creek, a tributary of the Chickahominy. Close-range fire from well-sited batteries and accurate volleys from the infantry ripped into the Rebels as they bravely struggled again and again to assail the Federals. By nightfall, A.P. Hill had lost more than 1,600 soldiers; Porter still occupied the formidable position from which he should have been evicted by Jackson coming in on his right flank and rear.

However, Jackson and his 18,500 men, exhausted from their marches in the Shenandoah Valley, were two and a half miles from the battlefield. They had started late and progressed slowly over unfamiliar country dotted with obstacles placed in their path by Federal cavalry.

Despite this Union success, McClellan

ROBERT EDWARD LEE (1807–70)

Lee, whose daring tactics during the Civil War put him among the ranks of the world's greatest generals, came from the Virginia aristocracy. His father was General Henry "Light-Horse Harry" Lee, a Revolutionary War hero and friend of George Washington.

Robert followed his father into the army, going to West Point in 1825, and then entering the Corps of Engineers. Captain Lee first saw active service in the Mexican War, when he joined the staff of the commanding general, Winfield Scott, and won himself a brevet colonelcy.

After the war, he returned to military engineering until he was appointed superintendent of West Point in 1852. Promotions followed and, in March, 1861, he became colonel of the US 1st Cavalry. By this time, Lee had come to public notice for, in October, 1859, he commanded the government forces which captured the abolitionist John Brown and his followers during their abortive raid on the Harpers Ferry arsenal.

When the Civil War broke out in 1861, Lee was offered command of the US Army; he declined, and, on April 20, resigned his commission, and offered his services to Virginia. Lee was made a general in the Confederate States Army, but, for a year, his talents were wasted in a series of minor appointments, culminating in his becoming military adviser to President Jefferson Davis.

The wounding of General Joseph E. Johnston at Seven Pines on May 31, 1862, provided Lee with his first important field command. From the various forces scattered around Richmond, he fashioned the legendary Army of Northern Virginia. In many great battles, Lee took on and beat stronger, and better fed and equipped, Union forces. It was the manpower shortage, more than inadequate leadership, that sealed the fate of the South.

In February, 1865, Lee was made commander in chief of all Confederate troops. But the promotion failed to save the Rebel cause. Two months later, on April 9, Lee surrendered his army to Lieutenant General Ulysses S. Grant to avoid further unnecessary bloodshed. After the war, Lee became president of Washington College, Lexington, Virginia, a post he held until his death on October 12, 1870.

MALVERN HILL: CHARGING THE FEDERAL GUNS

The battle for Malvern Hill brought to an end the week of brutal fighting that was named the Seven Days. The Federals occupied the 150-foot-high plateau on June 30. Here, they carefully sited about 100 pieces of artillery, and prepared themselves to fight a delaying action to cover their retreat to the new fortified Union base at Harrison's Landing on the James River. Despite the awesome task of taking such a strong and well-defended position, this was General Robert E. Lee's last chance to destroy the Army of the Potomac before it reached the safety of base camp.

At 8 p.m. on July 1, 1862, the final stages of the Rebels' struggle for Malvern Hill were in progress. Since early afternoon they had been trying to wrest control of the high ground from the Federals. Now, as the light of a hot summer's day was fading, the Rebel attacks became even more frenzied and desperate.

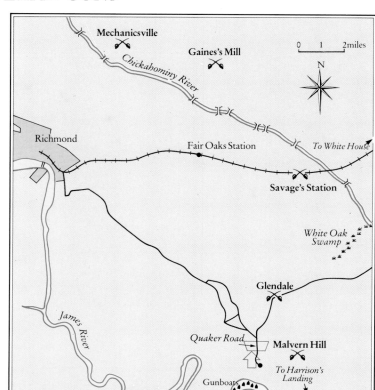

The battlefield

The Federals had more than 100 guns (**7**)—3-inch Rodman rifles, 10-pound Parrotts and 12-pound Napoleons—ranged along the crest of the hill (**8**). From the start of the fighting, the guns had poured an unrelenting fire into the advancing Rebel lines.

At about 5 p.m., Major General D.H. Hill had thrown his Rebel division into the attack; it was met by a terrifying barrage of shot and shell. The Union gun crews worked fast and accurately throughout the battle.

The Rebel attack had been piecemeal, with only 14 brigades engaged; the rest remained in the woods (**4**). Casualties were heavy, especially on the exposed fields of the hill's northern slope. Also, D.H. Hill's men lacked the protection of the ravines (**1**) afforded to troops on the Rebel right wing.

After three hours of fighting, Hill's troops (**3**) attacked the Union line with renewed vigor and ferocity.

Those who managed to get near the guns were picked off by Federal infantry (**5**), near West House (**6**), or by Berdan's green-clad sharpshooters (**2**), crouching behind shocks of wheat.

Throughout the battle, Federal Colonel Henry Hunt (**9**) had controlled his guns expertly and remained calm, despite having three horses shot from under him. The murderous effect of the Union artillery was described by a Union officer, who saw the battlefield the next day: "Over five thousand dead and wounded men were on the ground, in every attitude of distress. A third of

them were dead or dying, but enough were alive and moving to give to the field a singular crawling effect."

The Confederate assault had failed, and during the night McClellan's men moved off toward the protection of Harrison's Landing.

Allan Pinkerton and intelligence gathering

Generals in both the North and the South were well aware of the importance of gathering intelligence about the opposition's strength and intentions, but some commanders were better served than others. Both sides employed civilian spies. These men and women risked the death penalty if caught and, indeed, many were hanged. Newspapers and journals also played an important part in unwittingly providing valuable information to the enemy's armies: since a rigorous system of censorship did not exist, newspapers printed whatever they wished, and commanders were quick to use the military facts divulged in this way.

General Lee relied heavily on the cavalry to watch the enemy and bring back information about troop movements and numbers. For the most part, this traditional practice served the South well enough. There were times, however, when the Rebel horse failed to provide timely warnings—during the Gettysburg campaign, for example—and seriously affected the conduct of some battles. Despite these shortcomings, the Confederacy never attempted to organize a central intelligence-gathering bureau.

By contrast, the Union, at an early stage in the war, secured the services of a successful Chicago-based private detective agency run by Allan Pinkerton. A Scots-man by birth, Pinkerton arrived incognito in Washington under the alias of Major Allen. He was a good friend of Major General McClellan, whom he supplied with most of his intelligence. Unfortunately, the Pinkerton agents were inept at estimating numbers, and always filed wildly inflated estimates of Confederate strength. This faulty information induced undue caution in McClellan, and contributed significantly to the failure of his Peninsula Campaign.

When McClellan was retired after the Battle of Antietam in September, 1862, Pinkerton refused to do any further work for the army. Federal intelligence gathering remained in limbo until March, 1863, when Major General Joseph Hooker appointed Colonel George H. Sharpe of the 120th New York Regiment to create and lead the Bureau of Military Information.

A native of Scotland, Allan Pinkerton (*below right*) used his detective agency to provide military intelligence for the Union. In a photograph (*below left*) taken in May, 1862, Pinkerton's agents sit around a table while, behind them, their chief smokes his pipe.

resolved to give up his vulnerable White House base and move to Harrison's Landing on the James River, about 20 miles south. There, under the protection of gunboats, he would regroup his army, ready for another attempt on Richmond.

McClellan desperately needed to buy time to prepare for the retreat. To this end, he ordered Porter to fall back six miles during the early hours of June 27 to a reinforced position near Gaines's Mill. If Porter could hold the Confederates off, it would allow McClellan to withdraw across the Chickahominy bridges.

A.P. Hill's division led the Confederate pursuit and, in the early afternoon, advanced in line of battle against Porter's command. The latter occupied crude breastworks and gun emplacements strung out along a two-mile arc of high ground behind a marshy stream called Boatswain's Swamp, another tributary of the Chickahominy. Although Hill's regiments suffered terrible casualties as they moved slowly across open fields and down into the swamp, they also dealt heavy losses to the Federals.

Meanwhile, Longstreet had come up on A.P. Hill's right, and D.H. Hill was beginning to press Porter's right flank. But between the two Hills was a gap that Jackson was supposed to fill. Jackson, however, did not reach the field until late afternoon, by which time the Confederates had been beaten back in a series of uncoordinated assaults.

As evening drew on, Lee finally ordered a general assault all along the line. The Union center was broken and the victorious Confederates swarmed over the smoke-filled plateau, which was bathed in an eerie glow by the setting sun. Two fresh Federal brigades covered Porter's retreat over the Chickahominy bridges, which were then destroyed. Although the Confederates had lost 8,300 men compared with the Union's 6,800 at Gaines's Mill, they had won 22 guns and large amounts of much-needed weapons and equipment.

Now that Lee had cut McClellan's communications with his supply base, it remained to be seen what the Union commander would do to extricate him-

The pursuit to Harrison's Landing

On July 1, 1862, after five days of desperate fighting, General Robert E. Lee's Rebel army, chasing the Army of the Potomac to its new base at Harrison's Landing, was now confronted with a line of 100 Union cannon (6) on the crest of Malvern Hill. Here, the Federal gunners covered the open ground in front with a deadly fire, while Union gunboats on the James River (1) added to the bombardment.

Lee and General James Longstreet realized that a barrage from their own guns was desirable to support an assault; but the Rebel artillery (5) was soon put out of action by the Federal cannon. Nevertheless,

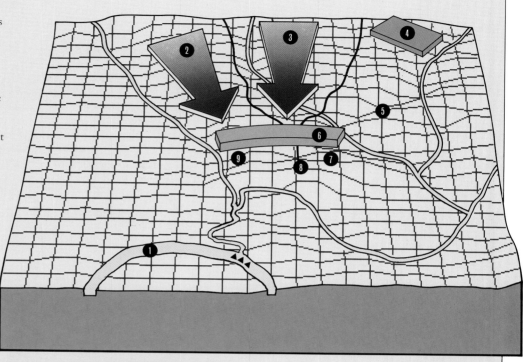

Union troops are greeted by the campfires of Harrison's Landing.

Lee decided to go ahead with a powerful frontal charge on the strong Federal position.

At about 5.00 p.m., the Rebel right wing (2) advanced across the broken ground toward Crew House (9). Some Rebel units were soon pinned down in ravines for the rest of the fighting by fierce Federal fire; others, however, managed to penetrate the Union line near the close of battle. But by then it was too late.

Meanwhile, in the Rebel center (3), Major General D.H. Hill had taken this advance of the Rebel right to be the prearranged signal for launching his own division toward West House (7). But, though wave after wave of Hill's troops recklessly charged the Federal guns until dark, they gained nothing, and lost hundreds of dead and wounded.

By the time the uncommitted Rebel infantry (4) was belatedly brought forward, their army had been beaten.

After the battle, the Federals retreated along the Quaker Road, which ended at Malvern House (8), then struck south for their new base.

self. On the 28th, Lee learned that the Federals had destroyed their White House base. Suspecting that clouds of dust on the south side of the river indicated troop movements, Lee ordered Magruder to keep a sharp watch on McClellan and report what was happening.

Evading Magruder's surveillance, Little Mac, as the Union commander was known, sent his army on a flank march toward the James. It was not until the 29th that the Confederates realized the siege of Richmond had been lifted. Magruder was ordered to pursue while Lee moved his divisions across the Chickahominy. Magruder caught up with the Union rear guard at Savage's Station and a fight ensued, which continued after darkness fell. Finally, the Federals broke off the action and continued to fall back, leaving behind great heaps of burning stores as well as field hospital containing 2,500 sick and wounded.

By now, Lee was across the Chickahominy and had finally concluded that McClellan was heading for the James, not back down the peninsula. Lee, therefore, split his command into five columns and followed the Union retreat as quickly as possible. On June 30, Lee brought McClellan's troops to battle at Glendale crossroads, about halfway between the Chickahominy and the James.

But Lee's plan to smash the Federals with a combined force in excess of 70,000 men misfired. Jackson once again failed to be in the right place at the right time. Maps were inadequate and staffwork was poor. So, a decisive hammerblow in the morning was reduced to desperate fighting in the afternoon and evening between 18,000 men from Longstreet's and A.P. Hill's commands and some 40,000 Union troops. The Confederates did well, breaking into the Federal position and taking many prisoners; but the bulk of the Union army was able to make its escape under the cover of darkness.

On the next day, July 1, the Federals were in a position of great strength on Malvern Hill, just north of Harrison's Landing, where a great new Union supply depot was burgeoning. With their flanks protected by streams, and supported by gunboats on the nearby James River, the Union infantry commanded the north and west faces of the hill, which was studded with carefully sited batteries covering the Rebels' only possible approach, across open fields to the front.

For once, Lee had all his troops around him as he converged on Malvern Hill that afternoon. Between 2 and 3 p.m., Confederate assault parties began to probe all along the Union lines. After 4 p.m., a lull descended while Lee considered his tactics. He opted for a grand, head-on attack which was signaled to begin at 5.30 p.m. To his disappointment, it was delivered spasmodically in the face of concentrated Union artillery fire, which caused dreadful losses in his ranks. Major General D.H. Hill summarized this situation:

"It was not war—it was murder." Time after time, Rebel regiments charged toward the hill with reckless bravado, only to be repulsed. Firing continued after darkness fell, but Lee's decimated troops found it impossible to breach the sturdy defenses: 5,000 dead and wounded lay in the open fields in front of the hill.

Union troops run a burning ammunition train (*top*) into the Chickahominy River rather than allow its valuable cargo to fall into Rebel hands.

After the Battle of Gaines's Mill, Porter took his battered troops across the Chickahominy to join McClellan's main army in readiness for a withdrawal to a new base at Harrison's Landing.

Federal Brigadier General Fitz-John Porter, the commander of V Corps, points toward the woods in the distance at the Battle of Gaines's Mill (*above*), on June 27, while speaking to his fellow officers.

During the battle, nearly 50,000 Rebels charged on 35,000 Federals, and, in Porter's own words: "At each repulse they [the Rebels] advanced new troops upon our diminishing forces, and in such numbers and so rapidly that it appeared as though their reserves were inexhaustible."

Lines of wagons and troops of the Army of the Potomac cross a creek near White Oak Swamp during the Federal retreat to Harrison's Landing. By and large, McClellan's men conducted themselves

Some of Lee's units were so badly cut up they feared they would not be able to withstand McClellan should he attack at first light. Little Mac, however, had no intention of going on the offensive. He considered the Battle of Malvern Hill to be no more than another holding action to cover the consolidation of his new base. By the morning of July 2, his army had resumed its withdrawal to Harrison's Landing, which had by then been strongly fortified.

Lee, for his part, decided not to expose his troops further to what would have been another bloody and futile assault. For the moment, Richmond was safe.

well as they marched south over a difficult terrain, with Lee's Rebels in hot pursuit.

According to Federal Major General William B. Franklin, the Federals "had no food but that which was carried in their haversacks, and the hot weather soon rendered that uneatable. Sleep was out of the question, and the only rest obtained was while lying down awaiting an attack, or sheltering themselves from shot and shell. They had been soldiers for less than a year, yet their conduct could not have been more soldierly had they seen ten years of service."

The aftermath

The Battle of Malvern Hill ended the fighting around Richmond that became known as the Seven Days. The Army of the Potomac reached the safety of Harrison's Landing which by then had been strongly fortified. Lee chose not to commit his troops to further bloodshed. They had fought with great courage, but now the Federal position was too formidable.

Lee's losses of 20,141 from an estimated strength of 80,000 to 90,000 men were greater than McClellan's 15,849 from a total of 105,445 men present on June 20. But Lee had raised the siege of Richmond, forced a stronger, better-equipped army than his own to retreat, and ruined McClellan's Peninsula Campaign: President Lincoln, impatient with McClellan's apparent lack of initiative, soon ordered Little Mac to evacuate the Virginia Peninsula.

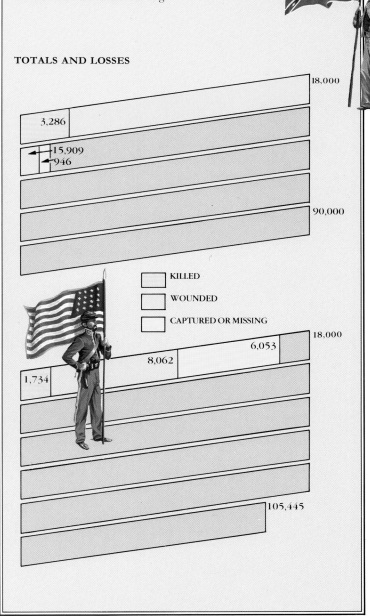

TOTALS AND LOSSES

18,000

3,286

15,909
946

90,000

KILLED

WOUNDED

CAPTURED OR MISSING

18,000

6,053

8,062

1,734

105,445

Second Bull Run

"Evidently Pope supposed that I was gone, as he was ignoring me entirely.
His whole army seemed to surge up against Jackson as if to crush him. . . ."

LIEUTENANT GENERAL JAMES LONGSTREET, CSA, after the battle

WHILE THE BATTLE of the Seven Days was being fought around Richmond, the Lincoln administration began to assemble a new striking force from units stationed around Washington and in the Shenandoah Valley. This was, in effect, a vote of no confidence in Major General George B. McClellan's Peninsula Campaign.

The Army of Virginia, as this Union force was called, initially numbered 40,000 men. It was placed under the command of Major General John Pope, who had led the Army of the Mississippi in the western theater with considerable success. Pope immediately made himself unpopular with his troops when, in an ill-judged address to his new army, he stated:

"I have come from the West where we have always seen the backs of our enemies."

He also introduced harsh measures, even more stringent than martial law, against civilians living in Union-occupied northern Virginia.

Pope then boasted to influential people in Washington, including Lincoln, that, if he had McClellan's army as well, he could defeat Lee and capture Richmond. Gullible politicians, hungry for a great Union victory, believed him; so did Major General Henry W. Halleck, newly transferred from overall command in the west to be general in chief of US land forces.

While the Federal hierarchy considered abandoning McClellan's operations in favor of an overland attack on Richmond, from the north, Pope became impatient, and he began to move on the Confederates on July 12. Lee guessed that McClellan would soon be recalled and, therefore, did not present a threat, so he sent Major General Thomas J. "Stonewall" Jackson north with 11,000 men to hinder Pope.

Meanwhile, Lee and the rest of his army watched "Little Mac" McClellan.

Lee was waiting to see whether or not McClellan would be ordered north from Harrison's Landing to join up with Pope. Since McClellan showed no sign of moving, Lee sent more and more troops to Jackson, who, within a few weeks, mustered a corps of 24,000. Eventually, on August 3, Halleck ordered McClellan to join Pope.

Lee realized that he had to gamble on leaving only a skeleton force in the

Richmond lines, while he moved north with Longstreet's corps of 28,000 men. They needed to unite with Jackson and bring Pope to battle before the latter could be reinforced by McClellan and the Army of the Potomac; everything depended on perfect timing.

On August 9, Jackson met Pope's leading corps at Cedar Mountain, defeated it, and obliged Pope to regroup and bring up reinforcements from a position behind the Rapidan River. Lee wasted this opportunity to cross the Rapidan and intercept the Federals as they retired. In the interim, Pope learned of Lee's presence and moved to the less vulnerable north bank of the Rappahannock River.

Union reinforcements were now beginning to arrive from McClellan, so Lee put into action a plan to maneuver Pope out of his strong position, cut his railroad supply line from Washington and Alexandria, and attack him on a field of his own choosing. Lee audaciously divided his army in the face of an enemy now more than 70,000 strong. On August 25, Jackson started out on a flank march northward to position himself in the rear of Pope and cut his lines of communication, while Lee and Longstreet remained on the Rappahannock. Lee believed that Pope would chase Jackson, whom he would then join with the remainder of the Army of Northern Virginia.

Pope knew that Jackson was on the move, but he dismissed this as a raid into the Shenandoah Valley and devoted all his attention to Longstreet. By this time, Jackson had force-marched his men on a looping route north. They crossed the headwaters of the Rappahannock, proceeded west of the Bull Run Mountains and through Thoroughfare Gap which brought them out onto the Manassas plain on August 26. By nightfall they were

JOHN POPE (1822–92)

THOMAS JONATHAN "STONEWALL" JACKSON
(1824–63)

Pope, the commander of the Army of Virginia at Second Bull Run, was a professional soldier all his life, and gained a reputation among his troops for insensitivity and bullying. A native of Kentucky, he left West Point in 1842, joined the topographical department of the Corps of Engineers, and took part in surveying assignments, until seeing active service in the Mexican War.

At the start of the Civil War, Captain Pope became a brigadier general of US Volunteers and served in Missouri as a district and divisional commander. He was given command of the army of the Mississippi in February, 1862, and came to notice for his service in actions at New Madrid, Island No. 10, and Corinth.

Promoted to major general in March, 1862, Pope was President Lincoln's personal choice to lead the new Federal Army of Virginia, which began forming in June. However, Pope's tactless and condescending address to his new troops on July 14 upset them; and the draconian treatment that he prescribed for enemy civilians earned him the hatred of Southern soldiers.

Pope, who had boasted that he had always seen the backs of the enemy, was beaten by Lee in his first big battle, Second Bull Run. Although relieved of his command on September 2, Pope stayed on the active list, and commanded the Department of the Northwest for most of the rest of the war.

A devout Presbyterian, Jackson became revered in the South, and feared in the North, for his dynamism and leadership. A graduate of West Point, Jackson was born at Clarksburg, Virginia, and became a brevet major in the US 1st Artillery after fighting in the Mexican War.

Later, Jackson left the army and became professor of philosophy and artillery tactics at the Virginia Military Institute, Lexington, until the outbreak of the Civil War, when he joined the Rebel cause. As a brigadier general at First Bull Run, he won the nickname "Stonewall" for his steadfastness.

The next year, Jackson's daring and clever tactics gained him fame in the Shenandoah Valley, when his outnumbered, fast-moving "foot cavalry" defeated the Federals five times. General Robert E. Lee then called on Jackson to assist him in the battles of the Seven Days. Although Jackson did not perform well, Lee retained his faith in him and in July sent him north to operate against a new threat from General Pope's Army of Virginia. When Lee joined him later with the rest of the Rebel army, the two generals formed a close and brilliant association. Their combined prowess shone at Second Bull Run, Antietam, Fredericksburg and—last and most brilliantly—at Chancellorsville, where Jackson, now a lieutenant general, was mortally wounded by his own troops. He died on May 10, 1863.

In the early afternoon of August 29, Major General Stonewall Jackson's Rebel line was positioned along an unfinished railroad track, with his left flank resting on Bull Run stream. Although outnumbered by three to one, the Rebels managed to repel the piecemeal assault made by Major General John Pope's Federals. The gallant stand by Jackson's corps preoccupied Pope and allowed Major General Longstreet's 25,000 men—the rest of General Robert E. Lee's Army of Northern Virginia— to fall into position, unmolested, on Jackson's right.

On August 30, a hot summer's day, Pope renewed his attempt to smash Jackson's line. He concentrated all his forces on his right wing, ignoring reports that Longstreet was now in the area. By 4 p.m., Jackson, unable to fight off the Federals any longer, appealed to Lee for help: Longstreet immediately brought his guns into action, and, within 15 minutes, reversed the course of the battle.

The battlefield

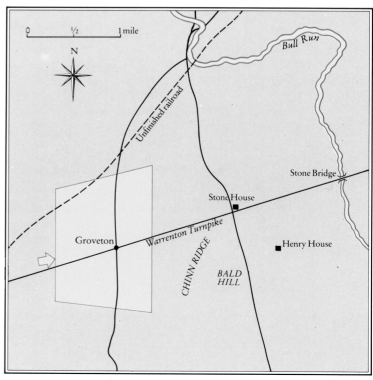

Since 1 p.m. on the 30th, the Federals (2) had advanced beyond Groveton (4) and repeatedly charged at Jackson's tiring men. When Longstreet's powerful artillery barrage (7), north of the Warrenton Turnpike (6), began, the Federals at first withstood the enfilading fire, and re-formed three times. However, they finally began to retreat as the Rebel cannonade tore huge gaps in their dense lines.

For almost two days Jackson's corps had fought from behind the protective embankment (1) of an unfinished railroad. In a single, two-mile line, about three ranks deep, they had fought off repeated Union assaults.

By the afternoon of the 30th, Jackson's infantrymen had used most of their ammunition—with some units resorting to hurling rocks at the oncoming Federals. Only timely artillery support from Longstreet prevented Jackson from being overrun.

About 15 minutes after the start of the Rebel enfilade, Longstreet ordered his entire infantry corps (5) of 25,000 men into an all-out attack.

When Longstreet's assault began, Pope was taken by surprise. Thinking that there were no Rebels in that area, Pope had moved troops north against Jackson's line; now, he was unable to send much help to his exposed left wing. Although they met some resistance, the Rebels eventually rolled back the Union flank. The Federal 5th New York Zouaves on the Union far left stood firm against the Rebel charge, and sustained the highest fatalities of any infantry regiment in the war. One Zouave described the horror of the battle there: "Where the regiment stood that day was the very vortex of Hell."

As Longstreet crushed the left of the Federal three-mile line, Jackson's men emerged from the railroad entrenchment to attack the Federal right. However, exhausted by the two days' fighting, Jackson was unable to cut off the Union retreat.

During the course of the battle only 20,000 of Pope's total force of about 60,000 men took part in the fighting. The rest remained in the woods (3) and hills to the east.

astride the Orange & Alexandria Railroad, the Union's main supply route, only seven miles from Manassas Junction, a huge depot which Major General J.E.B. Stuart was sent to capture with his cavalry.

Next morning, most of Jackson's command arrived at Manassas Junction and, for a few hours, the starving, ragged Confederates were allowed to clothe and feed themselves at Federal expense. Because he had no transport with him, Jackson had no alternative but to destroy anything that his men could not carry away.

Pope, who had been slow to appreciate that Jackson was operating in his rear, finally took Lee's bait and moved away from the Rappahannock, issuing orders to surround the Confederates at Manassas Junction. Lee and Longstreet left just one division on the south bank of the river, then set off in the footsteps of Jackson's march, with the intention of joining their comrades as quickly as possible.

When Pope's scattered corps converged on Manassas Junction on August 28, they were bewildered to find no Confederates there, nor to the east or west. In fact, Jackson had moved farther north, which placed him in a powerful position just eight miles east of Thoroughfare Gap, where Lee and Longstreet would join him.

That evening, in a deliberate diversion to attract Pope's attention, Jackson attacked Brigadier General Rufus King's division as it marched eastward along the Warrenton Turnpike. A sharp action ensued until nightfall. Pope, as Jackson expected, ordered his troops to gather at the village of Groveton in the morning to move against the Confederates. The latter

were ensconced close by—and behind an unfinished railroad grade. This spurred north from the Manassas Gap Railroad toward Sudley Springs, on the edge of the previous year's Bull Run battlefield.

Jackson's demonstration proved invaluable to the other half of the Army of Northern Virginia. Thoroughfare Gap had been blocked by the Federals which jeopardized Lee's plan. But Pope called in all units for the attack on Jackson, and thus left the way clear for the reunification of the Rebel forces.

Pope, fearful that Jackson might evade him again, pushed forward his skirmish lines just after dawn on the 29th. But even though he was outnumbered, Jackson waited for the rest of the Confederate army which the Union commander appeared to have forgotten about. Pope then launched his main assault against Jackson's front, but Major General Fitz-John Porter's corps from the Army of the Potomac failed to attack the right flank. Dust raised by J.E.B. Stuart's horsemen had duped Porter into thinking that overwhelming Rebel forces were marching toward him. This enabled Longstreet's corps to file unmolested into position on Jackson's right. Pope was furious with Porter, whom he subsequently had court-martialed for his failure to fight.

From early morning until late afternoon, Jackson's corps courageously warded off assault after assault. Severe fighting developed along most of his front, and the railroad cuts and fills were crammed with casualties, as were the woods in front of, and behind, them. Pope showed a callous streak when he ordered his artillery to fire into the trees, where it was known that wounded from

Major General Stonewall Jackson's hungry troops, having marched 56 miles in two days, eagerly pillage the Union supply depot at Manassas Junction on August 27, two days before the battle.

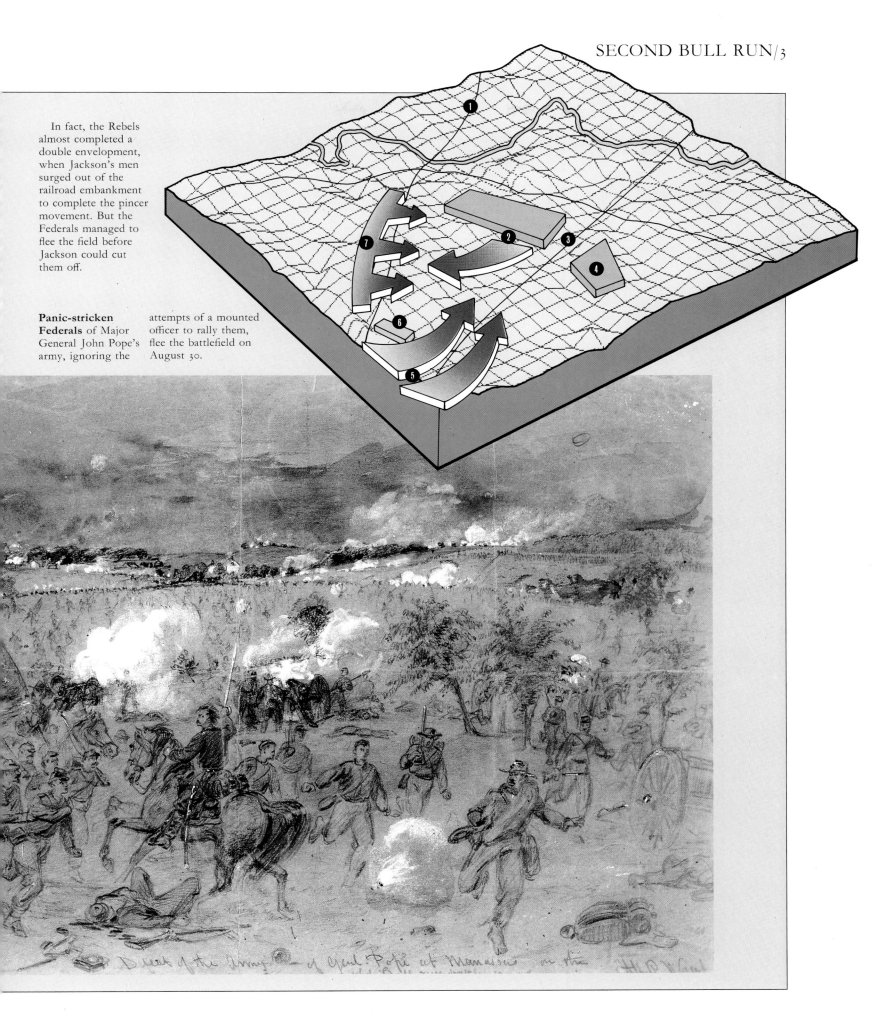

In fact, the Rebels almost completed a double envelopment, when Jackson's men surged out of the railroad embankment to complete the pincer movement. But the Federals managed to flee the field before Jackson could cut them off.

Panic-stricken Federals of Major General John Pope's army, ignoring the attempts of a mounted officer to rally them, flee the battlefield on August 30.

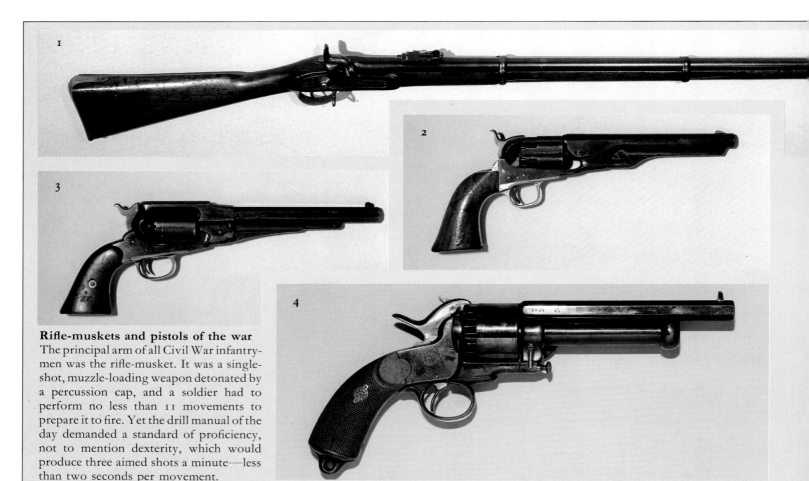

Rifle-muskets and pistols of the war

The principal arm of all Civil War infantry-men was the rifle-musket. It was a single-shot, muzzle-loading weapon detonated by a percussion cap, and a soldier had to perform no less than 11 movements to prepare it to fire. Yet the drill manual of the day demanded a standard of proficiency, not to mention dexterity, which would produce three aimed shots a minute—less than two seconds per movement.

Two rifle-muskets were most commonly used by both Union and Confederate infantry regiments: the US Springfield, Model 1861, which was captured by the South in large numbers on battlefields early in the war, and the British Enfield, Model 1853, which was imported by the governments in both Richmond and Washington.

As well as Enfields and Springfields, many different types of long-arms were to be seen in service. In the early part of the war, there were not enough weapons in America to arm the fast-growing armies of the Union and the Confederacy. Agents of both governments were dispatched to scour Europe for whatever weapons they could buy. Although they returned with some good rifle-muskets, notably the Austrian Lorenz, many of their newly acquired

arms represented the obsolete stock of arsenals from Russia to Italy. They were heavy, badly made, and came in a variety of non-standard calibers. The Union alone issued 79 different models to its troops.

Thousands of old-fashioned smooth-bore muskets, and even flintlocks, were also pressed into service in 1861. Three years later, Federal regiments could be found that were still armed with short-range smoothbore weapons, which were no match against rifle-muskets, and virtually useless in the face of troops armed with breechloading or repeating rifles.

Pistols of all shapes, sizes, makes, and calibers were carried by soldiers of both sides during the war, but the Army models produced by the Colt and Remington companies were by far the most popular.

The South had an extremely limited capacity for manufacturing small arms, although several small gunsmiths managed to produce copies of the Colt, or variations of it. On occasion they even resorted to using melted-down church bells to provide brass for the mountings. Such was the dearth of pistols in the Confederacy at the outbreak of war that units could be found armed with single-shot flintlock weapons of 1816 vintage.

One of the most formidable handguns of the war, the LeMat, was designed by a Confederate. Colonel Jean LeMat of Louisiana produced a hefty 9-shot cap and ball revolver in .40 caliber, the cylinder of which rotated around a second barrel containing a 16-gauge charge of buckshot. The LeMat was made in France.

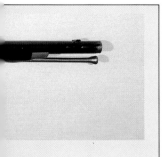

The US Springfield, Model 1861, a refinement of the M1855 **(5)**, was made at the United States armory of that name. It weighed $9\frac{3}{4}$ pounds and fired a .58 caliber conical bullet. Its range was slightly under 1,000 yards.

The British Enfield, Model 1853 **(1)** weighed 8 pounds $14\frac{1}{2}$ ounces. Its caliber was .577 and it was sighted to 1,100 yards.

The Colt New Army pistol (2) was a 6-shot cap and ball revolver in .44 caliber. This 8-inch round barreled pistol weighed 2 pounds 9 ounces and was accurate up to 50 yards.

The Remington New Army **(3)** was a .44 caliber, 6-shot revolver. It was 3 ounces heavier than the Colt and shared the same effective range.

The LeMat **(4)** had a two-position hammer requiring only a deft finger movement to switch from .40 caliber fire through the top barrel to the discharge of the "shotgun" barrel beneath it.

The aftermath

General Robert E. Lee's rout of the Federal Army of Virginia at Second Bull Run, or Second Manassas, as the South named it, was a severe setback for the Union. Lee's Army of Northern Virginia had exhibited excellent teamwork in the execution of a brilliant plan. But, from a total of, at most, 54,000 men they had lost 9,474 in all. In the short campaign, the discredited Pope suffered 14,462 casualties from at least 63,000 men.

Lee knew that a follow up attack on Washington was out of the question: it was far too strongly held. However, he decided it would make sense to carry the war into the North and invade Maryland, a border state which many Southerners thought would come over to the Confederacy if their forces were on its soil. On September 5–6, they were, and the Union dreaded to think what the outcome might be.

TOTALS AND LOSSES

10,000

7,812
109

1,553

54,000

☐ KILLED

☐ WOUNDED

☐ CAPTURED OR MISSING

10,000

8,452

1,747

4,263

63,000

both sides were sheltering, in case the Confederates were forming there. He later claimed that he did so in order to save thousands who were as yet un-wounded.

As the last furious assault died away, Jackson did not move from his position behind the railroad cut. But Pope thought he had won the fight and told his officers that he expected the Rebels to retreat during the night. Inexplicably, he completely failed to take account of Longstreet's uncommitted corps.

Next day, which was extremely hot, the Union army was camped on the old Bull Run battlefield. Pope made a reconnaissance of the Rebel lines and mistook realignment going on among some Confederate regiments for the start of a withdrawal. At midday, he ordered a general pursuit of Jackson, which was to be pressed until the Rebel line broke.

The Federals fell mainly upon the right flank of Jackson's corps, which was reduced to a single line and had little ammunition. Desperate fighting took place along the railroad grade and Lee allowed Pope's men to exhaust themselves in repeated attacks against Jackson's volleys. But once some of Jackson's units were reduced to throwing rocks at the Federals for want of cartridges, the odds grew too much—even for Jackson.

Longstreet's corps was lying nearly at a right angle to Jackson; a gap at the apex was filled with artillery. These guns now opened fire on the massed Federal ranks passing across their front, tearing great gaps in them. Several times the Union regiments closed up and crowded forward again until about 4 p.m., when Lee saw the Federal assault wavering. He then released Longstreet's three-deep battle line of fresh troops in a headlong charge which crumpled the Union left flank. Jackson's exhausted men moved forward in concert and together Lee's two corps drove the Federals from the field.

Pope's battered army fell back across the old Bull Run battlefield and a sharp rearguard action was fought on the plateau of Henry House Hill. This bought time to get most of the forces safely across Bull Run stream and on their way to Centreville, six miles up the road to Washington, where they halted for the night. There the defeated troops were reinforced by two more corps from McClellan's army. After more fighting on September 1 at Chantilly, the Union army fell back to the safety of the Washington defenses. There, McClellan was waiting to take command, reckoning that Lee would not attack such a strongly held city.

Antietam

=== SEPTEMBER 17, 1862 ===

*"Here is a paper with which if I cannot whip Bobbie Lee,
I will be willing to go home."*

MAJOR GENERAL GEORGE B. McCLELLAN, USA

AT THE BEGINNING of September 1862, General Robert E. Lee, whose victory at Second Bull Run had caused the Federals to leave Virginia, proposed that the Confederacy should abandon its policy of fighting only to protect its own soil. With the approval of President Jefferson Davis, Lee resolved to carry the war into the North, and quickly.

An invasion of Maryland seemed to offer the best option. Many Marylanders were already in the Rebel ranks, and the presence of a Southern army in that border state might be enough to bring it into the secession fold. Also, a victory in Union territory might well prompt the North, whose morale was at a low ebb, to offer peace overtures; and it might bring much-desired European recognition of the Confederacy. There was a logistical attraction, too: Lee's straitened commissariat would find it easier to raise food supplies in an area untouched by hard campaigning.

And so, on September 5, the dirty, ragged, hungry, but supremely confident Army of Northern Virginia splashed across the Potomac River fords above Leesburg to the strains of "Maryland, My Maryland" blared out by regimental bands. By September 7, the Confederates had gathered at Frederick. Here, Lee issued a proclamation to the people of Maryland, inviting them to espouse the Southern cause. He waited for a few days, but the Marylanders gave the Rebels a cool reception.

While Lee lingered at Frederick, he discovered that a large Federal garrison was occupying nearby Harpers Ferry, at the confluence of the Potomac and Shenandoah Rivers. Lee decided that this force would have to be neutralized, otherwise it would pose a serious threat to his lines of communication when he moved his army

deeper into Northern territory.

Because of the drubbing he had given General John Pope's Army of Virginia at Second Bull Run, Lee believed he was reasonably safe from Union pursuit for a while. He therefore divided his force of about 45,000 men: his Special Orders No. 191 detached Major General Stonewall Jackson with three columns to invest Harpers Ferry to the southeast; set Major General James Longstreet's corps on the

road over South Mountain, lying to the west of Frederick, to Boonsboro to the northwest; and charged Major General D.H. Hill's division with protecting the wagon and artillery trains.

Lee, however, had underestimated Major General George B. McClellan's organizing ability. With General Pope in eclipse, Little Mac—as McClellan was popularly known—had taken charge of the dislocated formations falling back on Washington. Within a few days, he had disbanded the short-lived Army of Virginia, incorporating its three corps into the Army of the Potomac, now nearly 90,000 strong, and was ready to take the field again. On September 8, McClellan, who had not officially been given operational command of the army, moved his men northwest toward the Confederates.

After a cautious advance, the Federal vanguard arrived at Frederick late on the 12th, just in time to skirmish with Lee's rear guard. Next day, McClellan had a real stroke of luck. A copy of Lee's Special Orders No. 191 was found wrapped around three cigars by a Union private in an abandoned Confederate campsite.

The orders soon reached a delighted McClellan who exclaimed:

"Here is a paper with which if I cannot whip Bobbie Lee, I will be willing to go home."

For once Little Mac abandoned the caution he normally adopted when in proximity to the enemy. Off went his cavalry to probe the South Mountain passes; preparations were made to send a relief column to Harpers Ferry and advance the rest of the army to a position between Lee's divided forces. It seemed as if the Army of Northern Virginia was about to be defeated in detail.

When, however, the battle for the South Mountain gaps began on the 14th,

AMBROSE POWELL HILL (1825–65)

It was A.P. Hill's timely arrival during the Battle of Antietam that saved the day for the Army of Northern Virginia. General Robert E. Lee told President Jefferson Davis after the battle that, Generals James Longstreet and Thomas J. Jackson excepted: "I consider General A.P. Hill the best commander with me. He fights his troops well and takes good care of them."

Hill graduated from West Point in 1847. He was commissioned into the US Artillery and served in Mexico in 1848—the last year of the war there. From then until the outbreak of the Civil War in 1861, he spent much of his time in garrison duty, with spells of active service in the Third Seminole War and on the frontier.

Promotion was slow in what became known as the "Old Army," and when Hill decided to offer his sword to his native state of Virginia in 1861, he did so as a first lieutenant. He was made colonel of the 13th Virginia, and served in the western part of the state before the first big battle of the war, First Bull Run, where his regiment was held in reserve.

In February, 1862, Hill was promoted to brigadier general in the Confederate army. He handled his brigade well in the early stages of the Peninsula Campaign, and within three months he was elevated to the rank of major general and given a division.

Hill excelled as a divisional commander, a position he held for a year. Between May, 1862, and May, 1863, his command, known as the Light Division for its prowess at rapid marching, was in the forefront of most of the big battles in the east, being led into action by Hill himself, resplendent in a red flannel "battle shirt."

After Stonewall Jackson was mortally wounded at Chancellorsville, in May, 1863, Hill, who was also wounded in that battle, was promoted to lieutenant general by Lee, and given command of the III Corps in his reorganized Army of Northern Virginia.

Hill, who suffered from ill health, seemed to find the responsibility of commanding a corps too much for him, and was often on the sick list. He was killed on April 2, 1865, at Petersburg.

General Robert E. Lee issued this proclamation to the people of Maryland in the hope that they might rally to the Southern cause. "It is for you to decide your destiny, freely and without constraint," Lee wrote. The Marylanders did just this, but overwhelmingly rejected Lee's invitation to ally themselves with the South.

The town of Harpers Ferry nestles below Maryland Heights, from where Federal soldiers survey the panoramic view.

Because Harpers Ferry, with its Union garrison, would prove a threat to Lee's line of communications as he advanced northward, the Rebel commander detached three columns under Stonewall Jackson to capture the town.

With the Rebels making effective use of their artillery, positioned on the surrounding heights, it was not long before the Federal garrison surrendered.

On September 15, more than 12,000 Federals were taken prisoner. Then, leaving Major General A.P. Hill to attend to the details of the surrender, Jackson himself set off with two divisions to join Lee at Sharpsburg.

McClellan's caution returned. As always, he overestimated enemy strength, believing that D.H. Hill had been reinforced by Longstreet's corps from nearby Boonsboro, where the captured orders placed him. It was not so. Longstreet had been 13 miles farther north, at Hagerstown near the Pennsylvania border, and was now hurrying back at Lee's insistence; but it would be late in the day before he could help Hill. Even then, only eight of his brigades went into the line.

By nightfall, the Confederate position on South Mountain had become untenable, but McClellan's hesitancy had bought Lee enough time to organize the concentration of his forces at Sharpsburg, six miles to the west, and close to a Potomac ford. On the morning of the 15th, Longstreet's corps, D.H. Hill's division, J.E.B. Stuart's cavalry, and the artillery were occupying rising ground west of Antietam Creek and awaiting the arrival of Jackson from Harpers Ferry.

Several hours before the leading elements of McClellan's army began to appear east of the Antietam, Lee learned that Harpers Ferry had only just surrendered; that meant the other half of his force would not be joining him that day. But, knowing how much his chief needed him, the redoubtable Jackson set off with part of his command on a night march;

two divisions were to start for Sharpsburg first thing on the 16th; and A.P. Hill's division was to follow as quickly as it could after tidying up the details of the Harpers Ferry capitulation, which included more than 11,000 prisoners, 13,000 small-arms, and 73 cannon.

Fortunately for Lee, Little Mac was taking his time. There was no fighting on the 15th, and the 16th passed with only long-range artillery dueling and some sharp skirmishing as General Joseph Hooker, on the right of the Union line, moved his I Corps across the Antietam and encountered Confederate pickets. But, as darkness descended, both sides knew that the next day would bring a great battle.

At dawn on September 17, about 30,000 men of the Army of Northern Virginia, excluding A.P. Hill's division, lined a three-mile front: Longstreet's corps and D.H. Hill's division held the right and center respectively, with most of the artillery; the left was the responsibility of Jackson's corps and Stuart's cavalry and horse artillery.

Opposing them, McClellan had five corps—about 60,000 men—and another corps was expected later that morning. He also possessed 49 batteries of artillery, which included many pieces of heavier calibers than those of the Rebels. His

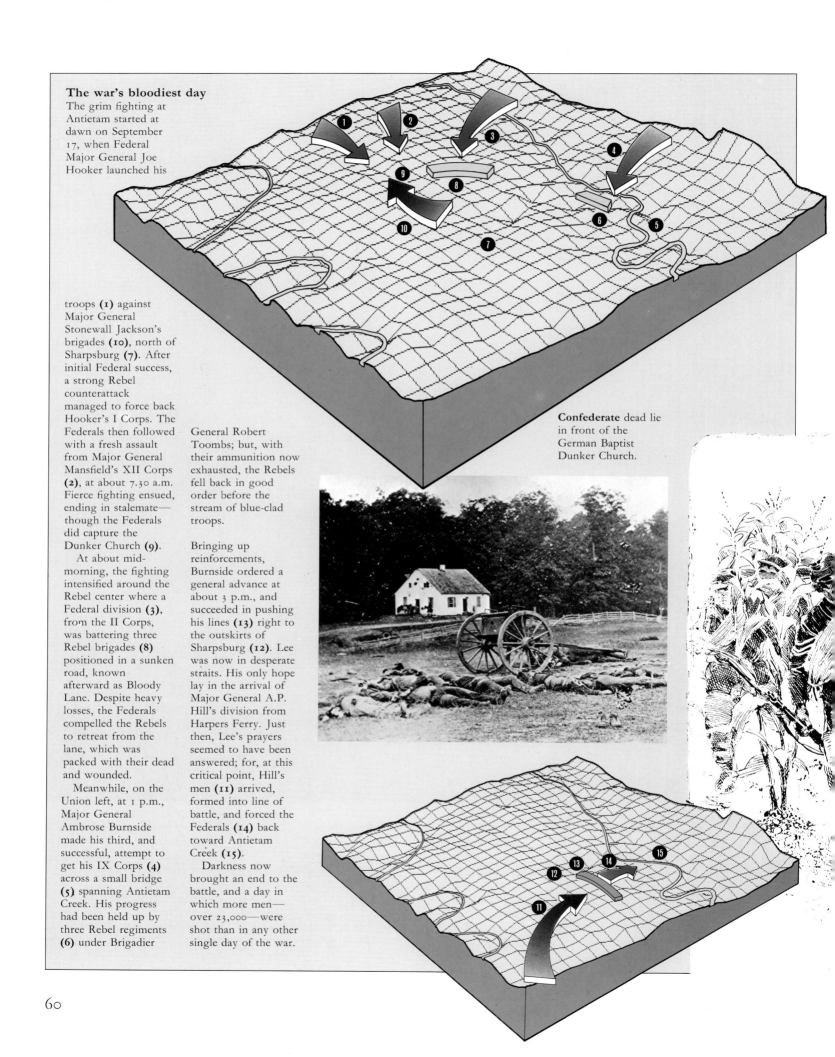

The war's bloodiest day

The grim fighting at Antietam started at dawn on September 17, when Federal Major General Joe Hooker launched his troops (1) against Major General Stonewall Jackson's brigades (10), north of Sharpsburg (7). After initial Federal success, a strong Rebel counterattack managed to force back Hooker's I Corps. The Federals then followed with a fresh assault from Major General Mansfield's XII Corps (2), at about 7.30 a.m. Fierce fighting ensued, ending in stalemate—though the Federals did capture the Dunker Church (9).

At about mid-morning, the fighting intensified around the Rebel center where a Federal division (3), from the II Corps, was battering three Rebel brigades (8) positioned in a sunken road, known afterward as Bloody Lane. Despite heavy losses, the Federals compelled the Rebels to retreat from the lane, which was packed with their dead and wounded.

Meanwhile, on the Union left, at 1 p.m., Major General Ambrose Burnside made his third, and successful, attempt to get his IX Corps (4) across a small bridge (5) spanning Antietam Creek. His progress had been held up by three Rebel regiments (6) under Brigadier General Robert Toombs; but, with their ammunition now exhausted, the Rebels fell back in good order before the stream of blue-clad troops.

Bringing up reinforcements, Burnside ordered a general advance at about 3 p.m., and succeeded in pushing his lines (13) right to the outskirts of Sharpsburg (12). Lee was now in desperate straits. His only hope lay in the arrival of Major General A.P. Hill's division from Harpers Ferry. Just then, Lee's prayers seemed to have been answered; for, at this critical point, Hill's men (11) arrived, formed into line of battle, and forced the Federals (14) back toward Antietam Creek (15).

Darkness now brought an end to the battle, and a day in which more men— over 23,000—were shot than in any other single day of the war.

Confederate dead lie in front of the German Baptist Dunker Church.

dispositions comprised Hooker's I Corps and the XII Corps, under Major General Joseph F.K. Mansfield, on the right, holding ground on the west side of the Antietam and to the north of Sharpsburg; Major General Edwin V. Sumner's II Corps (later to be reinforced by Major General William Franklin's VII Corps) in the center, still on the east bank; and Major General Ambrose Burnside's IX Corps forming the left to the east of a bridge over the creek, a mile southeast of Sharpsburg and closely guarded by the Rebels. Major General Fitz-John Porter's V Corps lay in reserve.

What McClellan intended to do is set out in his preliminary report of the ensuing action:

"The design was to make the main attack upon the enemy's left—at least to create a diversion in favor of the main attack, with the hope of something more, by assailing the enemy's right—and, as soon as one or both of the flank movements were fully successful, to attack their center with any reserve I might then have in hand."

Cannonading began at first light. Soon, the first real fighting of the battle began on the Confederate left around the woods and fields just north of Sharpsburg when, at about 6 a.m., Hooker unleashed his infantry. Leaving the shelter of the North Woods and the undulating ground to the east, the Federals dashed through a large cornfield between another two forested areas, known as the East and West Woods, with the object of taking the high ground, crowned by the German Baptist Dunker Church, to their front.

The charging Federals were met and checked by the divisions of both Brigadier General A.R. Lawton and Brigadier General J.R. Jones, who later counterattacked and were savaged by fresh I Corps units. Jackson then sent in Brigadier General John B. Hood's understrength division, which chased the Union infantry right back to their gun line, suffering heavy casualties in the process.

As Hood's Confederates retired and the Union I Corps was left reeling, Mansfield's XII Corps came up and occupied the East Woods. Jackson quickly called in three of D.H. Hill's brigades from the center to ward off the threat from the fresh Union corps, whose commander was fatally wounded before their part of the battle had properly begun. For the next hour and a half, Hill's and Hood's men grappled with most of the XII Corps in the fields between the East and West

Federals of Major General Joseph Hooker's I Corps encounter fierce Confederate fire as they charge through the cornfield between East and West Woods, during the morning of the battle. Hooker's men were eventually pushed back to their gun line by General John B. Hood's Rebel division.

THE STORMING OF "BURNSIDE'S BRIDGE"

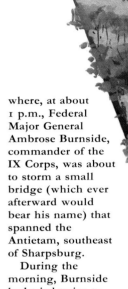

During the morning of September 17, Major General George McClellan, commanding the Army of the Potomac, hurled his troops against Rebel General Robert E. Lee's Army of Northern Virginia, positioned around the town of Sharpsburg.

First, Federal Major General Joe Hooker, the I Corps commander, tried, but failed, to break the Rebel left.

Then, during the middle of the morning, desperate fighting took place between Rebels positioned in a sunken farm lane, and two divisions from Major General Edwin V. Sumner's II Corps. Sumner's men eventually drove the Rebels out of what became known afterward as Bloody Lane.

The scene of the fighting now shifted to the Union left,

where, at about 1 p.m., Federal Major General Ambrose Burnside, commander of the IX Corps, was about to storm a small bridge (which ever afterward would bear his name) that spanned the Antietam, southeast of Sharpsburg.

During the morning, Burnside had tried twice to get his troops across the creek, but had been frustrated by a small force of Rebels, under Brigadier General Robert Toombs, on the west bank of the Antietam. Burnside was now determined to succeed at the third attempt.

The battlefield

For three hours, Toombs's 550 men from three Georgia regiments had stalled the advance of some 11,000 Federals.

Just before 1 p.m., Toombs realized that his troops could not stop a third Union assault on the bridge. The fact that the Georgians had accomplished as much

as they had was largely due to their position on a 100-foot-high bluff commanding the bridge. Here, taking shelter behind trees and boulders, the Confederate infantry and sharpshooters had delivered an accurate and withering fire on any approaching Federal troops. As a

result, despite the support of a battery of 20-pounders (3), two previous Federal assaults had collapsed.

But now, with ammunition running low, and the Federals again advancing toward the bridge, Toombs ordered the Georgians (5) to retire to a position half a mile in the rear.

The Federal regiments chosen to spearhead the third assault were the 51st New York and the 51st Pennsylvania, under the command of Colonel Edward Ferrero. The two regiments formed side by side and advanced toward the bridge, intending to cross it four abreast.

However, the Rebel rifle fire broke up their formation as they approached, and the Federals were forced to take shelter as best they could.

But, as the Rebel fire began to diminish just before 1 p.m., the Federals, following the lead of a captain, suddenly rushed across the bridge **(4)** in a great surge of blue. As they reached the other side, the troops streamed off to the right and left.

Burnside had at last gotten his men across the creek; but he had suffered more than 500 casualties, compared with only 160 Rebel losses.

With the bridge secured, Burnside used up two precious hours in crossing the entire IX Corps, and in replenishing ammunition. It was 3 p.m. before he ordered an advance against the Rebel right, comprising Brigadier General D.R. Jones's division. Lee had previously stripped his right wing to bolster his left. So Burnside, had he known it, faced only about 2,500 Rebels, positioned south of Sharpsburg **(1)** and the Rebel batteries **(2)** on Cemetery Hill.

With a great superiority in numbers, Burnside's troops pushed back the Rebels to the very outskirts of Sharpsburg. But, at this critical moment, Confederate Major General A.P. Hill's division arrived from Harpers Ferry, stopped the Federals in their tracks, and then pushed them back to the Antietam, bringing the battle to a close.

Confederate dead lie in the sunken road, afterward known as Bloody Lane, where some of the fiercest fighting at Antietam took place. Alexander Gardner's photograph was one of a number displayed by Mathew Brady in his New York gallery, in October, 1862, which brought home to a shocked public the harsh realities of war.

"He [President Lincoln] told me that he was satisfied with all that I had done, that he would stand by me. He parted from me with utmost cordiality."

So reported Major General George B. McClellan, pictured (*below*) on President Lincoln's right, after the president's visit to Little Mac's Antietam headquarters two weeks after the battle. But Lincoln was far from satisfied with McClellan's apparent reluctance to follow Lee and his Rebel army into Virginia, and drily told a companion that the Army of the Potomac was "only McClellan's bodyguard."

Shortly after his return to the White House, Lincoln sent McClellan an order "to cross the Potomac and give battle to the enemy or drive him south."

woods, fighting each other to a standstill.

About 20 minutes passed without the crash of musketry, during which time reinforcements from the II Corps, sent across Antietam Creek by Major General Sumner, were negotiating the East Woods. Major General John Sedgwick's division of the II Corps deployed in line of battle, then advanced across the battle-scarred fields toward the West Woods: the Federals were expecting weak and demoralized opponents. The absence of opposition, as they gained the trees, heightened this belief.

What they did not realize was that the brigade of the Confederate Brigadier General Jubal Early was lying in front of them, and strong reinforcements from the divisions of Generals Lafayette McLaws and John G. Walker, plus Brigadier General G.B. Anderson's brigade, were marching up on their left flank. The Federals were surprised as the Confederate volleys caught them in enfilade. In less than 20 minutes, Sedgwick lost nearly half of his division, and the rest went streaming back the way they had come.

The worst of the fighting was now over on the Confederate left. Fierce combat, however, continued unabated in the center, where one of Sumner's II Corps divisions under Brigadier General William French had begun attacking three of D.H. Hill's brigades around 10 a.m. The Rebels occupied a strong position in a natural trench formed by a sunken farm track. As the exchanges of fire grew in intensity, two more divisions took the field here, one Union, under Major General Israel Richardson, and one Rebel, under Major General Richard Anderson.

The violent struggle lasted until 12.30 p.m., when the Federals managed to get astride the track, enfilade the Confederates, and render their position untenable. The Rebels fell back unopposed to a new line 600 yards away, leaving a track packed with dead and wounded, which ever after would be known as Bloody Lane. Union losses, too, had been high.

About this time, Major General Burnside succeeded on his third attempt to cross the bridge in front of the Rebel right, now in a weakened state after units had been siphoned off to support Jackson on the left. In an epic defense, three Confederate regiments had seriously delayed the advance of a Union corps over the bridge for three hours.

Now was McClellan's chance to attack the Rebel center, split the shattered Rebel army and score a decisive victory. He had the men—two fresh corps and all his cavalry—and, for a while, he had the

Under the headline "The Great Victory," *The New-York Times* (*top* and *inset*), September 21, 1862, gives an account of the Battle of Antietam calculated to fuel Northern patriotism.

The September 23 issue of the South's Richmond *Enquirer* (*left*), also claims victory—but for the Confederacy. It also comments acidly that the "reports in the Northern newspapers prove to have been sheer and shameless fabrications. . . ."

intention, but caution overruled him. He would not—could not—bring himself to commit everything he had against an opponent of Lee's caliber.

Fighting on Jackson's and D.H. Hill's fronts was now over for the rest of the day, but Longstreet, on the Confederate right, was under threat. Having carried the bridge at 1 p.m. after prolonged battling, Burnside did not, however, push straight on to attack the thinly held Rebel line on rising ground south of Sharpsburg. Two precious hours or more were wasted in replenishing ammunition and in transferring the entire IX Corps to the west bank of the Antietam.

About 3 p.m., Burnside's battle lines started moving forward and began to press hard against Brigadier David R. Jones's 2,500-strong division. As they hurried to get to grips with the enemy, the Union infantry were heartened to see another long blue-clad column marching along the road off to their left: reinforcements, they thought. In fact, it was A.P. Hill's Confederate division arriving after a forced march from Harpers Ferry, where his ragged troops had, out of necessity rather than as a *ruse de guerre*, put on captured new Union uniforms.

To the confusion of Burnside's men, the marchers turned to the right, delivered a devastating volley into their flank, then charged them. The US IX Corps started back toward the Antietam, and did not stop until the soldiers had reached the safety afforded by the heights west of the creek. Thus ended the Battle of Antietam or, as the South called it, Sharpsburg.

The next day, September 18, Lee shortened his lines and lay ready to renew the fight, even though his generals cautioned against exposing the battered and exhausted army to more combat. That night, however, Lee finally decided that, in the face of the Federals' overwhelming strength, there was nothing to gain—and much to lose—by staying any longer in Maryland. The state would not join the South and, though he was about to concede the field, he had nevertheless fought an army twice the size of his own to a standstill. It was time to go back to Virginia.

Lee got clean away, crossing the Potomac at Shepherdstown, before McClellan could do much about it. There was some rearguard skirmishing on September 19 and 20, but no real effort was made by Union forces to regain close contact with the Confederate main body. For the next five weeks, the Army of the Potomac remained in the Sharpsburg area, while McClellan set about reinforcing it.

The Emancipation Proclamation

President Lincoln had led the North into the war with the sole objective of preserving the Union. However, flagging fortunes during the spring and summer of 1862 obliged him to seek further inspiration for the Federal war effort. Lincoln, a moderate, found the spark he needed from the powerful, hard-driving abolitionist lobby. He resolved to turn the Federals' fight to crush the rebellion into a crusade against slavery. He hoped this would swing the abolitionists firmly behind his administration and give new impetus to the Union war effort; and that it would also end the threat of European intervention on behalf of the Confederacy. For, he argued, no Continental power would want to be seen as fighting to uphold slavery.

The timing of such a controversial announcement was critical: Lincoln heeded his advisers' warning not to issue it after a run of defeats, in case it should be construed as "our last shriek on the retreat." Instead, he seized on the Confederate withdrawal from the North after Antietam to unveil his new policy.

On September 22, Lincoln published his preliminary Emancipation Proclamation which, in effect, decreed that as of January 1, 1863, all slaves held in states in

rebellion against the Union would be "then, thenceforward and forever free."

In a way the proclamation was a nonsense, because it proclaimed freedom for slaves in areas where the North had no power. Equally, it permitted slavery to continue in the border slave states which remained loyal to the Union and, oddly enough, in parts of the Confederacy occupied by Federal forces before that date.

Complete abolition of slavery in the United States of America did not, in fact, arrive until the passage of the 13th Amendment to the Constitution in 1865. However, Lincoln's Emancipation Proclamation—inadequate and hypocritical as it may have been—served to declare an intention to end human bondage and, as such, had the desired effect of broadening the base of the war and keeping Europe out of the conflict.

In sharp contrast to the decorative Emancipation Proclamation (*left*) is the Southern cartoon (*below*) of President Lincoln drafting the proclamation with one foot on the Constitution. The large picture on the wall suggests the violent effect the proclamation will have on the slaves.

In fact, despite its flaws, the proclamation gave a ray of hope to blacks such as those (*above*) depicted coming into Union lines in North Carolina in 1863.

The aftermath

The bloodiest single day in American history; that is how the Battle of Antietam or Sharpsburg, as the South called it, has been described. In fact, the exact casualty figures have never been properly calculated for this costly battle, in which all of Lee's 45,000 troops were engaged against no more than 60,000 out of McClellan's available strength of 87,000. It is stated, however, that the Federals lost about 12,410 men in all, and the Confederates, 11,172.

Although he had turned the Southern invaders away, McClellan had not won the decisive victory that his government expected. Nor had he shown much enthusiasm for seeking and destroying Lee's retreating army: on November 7, McClellan was ordered to hand over his command to Major General Ambrose Burnside.

TOTALS AND LOSSES

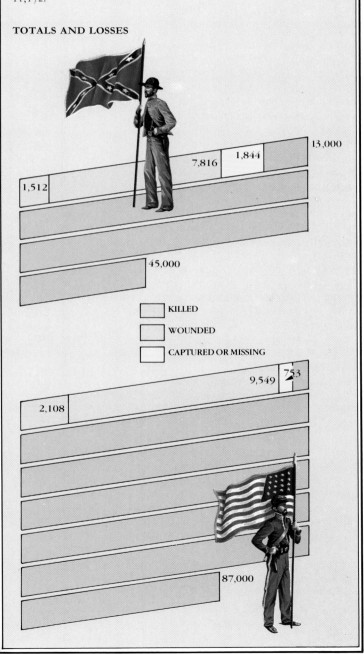

1,512
7,816
1,844
13,000

45,000

KILLED
WOUNDED
CAPTURED OR MISSING

2,108
9,549
753

87,000

Fredericksburg

DECEMBER 13, 1862

*"A chicken could not live on that field
when we open on it."*

LIEUTENANT COLONEL E. PORTER ALEXANDER, CSA

AFTER THE BATTLE OF Antietam in September 1862, President Abraham Lincoln was anxious for the Army of the Potomac to capitalize on its success by fighting the Confederates again as soon as possible. If the Federal army moved quickly enough, the Rebels might be crushed for good. However, Major General George B. McClellan, forever at odds with the Republican administration, judged his army not to be in a fit state to mount an immediate pursuit of General Robert E. Lee.

For several weeks after the battle, therefore, McClellan kept his troops around Sharpsburg and Harpers Ferry, rebuilding their strength and restoring their equipment. Meanwhile, he pondered whether eventually to march into Virginia by a direct route toward Richmond, ensuring that Washington was always covered by his forces, or to strike southwest into the fertile Shenandoah Valley, a major source of supply for the Rebels.

Having opted for a direct route to Richmond, Little Mac advanced to Warrenton; but he was too slow for Lincoln's liking. Thirty miles and the Rappahannock River still lay between the Army of the Potomac and the nearest element of the Army of Northern Virginia, Lieutenant General James Longstreet's I Corps at Culpeper Court House. Lieutenant General Thomas J. "Stonewall" Jackson and the II Corps were on the other side of the Blue Ridge Mountains, at Winchester, in the Shenandoah Valley, sent there by Lee to block McClellan should he choose that route to advance into the Confederacy. Prompt action was needed by the Union, and, to get it, the president decided that yet another change in command was necessary.

Lincoln's choice was Major General Ambrose E. Burnside, commander of the IX Corps, who had done well earlier that year while operating independently against coastal positions in North Carolina. Burnside, however, was not an obvious contender for the job, considering the number of more senior and more experienced officers available; and it was with reluctance that he stepped into Little Mac's shoes. But Burnside did have the reputation for being a fighter, and that was precisely what Lincoln needed.

The presidential order authorizing the changeover was signed on November 5, 1862—nearly two months after Antietam—and delivered to McClellan two days later. When the Army of the Potomac learned of the change in command, there were widespread protestations at the apparently peremptory removal of its beloved chief.

In an emotional farewell on November 10, McClellan bade his troops extend the same loyalty to Burnside as they had done to him. Then he departed for what was to prove permanent military retirement. Thereafter, the soldiers fought well for Burnside—and all the other commanders placed at their head before the war's end—but never again did they idolize a general as they had idolized Little Mac.

The new commanding general took over with only one aim—to get to grips with Lee and win a decisive victory: it was what Lincoln and his government and, indeed, the entire North desperately wanted. Burnside hurriedly reorganized the Army of the Potomac into three grand divisions—the Left Grand Division, under Major General William Franklin, the Center, under Major General Joseph Hooker, and the Right under Major General Edwin V. Sumner. Burnside then set his troops in the general direction of Richmond, the inclement late autumn weather notwithstanding.

Regiments of Sumner's Right Grand Division began to leave Warrenton on November 15. The Confederate cavalry were a little slow in detecting the move, and it was three days before Lee knew about it and could order Longstreet to intercept the Federals. After a series of forced marches, Longstreet arrived at Fredericksburg on the 21st and occupied the high ground behind the town, which

AMBROSE EVERETT BURNSIDE (1824–81)

A burly six-footer with bushy whiskers from which "sideburns" got their name, Burnside was born in Indiana, and led the Army of the Potomac at Fredericksburg. He graduated from West Point in 1847, and was commissioned into the artillery. He saw service, but no combat, in the Mexican War and against the Indians before resigning his commission in 1853 to start a firearms manufacturing company in Bristol, Rhode Island.

Three years later, he invented a breech-loading carbine which fired a metallic cartridge. It was a well-made but expensive weapon, which, in its fourth variation, armed some 55,000 troops during the Civil War. By that time, however, Burnside had gone into liquidation and the carbine was being turned out by his creditors.

From 1855–7, Burnside was major general of the Rhode Island militia, and, when the Civil War broke out in 1861, he became colonel of the 1st Rhode Island Volunteers. Promoted to brigadier general of US Volunteers after First Bull Run, he then won an independent command to raid Confederate installations in North Carolina and managed to make a success of it.

He returned to the Army of the Potomac as a major general (USV). Twice he declined President Lincoln's offer of command of that army, but the third time he was approached—in November, 1862, after the Battle of Antietam—he was persuaded to accept it. His subsequent Fredericksburg campaign was a disaster—"snatching defeat from the jaws of victory," as President Lincoln scathingly put it—and he was relieved of his command in early 1863.

Between March and December, 1863, Burnside commanded the Department of the Ohio in the western theater, with reasonable success. In 1864, he rejoined the Army of the Potomac as commander of the IX Corps, and saw action from the Wilderness to Petersburg. In mid-August, he was removed from his command for badly botching the Federal assault following the detonation of a mine under the Confederate line at Petersburg.

After the war, Burnside was a railroad executive, and also went into politics. He became governor of Rhode Island in 1866, and was twice reelected. He then represented Rhode Island in the US Senate until his death. Burnside was also the first president of the National Rifle Association.

lay on the west bank of the Rappahannock River. Across the river, on the 150-foot-high Stafford Heights and beyond, Burnside's army was encamped.

Because the Federals made no move to cross the Rappahannock, it was not clear to Lee exactly what Burnside's intentions were. Lee, therefore, decided that it was time to concentrate his forces at Fredericksburg. And so, with the prospect of a battle looming daily larger, the city's civilian population—predominantly old men, women and children—was evacuated. There are many testaments to the hardship suffered by these victims of circumstance who were obliged to leave their homes with only a few

personal belongings and journey through snow to try to find shelter and safety.

The pontoons that were needed for the Union advance across the Rappahannock had arrived by November 27, when the city was still unoccupied by the Confederates; but no immediate move was made to bridge the river. Days were allowed to pass while likely crossing points far downstream were reconnoitered, and all the time the Rebel positions were being strengthened.

Finally, Burnside made up his mind to throw three pontoons across the Rappahannock directly into Fredericksburg, and two pontoons about a mile and a half below the town. The Federals began to

build their bridges in the early hours of December 11, and the noise at once alerted the Rebels.

With three grand divisions totaling 116,683 effective men at his command, Burnside proposed to put a large force across to assault the Confederates in the hills behind Fredericksburg, while Franklin crossed the river lower down to turn the Rebels' right flank.

Lee, whose indomitable Army of Northern Virginia had been augmented since the rigors of the Antietam campaign, mustered 78,000 fighting men. They and their supporting artillery were spread in a five-mile crescent across rising ground behind Fredericksburg, the left

Pontoons: vital cogs of troop movement

Armies were not always able to rely on bridges or fords to cross the many rivers of the war zones. Sometimes, for example, the bridges were too heavily defended, or had been destroyed by a retreating enemy. The military answer to such difficulties was the pontoon bridge.

Although pontoon boats made of canvas, india rubber, gutta percha (a plastic-like substance), and corrugated iron saw service—some with more effect than others—it was the 21ft × 5ft 4in wooden punt-type which was most commonly used for military bridging. These wooden pontoons were transported on special wagons drawn by six mules; ancillary equipment

was carried in general service wagons. Some idea of the size of a pontoon train and the amount of room it took up on the road is indicated by the fact that the 15th and 50th New York Engineers arrived before Fredericksburg with 500 mules and enough pontoons to construct two bridges, each 420 feet long.

At the river's edge, the pontoons were manhandled into the water by the pontoniers (as this branch of the Engineer service was known), rowed into position, and anchored parallel to each other, about six feet apart, until the far bank was reached. Planking was then lashed across them and the result was a roadway 11 feet wide.

Wooden pontoon boats, like the one shown (*bottom*), were used, especially by the North, to make bridges such as those photographed (*below*) across the Rappahannock.

In the painting (*right*), Federal pontoniers encounter fierce rifle fire from Rebels trying to stop Burnside's army from crossing the Rappahannock into Fredericksburg.

flank anchored on the river. Longstreet's corps, dug in along Taylor's Hill, Marye's Heights and Telegraph Hill, held the left and center; Jackson's corps was on the right, unfortified on the gentle wooded slopes around Hamilton's Crossing where a railroad passed through a gap in the hills.

As the Federal pontoniers got to work, those trying to lay bridges over to the town found themselves under heavy and accurate rifle fire from Brigadier General William Barksdale's Mississippi Brigade, reinforced by some Floridians, who were concealed in brick houses and rifle pits along the south bank.

Efforts by Union batteries to support the exposed engineers were ineffectual, and time and again the pontoon laying had to be suspended. Fuming with impatience at the delay, Burnside, at 12.30 p.m., ordered a general bombardment of the town by all the artillery on Stafford Heights—147 guns of mixed calibers.

Lieutenant General Longstreet, who witnessed the Federal barrage, described it as follows:

"From our position on the heights we saw the batteries hurling an avalanche upon the town whose only offense was that near its edge in a snug retreat nestled three thousand Confederate hornets that were stinging the Army of the Potomac into a frenzy. It was terrific, the pandemonium which that little squad of Confederates had provoked. The town caught fire in several places, shells crashed and burst, and solid shot rained like hail. In the midst of the successive crashes could be heard the shouts and yells of those engaged in the struggle, while the smoke rose from the burning city and the flames leaped about, making a scene which can never be effaced from the memory of those who saw it."

But, despite this two-hour onslaught on the town, Barksdale and his men were

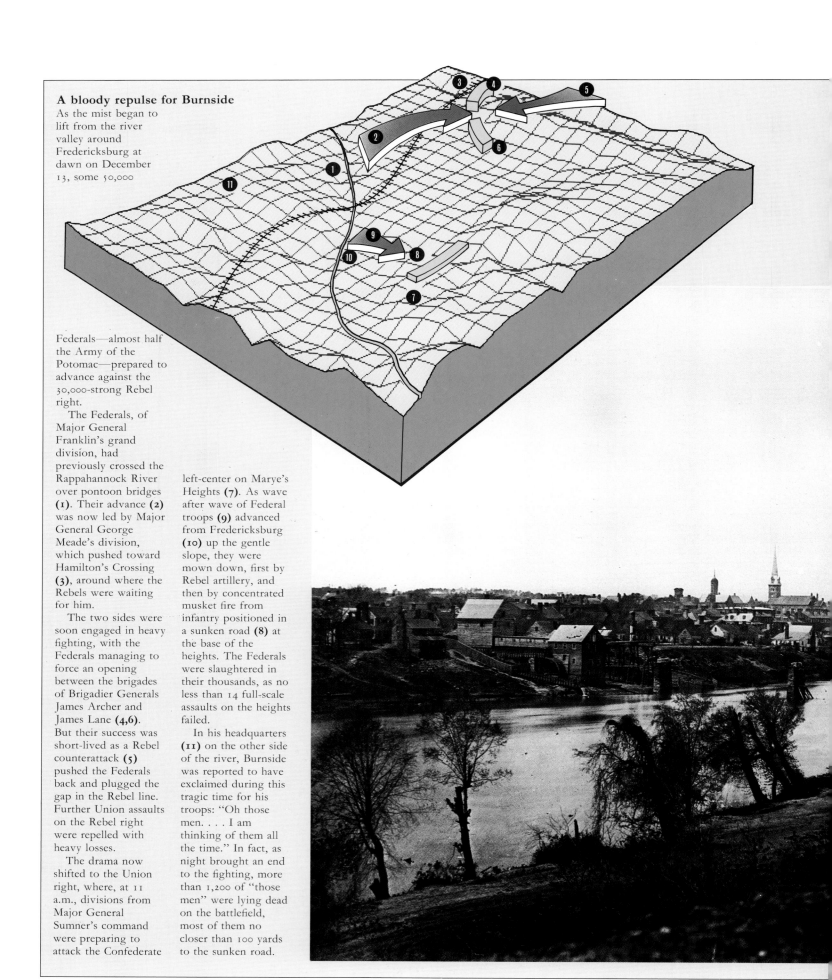

A bloody repulse for Burnside

As the mist began to lift from the river valley around Fredericksburg at dawn on December 13, some 50,000 Federals—almost half the Army of the Potomac—prepared to advance against the 30,000-strong Rebel right.

The Federals, of Major General Franklin's grand division, had previously crossed the Rappahannock River over pontoon bridges (1). Their advance (2) was now led by Major General George Meade's division, which pushed toward Hamilton's Crossing (3), around where the Rebels were waiting for him.

The two sides were soon engaged in heavy fighting, with the Federals managing to force an opening between the brigades of Brigadier Generals James Archer and James Lane (4,6). But their success was short-lived as a Rebel counterattack (5) pushed the Federals back and plugged the gap in the Rebel line. Further Union assaults on the Rebel right were repelled with heavy losses.

The drama now shifted to the Union right, where, at 11 a.m., divisions from Major General Sumner's command were preparing to attack the Confederate left-center on Marye's Heights (7). As wave after wave of Federal troops (9) advanced from Fredericksburg (10) up the gentle slope, they were mown down, first by Rebel artillery, and then by concentrated musket fire from infantry positioned in a sunken road (8) at the base of the heights. The Federals were slaughtered in their thousands, as no less than 14 full-scale assaults on the heights failed.

In his headquarters (11) on the other side of the river, Burnside was reported to have exclaimed during this tragic time for his troops: "Oh those men. . . . I am thinking of them all the time." In fact, as night brought an end to the fighting, more than 1,200 of "those men" were lying dead on the battlefield, most of them no closer than 100 yards to the sunken road.

Rebel sharpshooters
(*below*)—"hornets . . .
stinging the Army of
the Potomac into a
frenzy"—fire at the

Rebel sharpshooters
(*below*)—"hornets . . .
stinging the Army of
the Potomac into a
frenzy"—fire at the
Federals as they
attempt, on December
11, to cross the
Rappahannock into
Fredericksburg (*bottom*).

not dislodged. As a last resort, Union soldiers bravely piled into pontoon boats and ran the gauntlet of Rebel sharpshooters to establish a bridgehead in the town, and allow the vital crossings to be completed. Fierce clashes took place in the streets as more and more Union infantry came over, then Barksdale was ordered to disengage and fall back to the main Confederate line. Burnside then spent what little was left of the 11th and the following day getting troops across the Rappahannock and preparing for battle.

At dawn on the 13th, mist shrouded the river valley, but around 10 a.m., it began to clear, revealing to the Confederates the spectacle of Franklin's grand division, soon to be reinforced by two divisions of Hooker's command—some 50,000 men—deployed on the plain in front of their right wing. On the face of it, the principal Federal assault looked as if it was to be made against Jackson; but it was not. Many Union troops had already crossed the town pontoons and were concealed in dead ground and throughout the built-up area ready to attack the Rebel center. On the north bank, waiting to join them, were many more.

The Battle of Fredericksburg opened on the Confederate right. Burnside apparently still retained hopes of turning Lee's flank and levering him out of his entrenched position, even though the element of surprise had disappeared. And so he ordered Franklin to hold most of his command in readiness to move down the Old Richmond Road, which ran parallel with the river, and get around the Confederates, while the remainder "seized" rising ground around Hamilton's Crossing.

Franklin, therefore, sent Major General George G. Meade's division, supported by Brigadier General John Gibbon's division, in lines of battle through the dispersing mist toward the wooded area around the crossing, which concealed 30,000 men under Stonewall Jackson.

The Confederates waited until the first line neared them, then crippled it with shattering volleys. The Federals reformed and, in the heavy fighting which followed, forced a wedge between the brigades of Brigadier General James Lane and Brigadier General James Archer. Rebel reinforcements rushed to defend this threatened sector and Jackson's front line was reestablished.

The Union assaults were repelled with considerable loss, and the engagement was finally broken off without any ground being gained by Meade's and Gibbon's battered divisions. Franklin had done his best to obey Burnside's instructions to the letter. Later, the Union commander admitted that he *should* have ordered the Left Grand Division to take Hamilton's Crossing at all hazards. Under the circumstances, such a move would

Unruly elements of
Burnside's army are
sketched here looting
Fredericksburg after
the city had been
taken by the Federals.

THE CARNAGE BELOW MARYE'S HEIGHTS

As the dawn mist cleared on December 13, the Federal Army of the Potomac braced itself to advance from its positions around the city of Fredericksburg. Its objective was to dislodge the seasoned veterans of General Robert E. Lee's Army of Northern Virginia, entrenched on rising ground to the south of the city.

From 10 a.m., for several hours, heavy fighting took place on the Rebel right, but the Federals were unable to break Lieutenant General Stonewall Jackson's line.

Later that morning, as the fighting on the Union left was still going on, thousands more Federal troops began to gird themselves for an assault on the Rebel left-center, positioned on and at the base of a gently rising hill called Marye's Heights.

The Confederates here had a formidable defensive position: artillery from the crest of the heights commanded the open ground that stretched toward the city. Running along the base of the heights was a worn-away track, known afterward as the Sunken Road. This was protected on its forward edge by a stone wall. Behind this, the Rebel infantry could fire on the enemy with minimum exposure.

Thus, as Federal troops mounted continuous attacks throughout the afternoon, they were met by a "sheet of fire" as volley after volley of rifle bullets tore into their ranks. Despite the terrible carnage, Major General Ambrose Burnside, who was across the river away from the slaughter, ordered that the assault should continue. At about 5 p.m., it was the turn of Brigadier General George W. Getty's division from the IX Corps to be ordered into the attack.

In the fading light of a bitterly cold December day, the gallant Federals of Colonel Rush Hawkins' brigade (6), emerged from the gloom, at first undetected by the Confederates. They then charged over the open ground, which lay in front of the spires and buildings of Fredericksburg (2), and which was now littered with thousands of their dead and wounded comrades.

The terrain between the city and the Confederate positions afforded little protection for the dense ranks of Union troops. A few houses, especially near Hanover Street (3), gave shelter, but the muddy ground and various fences slowed the momentum of the attack.

Facing the onrush of Federals at the Sunken Road, the Confederates (5), from the brigades of Brigadier Generals Thomas R.R. Cobb and Joseph B. Kershaw, unleashed murderous volleys from behind a stone wall which was banked with earth.

According to Confederate Major General Lafayette McLaws, at this stage of the battle the Rebel line was "four deep throughout the whole Sunken Road, and beyond the right flank." The ranks shot in rotation so that the fire was, according to Kershaw, "the most rapid and continuous that I have ever witnessed." By this time, Kershaw had taken command of the troops in the Sunken Road after Cobb had been shot in the thigh and bled to death.

The Confederate guns (4), to the right of Marye's Mansion (1) had played a crucial role in the successive repulses of the Union infantry throughout the day. Typical of what happened was described by First Lieutenant William Owen of the Rebel Washington Artillery: "We could see our shells bursting in their ranks, making great gaps; but on they came, as though they would go straight through and over us. Now we gave them canister, and that staggered them."

But, as the day wore on, accurate Federal sharpshooting took its toll of the artillerymen. Not only that, but at about 5 p.m., as Owen reported, the Rebel guns were nearly out of ammunition and "were reduced to a few solid shot only."

The battlefield

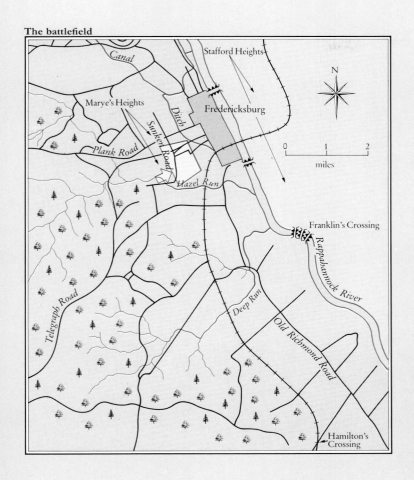

Canal
Stafford Heights
Marye's Heights
Fredericksburg
Ditch
Sunken Road
Plank Road
Hazel Run
Franklin's Crossing
Telegraph Road
Deep Run
Rappahannock River
Old Richmond Road
Hamilton's Crossing

N

0   1   2
miles

Hawkins' Federals advanced, effectively unhindered by the Rebel guns; at first, the progress of the men from New Hampshire, New Jersey, and New York was rapid as the fading light concealed their movement from the enemy; but, as they opened fire, the flashes from their rifles gave their positions away and attracted deadly volleys from the Southerners.

Crumbling under the intensity of the firing, Hawkins' lines broke. Of his brigade, 225 men lay on the field along with thousands of other blue-clad soldiers. Most fell at least 100 yards from the Sunken Road. Only one Union officer got within 30 yards of the Rebel positions.

The night after the battle brought further terrible suffering to the Federals still on the battlefield, holding the front line. Exposure to the bitter cold hastened the death of many of the wounded. Frozen corpses were used as shelter by the living, and some were positioned to resemble sentries.

Burnside had led his army to a bloody defeat—7,000 of the cream of his men lay on the open ground between the city and Marye's Heights. Although he tried to appear cheerful to some of his officers, Burnside knew what terrible carnage his orders had brought. Major General Darius Couch saw him at 2 a.m., after the battle, and later wrote: ". . . one knowing him so long and well as myself could see that he wished his body was also lying in front of Marye's Heights. I never felt so badly for a man in my life."

Retreating into winter quarters

Campaigning in the Civil War was generally confined to those months of the year when roads were in reasonable condition. When frost and snow arrived, Union and Confederate field armies would back off from each other and move into winter quarters until spring warmed the air and dried out the ground.

The principal enemy during these wintering periods, which often lasted three months or more, was the cold. However, soldiers on both sides contrived to make themselves as snug as possible—at the expense of great swathes of woodland in the vicinity of their camps.

Sprawling cities of little log cabins, arranged in regimental streets, would spring up. Each hut housed four to six men, who ate, slept, and spent their off-duty moments there. Much ingenuity was put into making these rough shacks homey and comfortable. Chairs, tables, shelves, and cots were constructed, and most cabins boasted an open fireplace. Empty barrels from the quartermasters were prized for making efficient chimneys. Troops who were unable to obtain enough wood to build cabins would pitch their tents and put timber around the sides to keep out the worst of the drafts.

have been much more effective.

Meanwhile, Lee, watching the battle's progress from Telegraph Hill in the middle of his line, had anticipated that any attack on his left center would fall on Marye's Heights. The terrain there, nearest the town, was not so rugged as the rest of his center and left; but it was well-fortified. A sunken lane at the base of Marye's Heights in particular provided a formidable defensive position. Lying in wait under cover of a shoulder-high stone wall which edged the north side of this lane were veteran infantrymen from Longstreet's corps.

Also, the open ground in front of Marye's Heights, glistening under a light dusting of snow, was so well bracketed by Rebel guns that Lieutenant Colonel E. Porter Alexander, an artillery chief, was not boasting when he assured Longstreet:

"A chicken could not live on that field when we open on it."

About 11 a.m., the first indications came that a major Federal attack was coming from the direction of the town. Long lines of Union troops from Brigadier General William French's division filed out and deployed in three brigade lines, 200 yards apart. In support was

Lee thanks his troops

Since its constitution in June, 1862, the Confederate Army of Northern Virginia had performed nobly under the leadership of General Robert E. Lee. That great commander was justly proud of his men's endeavors over four months of hard campaigning, and when he got a breathing space in the aftermath of Antietam, he took the opportunity to tell them so:

"In reviewing the achievements of the army during the present campaign, the commanding general cannot withhold the expression of his admiration of the indomitable courage it has displayed in battle and its cheerful endurance of privation and hardships on the march.

"Since your great victories around Richmond you have defeated the enemy at Cedar Mountain, expelled him from the Rappahannock, and after a conflict of three days utterly repulsed him on the plains of Manassas and forced him to take shelter within the fortifications around his capital. Without halting for repose, you crossed the Potomac, stormed the heights of Harpers Ferry, made prisoners of more than 11,600 men, and captured upward of seventy pieces of artillery, all their small-arms, and other munitions of war. While one corps of the army was thus engaged the other ensured its success by arresting at Boonsboro' the combined armies of the enemy, advancing under their favorite general to the relief of their beleaguered comrades.

"On the field of Sharpsburg, with less than one-third his numbers, you resisted from daylight until dark the whole army of the enemy, and repulsed every attack along his entire front of more than four miles in extent.

"The whole of the following day you stood prepared to resume the conflict on the same ground, and retired next morning without molestation across the Potomac.

"Two attempts subsequently made by the enemy to follow you across the river have resulted in his complete discomfiture and his being driven back with loss. Achievements such as these demanded much valor and patriotism. History records fewer examples of greater fortitude and endurance than this army has exhibited, and I am commissioned by the President to thank you in the name of the Confederate States for the undying fame you have won for their arms.

"Much as you have done, much more remains to be accomplished. The enemy again threatens us with invasion, and to your tried valor and patriotism the country looks with confidence for deliverance and safety. Your past exploits give assurance that this confidence is not misplaced."

Parading in front of a Federal camp (*above*) near Brandy Station are the men of the 114th Pennsylvania Regiment, in their role as guard to the headquarters of the Army of the Potomac.

Soldiers' huts, with their distinctive barrel chimneys, can be seen just behind the troops; and on the rising ground by the trees are larger huts belonging to officers. To the right, separate from the main body of the camp, can be seen a sutler's tent.

In a relaxed mood, Union soldiers pose before the camera in a deserted camp (*left*) near Fredericksburg. Although dilapidated, the camp still shows the care with which it was constructed.

Soldiers also took pride in making the interiors of their huts as comfortable as possible; an open fire (*far left*) did much to make the winter months more bearable.

With pickax and spade, Union soldiers begin the grim task of burying their dead on the Fredericksburg battlefield. Many of the corpses had had their clothes stripped off during the night by poorly clad Rebels suffering from the bitter cold.

Brigadier General Winfield Scott Hancock's division. Their object was to storm Marye's Heights. But, as soon as the Union ranks began to advance across the flat ground, they were mown down by scything artillery fire and deadly volleys from the reinforced brigade of Brigadier General Thomas R. R. Cobb (who was later mortally wounded), concealed behind the stone wall of the sunken lane.

Although their casualties soared, the Federal infantry kept returning to the attack with reckless obstinacy. Their courage in the face of such devastating fire was exemplary. Major General Darius N. Couch, commanding the Union II Corps, climbed the steeple of the city courthouse to survey the battlefield:

"I remember that the whole plain was covered with men, prostrate and dropping, the live men running here and there, and in front closing upon each other, and the wounded coming back. The commands seemed to be mixed up. I have never before seen fighting like that, nothing approaching it in terrible uproar and destruction. There was no cheering on the part of the men, but a stubborn determination to obey orders and do their duty. I don't think there was much feeling of success. As they charged, the artillery fire would break their formation and they would get mixed; then they would close up, go forward, receive the withering infantry fire, and those who were able would run to the houses and fight as best they could; and then the next brigade coming up in succession would do its duty and melt like snow coming down on warm ground."

Throughout that bloody afternoon and evening, no less than 14 full-scale assaults were made on the sunken lane, which had been reinforced by regiments from Brigadier Generals Joseph Kershaw's, John R. Cooke's, and Robert Ransom's brigades. Confederate riflemen now stood four deep in the shelter of the sunken lane, and were thus able to maintain virtually uninterrupted fire. Only one Union soldier, an officer, reached within 30 yards of the wall before being shot down; the majority of his comrades—numbered in thousands—fell 100 yards out. Only gathering darkness brought an end to the futile slaughter.

In the early hours of the next morning, Burnside, realizing that a disaster had befallen him, talked about trying to recoup the situation by personally leading his old IX Corps in an attack on the morrow. However, his top commanders, including Sumner, Hooker, and Franklin, met his proposal with silence, and then pointed out the futility of mounting another assault on the strong Confederate positions. Burnside took heed of his commanders' advice and dropped his plan to attack: there would be no repeat of the terrible bloodshed of the previous day.

As a new gloom settled over the North following yet another humiliating defeat at the hands of Lee, the Army of the Potomac retired across the Rappahannock and went into winter quarters, with its confidence in Burnside badly shaken.

After his defeat at Fredericksburg, Major General Burnside began making fresh plans to tackle Lee.

This time, his scheme was to put troops across the Rappahannock river at Banks' Ford, three miles upstream, to catch the Rebels in their left and rear.

The grand divisions of Franklin and Hooker moved out and camped for the night of January 20 near Banks' Ford. But torrential rain began to turn the clay soil into a sea of oozing mud. Pontoon trains, ammunition and supply wagons, and artillery sank up to their axles, and the soaked, cursing soldiers found the going almost impossible. What became known as the "Mud March," (*below*), failed, and the troops made their way back to their winter quarters as best they could. Along the Fredericksburg shore, the Confederates pinned up jeering notices proclaiming: "Burnside's stuck in the mud."

The aftermath

The Union losses of 12,653 at Fredericksburg were extremely heavy, considering that the brunt of the fighting was borne by only five divisions out of an army of more than 116,000 men.

Most of the Federal dead lay in front of the Sunken Road beneath Marye's Heights—a testimony to the bravery, and futility, of the Union assaults made upon that position. Confederate casualties were relatively light, with a total of 5,377 out of an army of about 78,000 men.

After his attempt to redeem himself had failed in the farcical "Mud March," Major General Ambrose Burnside lost the confidence of President Lincoln. Consequently, in early 1863, Burnside was replaced as commander of the Army of the Potomac by his subordinate and bitter rival Major General "Fighting Joe" Hooker.

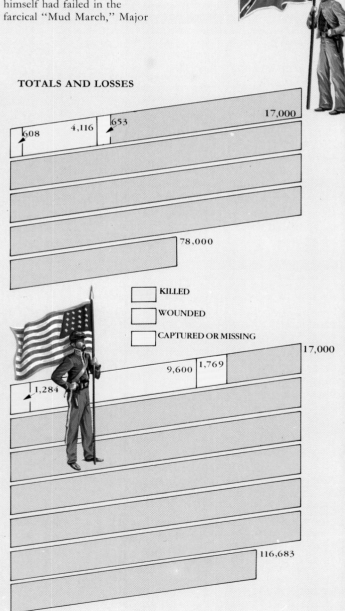

TOTALS AND LOSSES

608   4,116   653   17,000

78,000

☐ KILLED

☐ WOUNDED

☐ CAPTURED OR MISSING

1,284   9,600   1,769   17,000

116,683

Stones River

"The sheen of a bright moon revealed the sad carnage of the day, and the horrors of war became vividly distinct."

COLONEL DAVID URQUHART, CSA, after the first day of the battle

TOWARD THE END OF 1862, the Union was hoping at last to marshal its superiority in manpower and equipment for a concerted, irresistible push against the Confederacy. No less than three armies—one in the eastern theater and two in the west—were to begin offensives to break the straining Rebel war effort.

As Christmas approached, however, the Army of the Potomac under its new leader, Major General Ambrose E. Burnside, had dashed itself to defeat in the eastern theater at Fredericksburg, Virginia; and Major General Ulysses S. Grant's Army of the Tennessee was in difficulties on its march against Vicksburg on the eastern bank of the Mississippi. Only the newly designated Army of the Cumberland, led by Major General William S. Rosecrans, operating in middle Tennessee, seemed to offer any chance of a significant Federal victory before the year's end.

Rosecrans had been given command of the army after the Battle of Perryville in October. In that fight, the Confederate General Braxton Bragg had broken off the conflict and withdrawn his invading troops from Kentucky because he believed he was faced with overwhelming opposition. The Federal Major General Don Carlos Buell, with his Army of the Ohio, was slow to pursue and destroy him, and so forfeited his command.

The Army of the Ohio was then redesignated as the Army of the Cumberland and concentrated at Nashville, Tennessee, where Rosecrans spent several weeks reorganizing and refitting his divisions. Meanwhile, Bragg, from his headquarters at Knoxville in east Tennessee, had won President Jefferson Davis's approval for an advance into middle Tennessee. By November 24, the Confederate Army of Tennessee was lying at

Murfreesboro, on Stones River, about 30 miles southeast of Nashville.

In the weeks leading up to the second Christmas of the war, there was a lot of skirmishing between the forward patrols of the two armies, but nothing that looked like developing into a pitched battle. Rosecrans, however, urged on by Washington, decided to ignore the constant freezing rain, the poor roads, and the festive season: on December 26, he ordered his army to march on Murfreesboro.

The Union troops, who moved out in three corps, each traveling by a different road, found the going tough and the Confederates alert and active. It was not until late on the 29th that the first Union corps, under Major General Thomas Crittenden, arrived, cold and soaked, in the vicinity of Murfreesboro—and under

orders not to light fires in case they attracted attention. Major General George H. Thomas's corps came up a little later; and, by mid-morning of the 30th, Major General Alexander McCook's corps had arrived to complete the concentration.

Both sides spent December 30 drawing up their battle lines, with desultory artillery duels accompanying the movement of troops. Another bitterly cold night without the comfort of fires had to be endured by Rosecrans' 43,400-strong army, which was now aligned for the coming fight: Crittenden was on the left, Thomas in the center, with Alexander McCook on the right, facing southeast toward Murfreesboro, which lay about two miles away.

Bragg's dispositions fanned across all approaches to the town from the north and west. His right, which was east of Stones River, was held by Major General John C. Breckinridge's division of Lieutenant General William J. Hardee's corps. Lieutenant General Leonidas Polk's corps was in the center. The Rebel left was commanded by Hardee: it comprised the other division of his corps, under Major General Pat Cleburne, and the reserve division of Major General John P. McCown. In all, 37,712 Confederates were deployed.

In his battle plan, Rosecrans proposed to send Crittenden across Stones River to drive in the Rebel right, while Thomas moved against the center; McCook's corps was to hold the Confederate forces on its front and await the Union left and center to swing around behind them.

By coincidence, Bragg had decided on an almost identical plan: to send Hardee in against the Federal right, let Polk develop the attack, and hold Breckinridge in position. His idea was to push the Federals back against Stones River and

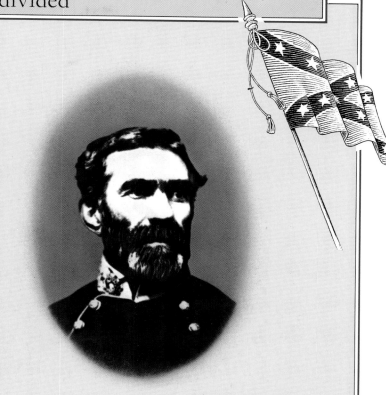

WILLIAM STARKE ROSECRANS (1819–98)

BRAXTON BRAGG (1817–76)

"Old Rosy" was an intelligent, tactically astute soldier who commanded the Army of the Cumberland at Stones River. Rosecrans, who came from Cincinnati, Ohio, joined the engineers after graduating from West Point in 1842.

When the Civil War broke out, Rosecrans was a colonel of engineers in the Ohio State militia. He then became colonel of the 23rd Ohio, and was later promoted to brigadier general.

In March, 1862, Rosecrans was named major general of US Volunteers. Three months later, he was transferred to command the Army of the Mississippi and won the Battles of Iuka and Corinth. In October, 1862, he became the commander of the Army of the Ohio, redesignated it the Army of the Cumberland, and went on the offensive in Tennessee. After the bloody struggle at Stones River, Rosecrans rested his army for six months before again seeking the enemy.

In late June and early July, 1863, Rosecrans skillfully maneuvered the Rebels out of middle Tennessee and into north Georgia. But, on September 19–20 of that year, he met the Confederates at Chickamauga and was defeated in the biggest battle of the war fought in the western theater. He was shortly replaced, left inactive for three months, then given command of the Department of the Missouri, where he remained until the end of the war.

Bragg, the Confederate commander at Stones River, was a testy, quarrelsome officer who seemed to have a predilection for withdrawal even when his forces were winning. A North Carolinian, Bragg graduated from West Point in 1837, and joined the artillery. He saw action in the Second Seminole War, the Mexican War, and on the frontier before resigning in 1856.

On the eve of secession, Bragg was a militia officer, then, in March, 1861, he was commissioned brigadier general in the Confederate States Army, with responsibility for guarding the coast between Pensacola and Mobile.

Bragg became a major general in September, 1861, and was transferred to the western theater. There he commanded the II Corps in General A.S. Johnston's army at the Battle of Shiloh in April, 1862. That same month he was promoted to full general. At the end of June, 1862, Bragg was given command of the Army of the Mississippi (soon to be redesignated the Army of Tennessee) and led it in action at Perryville, Stones River, Chickamauga and Chattanooga.

Not long after the Confederate defeat at Chattanooga in December, 1863, Bragg requested to be relieved of his command. He became military adviser to President Davis, a position he held until January 1865.

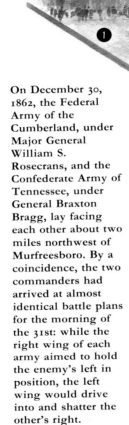

On December 30, 1862, the Federal Army of the Cumberland, under Major General William S. Rosecrans, and the Confederate Army of Tennessee, under General Braxton Bragg, lay facing each other about two miles northwest of Murfreesboro. By a coincidence, the two commanders had arrived at almost identical battle plans for the morning of the 31st: while the right wing of each army aimed to hold the enemy's left in position, the left wing would drive into and shatter the other's right.

As it turned out, at dawn on the 31st, Bragg's men moved first, with the troops of Lieutenant General Hardee's corps crashing into the unwary Federals. The Union far right was soon crumpled, with heavy casualties.

But, as disaster threatened Rosecrans' army, Federal Brigadier General Philip Sheridan, whose position lay on the Wilkinson Turnpike at a right angle to the main Union line, managed to stem the Rebel tide. He was forced to withdraw only when his men ran out of ammunition.

The Federal resistance, however, continued from troops of Major General L.H. Rousseau's and Brigadier General James Negley's divisions of Major General George Thomas's corps.

Just before noon on December 31, a bitterly cold winter's morning, a determined line of Federals, under Colonel J.F. Miller, of Negley's division, faced a head-on charge by Rebels under the command of Brigadier General J. Patton Anderson of Major General Withers' division.

As the 27th, 29th, and 30th Mississippi regiments (2, 3, 4, respectively) advanced from their own line, where the guns of Barrett's battery (1) had now fallen silent, their formation was disrupted not only by fierce Federal fire but also by the uneven terrain. As was typical of the clearings of the Stones River battlefield, the ground was scattered with boulders and tree stumps, and it had been softened by the previous night's rain.

As the Confederates neared Miller's line, positioned at the fringes of a dense patch of cedars, they were met by deadly rifle and artillery fire. While the men of Ellsworth's battery (7) worked their guns, the 21st Ohio (6) leveled their rifles and delivered a murderous volley into the Rebel ranks. Marshall's battery (5), with the 74th Ohio on their right, also wreaked heavy losses on the advancing enemy. To the right of the Ohioans, the 37th Indiana and the 74th Pennsylvania kept up the pressure on the Confederates.

Despite their valiant efforts, the Federals were forced into retreat—the official records are not entirely clear as to the details—and in doing so, both guns and men were captured by the Rebels.

But the Confederate success had been paid for in blood: according to Rebel corps commander Lieutenant General Leonidas Polk, the engagement here "was one of the points at which we encountered the most determined opposition." The 30th Mississippi alone lost 62 officers and men killed, and 139 wounded.

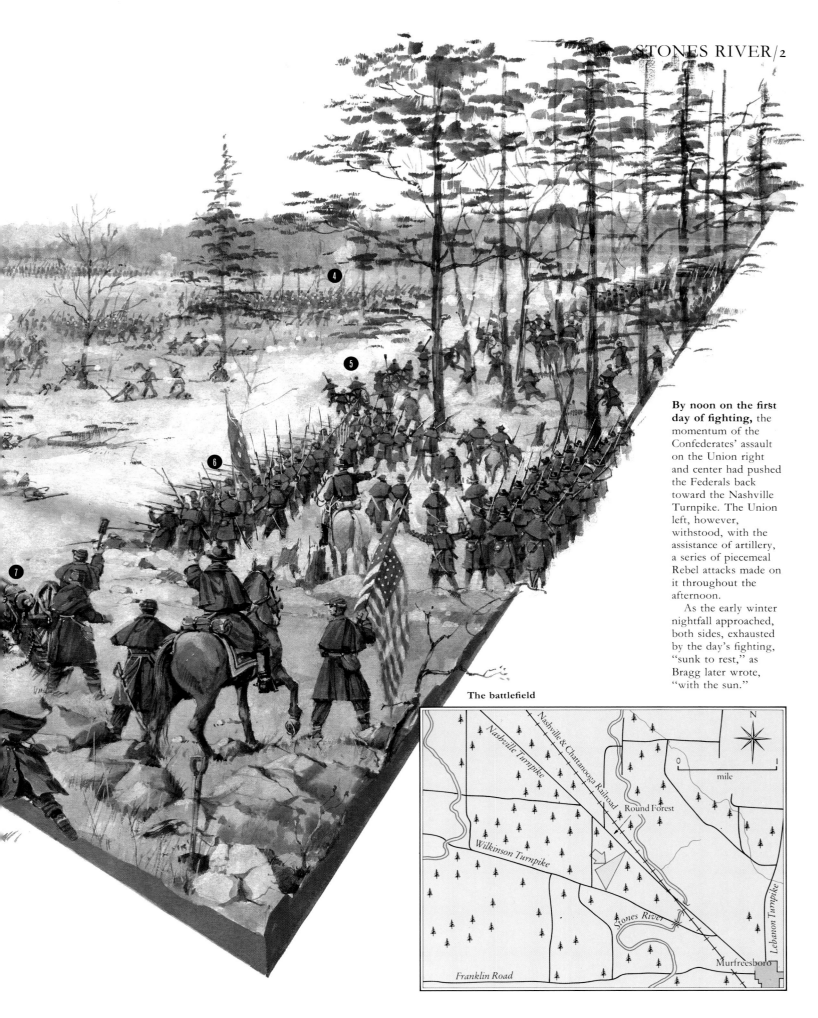

By noon on the first day of fighting, the momentum of the Confederates' assault on the Union right and center had pushed the Federals back toward the Nashville Turnpike. The Union left, however, withstood, with the assistance of artillery, a series of piecemeal Rebel attacks made on it throughout the afternoon.

As the early winter nightfall approached, both sides, exhausted by the day's fighting, "sunk to rest," as Bragg later wrote, "with the sun."

The battlefield

cut their lines of communication with Nashville, leaving them helpless. If the two plans had been executed at the same time, the two armies might have swung around like two opposite spokes on a wheel. However, Bragg beat Rosecrans' move by an hour.

As a cold dawn broke and Crittenden's troops were preparing to march one and a half miles to begin their attack, Hardee's battle line crashed across the few hundred yards separating it from the Union right, overran the pickets, and burst in on the surprised Federals. Brigadier General Richard Johnson's division, on the extreme right of Rosecrans' line, bore the brunt of the first onslaught, and was quickly scattered in confusion. As the Confederate attack developed, Federal Brigadier General Jefferson C. Davis's division was also pushed back with heavy casualties.

Rosecrans, at first unwilling to believe that such a disaster could have overtaken his right, ordered Brigadier General Philip H. Sheridan (who led the only intact division left in McCook's corps) and the remains of Davis's command to hold a position along the Wilkinson Turnpike at a right angle to the main line. Meanwhile Brigadier General Horatio Van Cleve's division of Crittenden's

corps was recalled from the other side of the river, and a new line was improvized on rising ground covering the Nashville Turnpike and the Nashville & Chattanooga Railroad at an acute angle to the rest of the Union left wing.

For much of the morning, fighting raged in the cedars between the Wilkinson and Nashville pikes. Batteries blasted each other at close range, and the musketry fire was so intense that regiments on both sides ran out of ammunition. Around 11 a.m., Sheridan was obliged to withdraw for lack of cartridges, but the fight was continued by troops from Major General Lovell Rousseau's and Brigadier General James Negley's divisions of Thomas's corps.

The fighting was fiercest in the cedar glades shielding the Nashville pike. As Hardee and Polk piled on the pressure, Bragg sent to Breckinridge for reinforcements, which he felt would break the enemy line. Breckinridge, however, declined to transfer two of his brigades as requested, because he thought—erroneously as it turned out—that he was still under threat of an attack by Crittenden.

As the battle progressed, a combination of Confederate infantry lapping around behind the exposed Union right flank and dwindling ammunition finally

forced the Union troops to retire on Van Cleve's line, which they did in good order. The battlefield situation at that moment is described by Colonel David Urquhart of Bragg's staff:

"Our attack had pivoted the Federals on their center, bending back their line, as one half-shuts a knife-blade. At 12 o'clock we had a large part of the field, with many prisoners, cannon, guns, ammunition, wagons, and the dead and wounded of both armies."

But, unknown to the Rebels, whose view was obscured by the trees, Rosecrans had massed half a dozen batteries on a low ridge behind his new line along the Nashville Turnpike. These guns played a big part in helping the hard-pressed Union infantry to hold off repeated Rebel attacks during the afternoon.

Federals of the 78th Pennsylvania
Regiment of Colonel John F. Miller's brigade storm a Confederate battery during the fighting on January 2.

Miller had launched a fierce counterattack against Rebel troops under Major General John Breckinridge, as they fled in retreat from the onslaught of massed Union artillery on the west bank of Stones River.

The Army of the Cumberland holds on

The Battle of Stones River opened at dawn on December 31, 1862, just northwest of Murfreesboro (7), when the left wing of the Rebel Army of Tennessee struck a powerful blow against the right of Major General William S. Rosecrans' Army of the Cumberland.

The initial Rebel onslaught threatened to shatter the entire Union right. But then Federals under Brigadier General Philip H. Sheridan and, a little later, under Major General Lovell H. Rousseau and Brigadier General James Negley, put up some stiff resistance.

Nevertheless, at about noon, the force of the Rebel attack (1) had pushed the Union line (2) back toward the Nashville Turnpike like the half-shut blade of a knife. With the Union center (3) withstanding fierce assaults from Lieutenant General Leonidas Polk's command (6), General Braxton Bragg ordered Major General John Breckinridge to send reinforcements from his division (5). Breckinridge, however, thought that he was about to face a Federal attack in his front, and declined to transfer any troops. In fact, Federal Brigadier General Horatio Van Cleve's division (4), which had been ordered across Stones River to attack the Rebel right, was soon after recalled to strengthen the Federals' own right flank.

With the help of massed artillery, Rosecrans' men managed to stave off defeat before darkness brought an end to the first day's fighting. No fighting took place on January 1, 1863. Next day, the two armies (8,9) still faced each other on the west side of Stones River (14). On the east bank, however, Bragg found that Federals from Van Cleve's division had been moved to the high ground and were threatening his right flank.

Bragg, therefore, ordered four brigades (13) under Breckinridge to attack the Federals. The Rebels stormed the slope successfully, and pushed the Federals (11) back to the river. However, massed Union guns from the west side of the river broke up the Rebel assault. Some 1,500 men fell within a few minutes. The survivors (12) made their way back to their own lines, so bringing the battle to a close.

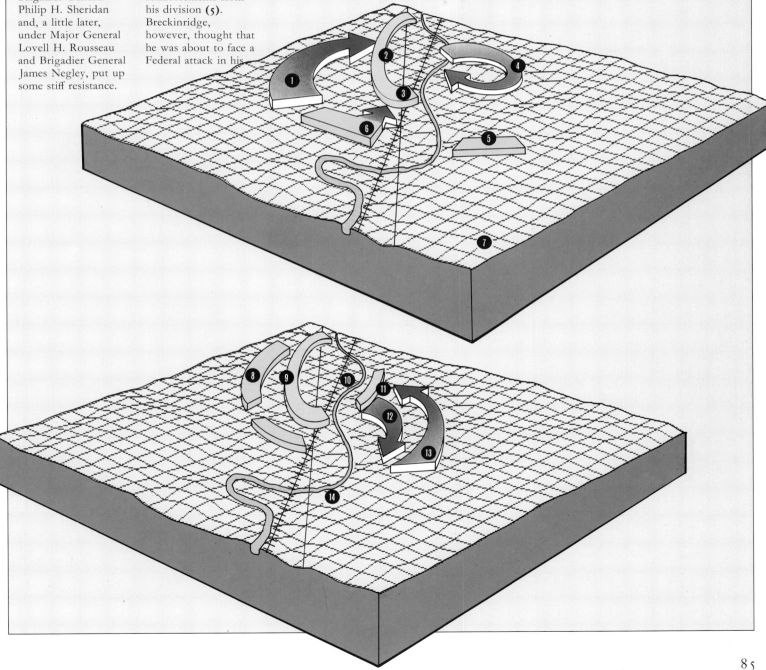

About 2 p.m., Bragg decided to make a last effort to smash the Federal line. A charge by two fresh brigades from Breckinridge was to drive in the Union left, so that what remained of Rosecrans' center and right, posted at a right angle to it along the Nashville pike, would be taken in front and rear. But the assault was delivered piecemeal in the face of terrific artillery fire and was driven back.

At 4 p.m., two fresh brigades of Breckinridge's division surged forward, but were repulsed by the Federals with daylight fading. As Bragg wrote later:

"Both armies, exhausted by a conflict of full ten hours' duration, rarely surpassed for its continued intensity and heavy losses sustained, sunk to rest with the sun."

As things stood on that bitterly cold New Year's Eve, the Confederates had had the best of the day's battle. Rosecrans knew it, and, at a council of war that night, there was talk of withdrawal. A retreat was rejected, however, because it was thought that the Rebel cavalry had blocked the Nashville pike between Nashville and the battlefield: they would stay and fight it out.

But the first day of 1863 passed quietly along Stones River, with both commanders redeploying and strengthening their respective positions. Bragg, who had confidently expected to find Rosecrans gone on January 1, was slower to reorganize his front than his opponent, and discovered that Van Cleve's division, now led by Colonel Samuel Beatty, was entrenched on the east bank of the river and in a position to enfilade his right.

Next day, Bragg sought to rid himself of this threat by launching a carefully timed assault. Major General Breckinridge with four brigades, supported by two batteries, was to go in at 4 p.m., an hour before dusk, carry the hill, and consolidate on its crest: the coming darkness would prevent a Federal counterattack.

At the appointed hour, Breckinridge's battle lines advanced and, after fierce fighting, stormed the slope. The plan was to stop and occupy the ridge, but the exhilarated troops hotly pursued the retreating Federals. Soon the massed Rebel infantry were beyond their artillery support and within short range of 57 Union guns on the other side of the river. The massacre was fearful: 1,500 of the cream of Bragg's army fell within a few minutes. The survivors returned to their lines, bringing to a close the bloody, but indecisive, Battle of Stones River, or as the South called it, Murfreesboro.

A colorful record of service for a Union soldier serving in the Army of the Cumberland.

Amusements and pastimes

Time could hang heavy on a soldier's hands, especially when he was off duty. During the day, reading newspapers and books—no matter how old or how crass—was a common pastime, as was playing cards or other games—often with money at stake. Writing to family and friends back home also helped to while away the hours. Some men, however, just lounged around, or slept.

In the evenings, beside campfires, there would be story-telling, music, theatricals, nostalgic songs, and an avid exchange of gossip, particularly concerning future movements of the army. It was also the time for visiting friends, or even relations,

The aftermath

The Battle of Stones River, or Murfreesboro, as the South called it, was an inconclusive, bloody struggle. Out of his 43,400-strong army, Rosecrans lost a total of 13,249 men. The Rebels lost 10,266 men out of a total of 37,712.

On January 3, 1863, Bragg ordered a withdrawal to Tullahoma, 36 miles south. There, the Rebels would wait some six months for the Federals to come at them again.

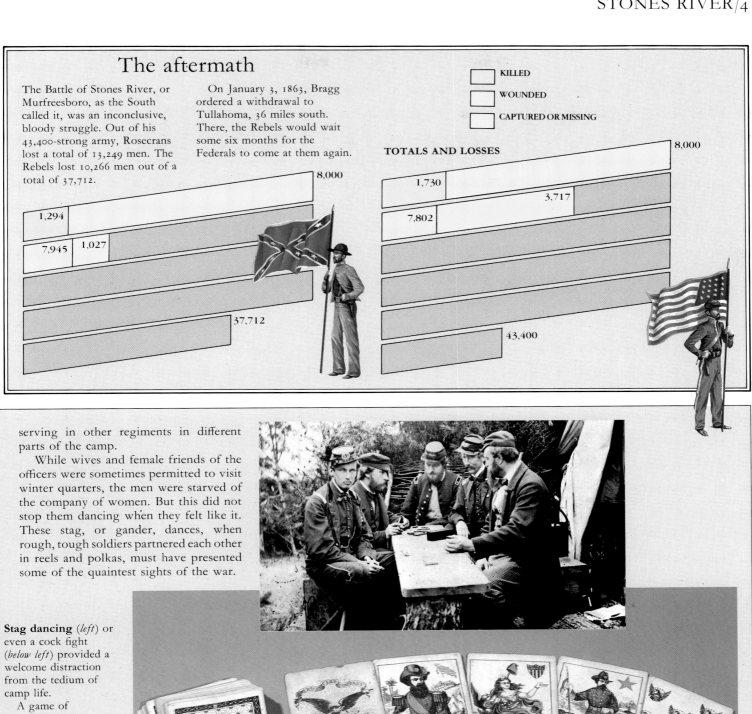

KILLED

WOUNDED

CAPTURED OR MISSING

1,294

7,945   1,027

37,712

8,000

TOTALS AND LOSSES

1,730

3,717

7,802

8,000

43,400

serving in other regiments in different parts of the camp.

While wives and female friends of the officers were sometimes permitted to visit winter quarters, the men were starved of the company of women. But this did not stop them dancing when they felt like it. These stag, or gander, dances, when rough, tough soldiers partnered each other in reels and polkas, must have presented some of the quaintest sights of the war.

Stag dancing (*left*) or even a cock fight (*below left*) provided a welcome distraction from the tedium of camp life.

A game of dominoes (*above right*) was another way of passing the time. And poker might be played with patriotic playing cards (*right*), below which are dice and an ivory poker chip. The latter was found with the coins in the leather purse which belonged to an Ohioan private. The carved pipe was made in France specifically for export to America.

Chancellorsville

MAY 1—4, 1863

". . . the attacking force emerged from the forest and rushed on . . . in such multitudes that our men went down before them like trees in a hurricane."

MAJOR GENERAL OLIVER O. HOWARD, USA, after the battle

AFTER HIS DEBACLE at Fredericksburg in December, 1862, Major General Burnside was removed from the command of the Federal Army of the Potomac on January 25, 1863. A period of quiet then descended along the banks of the Rappahannock River in Virginia, which lasted through the winter months.

The new Union commander, Major General Joseph Hooker, devoted his efforts to raising the morale of his troops, camped around Falmouth on the north side of the Rappahannock River. Meanwhile, the Confederate Army of Northern Virginia—not as well clad or fed as the Federals—kept watch from their lines in the hills behind Fredericksburg.

"Fighting Joe," as Hooker had been labeled by the press during McClellan's Peninsula Campaign, displayed an unforeseen talent for organizing and running a large army. Hooker replaced Burnside's ponderous grand division structure with a system in which his seven infantry corps commanders reported to him directly. The introduction of distinctive badges for all corps promoted a feeling of pride among their members. Hooker drastically curbed desertion and homesickness by arranging a system of furloughs. The neglected cavalry was detached from the infantry so that it could operate as an autonomous force. It was also brought up to strength and given a standard of training which at last put it on a par with the Rebel horse troops. By the time spring arrived, Hooker was confident that the 130,000-strong Army of the Potomac was once again ready to take the field against the Confederates.

Recalling Lincoln's advice in a letter to him,

"Beware of rashness, but with energy and sleepless vigilance go forward, and give us victories,"

Hooker carefully set about preparing an offensive which displayed genuine brilliance in its conception. "My plan is perfect," he immodestly proclaimed— and it nearly was.

The Union's 1863 campaign season in the eastern theater began on April 27 when the Union XI and XII Corps moved off, undetected by the Confederates, on a circuitous 27-mile march upriver to Kelly's Ford. The V Corps joined them on the 28th, and crossings began. While the Rappahannock was being forded upstream by this flanking force, Hooker ordered Major General John Sedgwick to take the I, III and VI Corps and move three miles downstream on April 29 to create a diversion.

This proved so successful that by noon, April 30, Hooker was able to move nearly four corps with cavalry and artillery support, wagons, and ambulances to their designated point of concentration. This was Chancellorsville crossroads, ten miles west of Fredericksburg and in the rear of General Robert E. Lee's army.

It was an exceedingly dangerous moment for the South, since Lee, with only about 60,000 troops and without Lieutenant General James Longstreet, who was on detached service with two divisions of his I Corps, was caught in the jaws of a vise: 45,000 Union soldiers were in front of him and 70,000 behind him. It was no wonder, then, that Hooker crowed:

"The Confederate army is now the legitimate property of the Army of the Potomac."

In an address to his troops, he added that:

"The enemy must either ingloriously fly or come out from behind his defenses and give us battle upon our own ground, where certain destruction awaits him."

Lee had no intention of either flying or being destroyed, no matter how disastrous the situation appeared. As a first measure, he had, on April 29, sent Major General Richard Anderson's division, less two brigades, six miles down the Fredericksburg Turnpike toward Chancellorsville. The troops had orders to dig in there, and hold any Union advance, even though they would be in the open. This was an unheard of practice, and

JOSEPH HOOKER (1814–79)

JAMES EWELL BROWN STUART (1833–64)

"Fighting Joe" Hooker, a spirited and aggressive soldier, was the Union commander at Chancellorsville. A native of Massachusetts, he graduated from West Point in 1837 to join the artillery, and served in both the Seminole and the Mexican Wars before resigning his commission in 1853.

Shortly after the outbreak of the Civil War, Hooker became a brigadier general of US Volunteers. By October, 1861, he was commanding a brigade in the Army of the Potomac. Six months later, he was promoted to major general (USV), and commanded a division in the III Corps of Major General Pope's ill-fated Army of Virginia. After Second Bull Run, Hooker was given the I Corps in the Army of the Potomac, and took part in Major General George McClellan's Antietam campaign, where he was wounded.

As commander of the Center Grand Division under Major General Burnside at Fredericksburg, Hooker schemed to obtain the leadership of the Army of the Potomac. His chance came in January, 1863. However, Hooker was defeated at Chancellorsville, and relieved of his command in June, 1863.

Hooker was then transferred to the western theater as a corps commander, and took part in Sherman's advance to Atlanta. When Hooker failed to achieve command of the Army of the Tennessee he requested that he be relieved.

A dashing soldier who wore a plumed hat and red-lined cape, "Jeb" Stuart, one of the best known cavalry leaders of the Civil War, was given command at Chancellorsville by General Robert E. Lee after Lieutenant General Stonewall Jackson and Major General A.P. Hill were wounded.

A Virginian and West Pointer, Stuart served in the mounted rifles and cavalry in the US Army, and was wounded fighting Indians on the frontier. Stuart resigned his commission in May, 1861, to follow his state, becoming colonel of the 1st Virginia Cavalry and seeing action at First Bull Run. He was then promoted to brigadier general, and led his cavalry against General McClellan on the peninsula.

Stuart rose to major general in July, 1862, and was given command of all cavalry in the Army of Northern Virginia. Raiding and scouting over wide areas, his troopers became Lee's "eyes and ears."

After a temporary command of an infantry corps at Chancellorsville, Stuart soon reverted to the role he knew best—leading cavalry. During the ensuing invasion of the North, he won the biggest cavalry engagement of the war at Brandy Station. By the spring of 1864, when Lieutenant General Grant began his thrust toward Richmond, Stuart's Cavalry Corps was past its best, being short of both men and horses. On May 11, 1864, at Yellow Tavern, on the outskirts of Richmond, Stuart was mortally wounded by Major General Philip Sheridan's troopers.

presaged the era of trench warfare that reached its peak in World War I.

After studying reconnaissance reports, Lee correctly decided that Sedgwick was making a feint, and that the principal attack would come from the direction of Chancellorsville. On the night of April 30, he ordered Major General Lafayette McLaws to move his division (less Brigadier General William Barksdale's brigade) to support Anderson; Lieutenant General Thomas J. Jackson's II Corps (less Major General Jubal Early's division) was to follow a few hours later. Only Early's division reinforced by Barksdale's and Brigadier General Cadmus Wilcox's brigades—about 12,000 men and 45 guns—were to remain in the Fredericksburg defenses to watch Sedgwick.

After considerable delays on the morning of May 1, Union columns began to advance eastward from Chancellorsville, through a vast, thickly wooded area known as the Wilderness. This dense second-growth forest of scrub, pine, and oak was difficult terrain, but the Federals managed to gain the advantageous high ground. Lee, commanding the Confederate front, moved to meet them, but before battle could be joined, Hooker halted and turned back.

Later, the Federal commander gave this explanation for this retrograde movement which so angered some of his subordinates:

"Before I had proceeded two miles the heads of my columns, while still upon the narrow roads in these interminable forests, where it was impossible to manoeuvre my forces, were met by Jackson with a full two-thirds of the entire Confederate army. I had no alternative but to turn back, as I had only a fragment of my command in hand, and take up the position about Chancellorsville which I had occupied during the night, as I was being rapidly outflanked upon my right, the enemy having open ground on which to operate."

Skirmishers were pushed forward by the Confederates to feel out the Union positions. It was discovered that Hooker's forces—now nearly five corps strong—were deployed behind two lines of breastworks facing south and east, at a right angle to each other, with the area in front of them cleared to a depth of 100 yards to give an unobstructed field of fire; artillery was positioned across the roads. The Confederate commander, when apprised of these strong defensive works,

Taking shelter
behind breastworks as best they can, Federal soldiers of the 29th Pennsylvania Regiment of the Second Brigade of Major General Henry W. Slocum's XII

Corps come under withering Confederate artillery fire during the fighting on May 3.

The reorganization of the Army of Northern Virginia

The Army of Northern Virginia was created by General Robert E. Lee in June, 1862, when he took over the Confederate forces in the Virginia Peninsula after General Joseph E. Johnston was wounded at Seven Pines.

Lee welded his command into a formidable fighting machine, with a flexibility on the battlefield which was to perplex many Union generals. He favored deploying his army in two wings, one under General James Longstreet—which usually held the enemy in front—and the other under General Stonewall Jackson, a master of daring flank marches and surprise attacks. It was a successful combination which came to an untimely end at Chancellorsville in May, 1863, when Jackson was mortally wounded.

"I know not how to replace him," Lee said on hearing that his "great lieutenant" had succumbed to pneumonia on May 10. Indeed, he could not replace the stricken general, for there was no officer available to match his tactical genius.

Lee resignedly accepted this misfortune as God's will, and set about rethinking the organization of the Army of Northern Virginia. The strength of his force lying at Fredericksburg was gradually built up until it numbered about 70,000 men, which he divided into three corps, each comprising three divisions. Longstreet had the I Corps, and Richard S. Ewell and Ambrose P. Hill, both promoted to lieutenant general, were given the II and III Corps respectively.

It was in this formation that, on June 3, 1863, the Army of Northern Virginia set out on the Gettysburg campaign; and it remained so composed until the end of the war. This most famous of Southern armies would continue to give a good account of itself against ever-increasing odds in the months and years following Chancellorsville; but it never again achieved the brilliant victories that resulted from the Lee–Jackson partnership.

General Robert E. Lee, creator of the Army of Northern Virginia, salutes his cheering troops as he rides alongside them on his favorite horse, Traveller.

accepted that it would be folly to attempt a frontal assault.

At that moment, Major General J.E.B. Stuart's Rebel cavalry, which had been probing the right of Hooker's position, reported that this flank was open to an attack from the west. The Union XI Corps, composed largely of German immigrants under Major General Oliver O. Howard, had been placed there because it was thought to be the least likely part of the line to see serious action. The XI Corps defenses faced south, conforming with those of the units on its left, but the extreme right was anchored on nothing stronger than the woods.

As Lee pondered how to take advantage of this situation, the Rev. B.F.C. Lacy, a chaplain in Jackson's command, came forward with the news that he knew the area well, and could point out a country road which would lead around the Union right.

On the night of May 1, Lee, who had already shown a disregard for traditional military rules by dividing his army in the face of a superior force, decided to take an even greater risk. He would retain Anderson's and McLaws's divisions of only 14,000 to face Hooker's 75,000 troops, while Jackson and his corps went on a flanking march across the Federals' front to fall on their exposed right. Everything depended upon "Stonewall" Jackson ex-

The remains of Union breastworks between Dowdall's Tavern and Chancellorsville a year after the battle. It was here that the troops of General Oliver O. Howard's XI Corps rallied during the Rebel onslaught of May 2, 1863.

ecuting his dangerous maneuver quickly and quietly.

At about 8 a.m. the next morning, the six-mile-long Confederate II Corps column, accouterments muffled, moved out on its roundabout journey, with Jackson urging them to maintain a good pace. Lee's meager forces were left to keep Hooker's attention focused on them. Part of Jackson's corps was observed by the Federals as it crossed a clearing on the southern leg of its march, and the Union commander came to the conclusion that Lee was attempting a flanking movement.

In the early afternoon Hooker ordered Major General Daniel Sickles, commanding the III Corps, to send forward two divisions, later reinforced by an XI Corps brigade, to interdict this enemy movement. The Union troops, however, were successfully held at bay by the Rebel rear guard. This skirmish not only provided a diversion which allowed Jackson through unhindered, but it made Hooker reappraise the situation. From the number of wagons and ambulances that had been seen in the Rebel column, he now thought that the Confederates must be in retreat. Despite later reports of Confederates massing on his right flank, Hooker refused to believe that an attack through the Wilderness was being planned.

Meanwhile, Jackson urged on the rest of his corps, arriving at Howard's extreme right flank at about 5.30 p.m. Jackson sent back a message to Lee that he was in position to attack, but this good news was tempered by alarming developments at Fredericksburg. Jubal Early, misunderstanding an order, had vacated the fortified lines and was marching toward Chancellorsville, leaving the Confederate rear open to Sedgwick. Lee sent Early hurrying back to Fredericksburg, then turned his attention to the impending battle.

At 6 p.m., a signal gun boomed away to the west, bugles rang out and Jackson's veterans charged out of the forest, which was so dense that some soldiers had their clothes ripped from them. They fell upon Howard's unsuspecting troops, inflicting 2,000 casualties and driving them off in confusion. Hooker immediately mustered Major General Hiram Berry's Second Division of the III Corps, as well as any other formed units he could rally in the vicinity, and supported them with the 22 guns in a clearing named Hazel Grove, immediately opposite Jackson's advancing right. In doing so, he succeeded in blunting the Confederate thrust.

As daylight failed and darkness came on, the advance lost its impetus, even

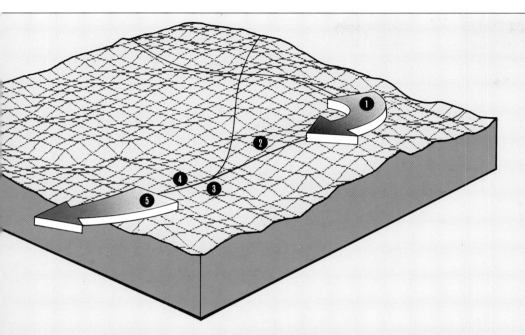

large numbers of Rebel wagons moving south, he wrongly supposed that the Confederates were in retreat.

When, on the evening of May 2, Jackson's men (1) charged into the Union right flank, it was a complete surprise.

The Federals had mistakenly thought that this part of the Wilderness, as the tangled region was known, was impenetrable enough to deter a large-scale attack.

The Union troops in this area were deployed along the Orange Turnpike, facing south, and were unaware of Jackson's presence until it was too late. The Union XI Corps did not have time to rally near Talley's Farm (2). But they did manage to put up stiffer resistance around the Wilderness Church (3), and, particularly, Dowdall's Tavern (4), where they had thrown up some breastworks.

The speed and ferocity of the Rebel attack swept all before it, and the area was soon the scene of a rout. Federal troops (5) fled toward the Union headquarters at Chancellorsville, where Hooker learned of his army's retreat.

Major General Darius N. Couch's Federal II Corps form a line of battle to cover the XI Corps' retreat from Stonewall Jackson's jubilant Rebels. The Federals were hampered by their wagons and animals, which blocked the road.

The Union commander of the Army of the Potomac, Major General Joe Hooker, thought that his outflanking maneuver on April 27 had put General Robert E. Lee's Army of Northern Virginia in a position from which it could not escape.

Hooker had led three corps on a 56-mile flanking march, bringing them onto the Rebel left and rear within four days. He had failed to press his advantage, however, and had given the Rebel commander time to devise a plan of his own.

Reconnaissance proved to Lee that the Federal right wing was unprotected, and together with Lieutenant General Stonewall Jackson, he devised a way to attack these Federals, but still remain undetected by the main body of the opposing army: while Lee held off 75,000 Federals with only 14,000 Rebels east of Chancellorsville, Jackson began a flank march with the rest of the army.

The area around Chancellorsville, where Hooker had established his headquarters, was known as the Wilderness. Dense second-growth forests extended for 20 miles from east to west and 15 miles from north to south, and were deemed to be impassable for large bodies of men. But the Rebels had been shown a route through, by way of the Brock Road, which looped southwest before joining the Orange Plank Road. This road led to the Orange Turnpike, along which the Federals were deployed.

It took Jackson's ten-mile column of infantry nine hours to complete their march on the warm spring day of May 2. Lee had taken a tremendous risk in dividing his army before a superior force; but his confidence in Jackson was not misplaced. For, when the Rebels burst upon the Federal right flank at about 5 p.m. that day, Lee not only released his army from the threat of an imminent encirclement, but also seized from Hooker a considerable victory, which the Federal commander had claimed prematurely.

Jackson's troops had covered 12 miles through the Wilderness before getting into position for their evening attack. But their day-long march had not exhausted them. As one Rebel soldier recorded: "For a moment all the troops seemed buried in the depths of the gloomy forest, and then suddenly the echoes waked and swept the country for miles . . . —the wild 'Rebel yell' of the long Confederate lines. Never was an assault delivered with greater enthusiasm. Fresh from the long winter's waiting . . . the troops were in fine condition and in high spirits . . . 'Old Jack' was there upon the road in their midst; there could be . . . no failure."

Three divisions led the attack along the Orange Turnpike. It took them half an hour to make their way to the first clearing in the forest, near Talley's Farm **(1)**, and their clothes were torn from scrabbling through the thickets. The men of Major General Oliver O. Howard's XI Corps were preparing a meal—their arms stacked on one side—when the Rebels surged out of the dense woods toward the Federal encampment **(2)** around Talley's Farm. The men here had no opportunity to stand and fight so they retreated along the road toward Wilderness Church **(5)** and Dowdall's Tavern **(6)**, where stronger breastworks could afford them a chance to fight under cover. They made an attempt to bring some artillery into action on the turnpike, but were soon overrun by the Rebel onslaught.

Hazel Grove **(9)**, a clearing to the southeast of Dowdall's Tavern, was the only area in which the Federals could establish an effective hold. This ridge of high ground was not more than 200 yards from the woods **(8)** at any point, and Union artillery was effectively deployed here.

Wagons, ambulances and frightened horses **(7)** soon blocked the eastward escape of the Federals along the road. Confusion reigned and slaughter was terrible, since the Federals **(4)** were unable to withstand the organized Rebel advance **(3)**. Howard described the Rebel movements: ". . . the men in front would halt and fire, and, while these were reloading, another set would run before them, halt and fire, in no regular line, but in such multitudes that our men went down before them like trees in a hurricane."

The Rebels won a decisive victory that night, but failed to consolidate it because darkness prevented further action in the dense forests. As darkness descended, Rebel soldiers were responsible for a tragic accident: they mistook their inspiring leader, Stonewall Jackson, for an enemy and shot and mortally wounded him.

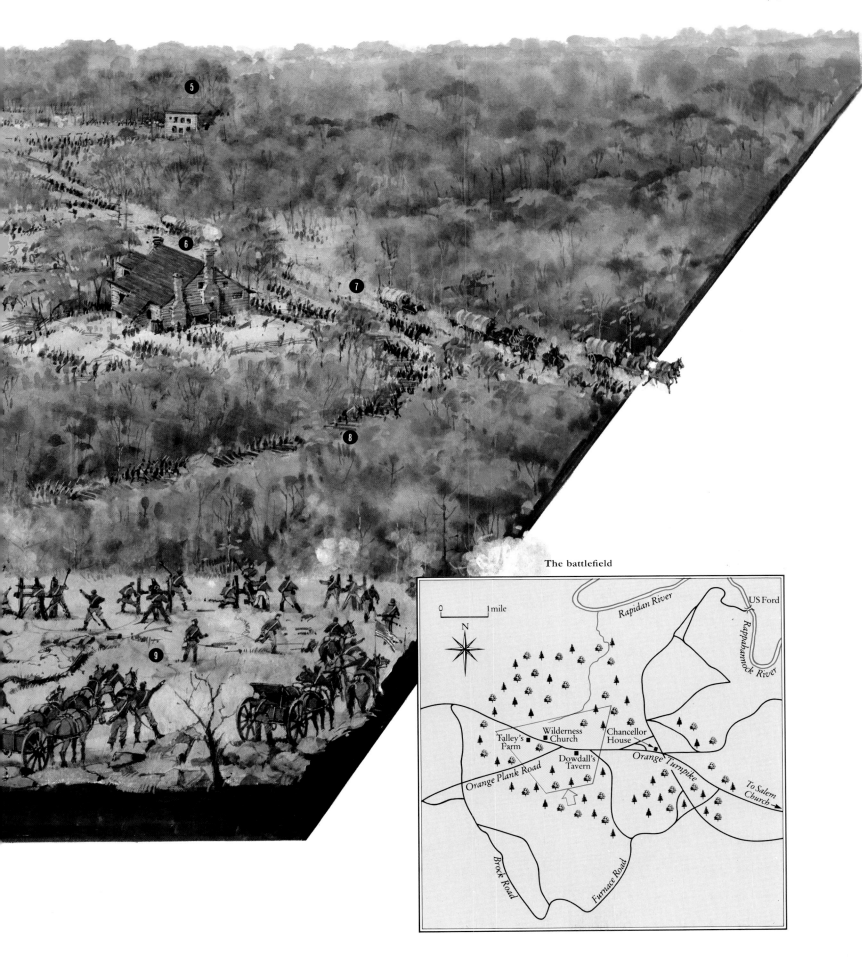

The battlefield

Caring for the sick and wounded

Both Union and Confederate authorities applied themselves to the enormous task of caring for the hundreds of thousands of sick and wounded who were casualties of the conflict. Nevertheless, many patients died and others suffered excruciatingly, chiefly because medical knowledge in the 1860s did not encompass the use of antiseptics and sterile dressings and instruments, nor did it recognize the importance of hygiene and sanitation.

The US Medical Department and the CSA Medical Service were each organized under the command of a Surgeon General, and each provided battlefield first aid, ambulance transport, field and general hospitals, plus day-to-day health care for the troops. Throughout the war, the Union employed 10,000 surgeons, and the Confederacy probably had around 4,000. Many of these doctors were deployed at or near the front and, though they were generally regarded as non-combatant, several were killed or wounded in the course of their humanitarian duty.

While a battle was raging, it was usual for a regiment's assistant surgeon to be close up in the center, immediately behind his unit. He was accompanied by a hospital steward, carrying a 20-pound hospital knapsack, and the infirmary detail—bandsmen or, later in the war, ambulance corpsmen—with stretchers to collect the badly wounded. The assistant surgeon applied temporary dressings and sent the casualties back to a field hospital set up by the surgeon about a mile to the rear in a convenient house or barn, or in tents.

After 1862, Federal field hospitals were organized on a division or corps basis. They were marked by a large yellow flag with a green border and a green H in the center; similar, though smaller, flags often signposted the route from the battle line to the field hospital. Here, on both sides of the line, and within the sound, if not the range, of gunfire, full medical treatments—including major operations—were carried out in filthy surroundings by surgeons with dirty hands, using instruments which may or may not have been given a cursory wipe between operations. Ignorant of the agents and causes of infection, they assumed that wounds would become inflamed and suppurate as a part of the healing process. Many men died as a result.

After big battles, and in much-fought-over zones, it was common for public buildings in nearby towns to be commandeered by the medical authorities and turned into hospitals. Transportation to these makeshift establishments, or to railheads or wharves where patients could be transferred to general hospitals in the rear, was carried out by ambulances, the best of which were padded and sprung four-wheel vehicles.

As the casualty lists lengthened and existing general hospitals overflowed,

many military hospitals were built. They were of single-story wood construction, well ventilated and heated, with clean beds, nourishing food, and attentive medical staff. In these surroundings, the sick and wounded stood the best chance of recovery. Chimborazo, the largest military hospital in the world at that time, was built by the Confederates at Richmond. By the end of the war, it had 150 wards, capable of housing a total of 4,500 patients; in all, some 76,000 men were admitted.

Because of its vast manufacturing capacity, the Union produced adequate medical supplies, including chloroform (though anesthesia was still imperfect and some surgeons preferred to operate without it).

The Confederacy bought many of its medical goods abroad, and brought them through the US Navy blockade. But, on occasion, vital drugs were smuggled through the lines from the North, sewn into the petticoats of women sympathetic to the Southern cause. Also, captured material helped stretch out limited supplies, as did the output of the few laboratories set up to manufacture herbal remedies.

The suffering of the Civil War wounded was increased by the relatively crude state of medicine. Field hospitals, such as the one at Savage's Station (*right*), dealt with casualties sent straight back from the firing line.

Amputations (*left*) were often done without anesthesia. Convalescents, such as those (*below left*) on Marye's Heights, Fredericksburg, stood a better chance of recovery if admitted to a military hospital—for example Armory Square (*below right*) in Washington.

though pockets of fierce fighting continued to break out among the thickets. Jackson ordered his reserve division, commanded by Major General A.P. Hill, to advance to the front and take over from those of Brigadier Generals R.E. Rodes and R.E. Colston, with a view to resuming his offensive.

Meanwhile, Hooker had been trying to rally his right wing, now pushed back two miles and forming a west-facing position perpendicular to its previous line. The Union army was thus deployed in a V-shaped salient narrowing around Chancellorsville crossroads, with part of Sickles' III Corps cut off outside its apex (though he later managed to rejoin the main body).

It was in this edgy, disorienting atmosphere that a serious blow was dealt to the Southern cause. Jackson and a small escort, returning in the gloom from a reconnaissance in front of the Confederate lines, were shot at by their own troops—the 18th North Carolina—who had mistaken them for Union cavalry. Two of the general's party were killed; Jackson himself was hit three times.

As Jackson was carried to the rear, Federal artillery opened a bombardment and his second-in-command, A.P. Hill, was wounded, too. "Stonewall," the II Corps' famed commander, had his left arm amputated and at first it was thought he would recover. Pneumonia set in, however, and eight days later he died.

That night, Lee was delighted to learn of the II Corps' success, but distressed at the incapacitation of Jackson, his "great lieutenant," and of A.P. Hill. He placed the command in the hands of the most senior general in the area, the cavalry leader J.E.B. Stuart (who had never before handled large numbers of infantry), with orders to press home the attack next morning, break the Federal lines, and link up with his forces pushing in from the east and southeast.

In the meantime, Hooker, who already possessed a large proportion of fresh troops lying between Chancellorsville and the Rappahannock, ordered Sedgwick to join him from Fredericksburg the following day. However, the purpose of this further reinforcement is still unclear, since the Federal commander never made full use of the reserves he had available when Lee and Stuart began to attack the salient around the crossroads at dawn.

Before long on that morning of May 3, a fearsome fight developed. Artillery shells set parts of the woods ablaze and the hideous shrieks of wounded being burned

The death of Stonewall Jackson

Late on the first day of the Battle of Chancellorsville, May 2, 1863, Lieutenant General Thomas J. "Stonewall" Jackson was accidentally shot by soldiers of the 18th North Carolina Regiment. The prognosis was that he would lose his left arm, the bones of which had been badly shattered by two bullets.

Initially, hopes were high that this great Confederate general would recover; there were, after all, many amputees around to prove that such an operation was not necessarily fatal.

But Jackson's general health was poor and, on May 7, he contracted pneumonia. Neither expert medical ministrations, nor the nursing of his wife, who had rushed to his bedside in the Chandler farmhouse at Guiney's Station, were enough to save this hero of the South. His condition worsened, and, on Sunday, May 10, Jackson died. His last words, uttered in delirium, were: "Order A.P. Hill to prepare for battle. Tell Major Hawks to advance the commissary train. Let us cross the river and rest in the shade."

Jackson's body was taken to Richmond, where it lay in state in the Hall of Representatives. Thousands, stunned by what President Davis described as "the great national calamity," came to pay their last respects. As was his wish, Jackson was buried at Lexington, where, before the war, he had been a professor at the Virginia Military Institute.

Jackson reviews his famous "foot cavalry" (*below*), whose swift marches during the Shenandoah Valley Campaign in 1862, insured resounding Confederate success, and enduring fame for their commander.

The death of Jackson, portrayed (*far right*) by J.A. Elder, shocked the South. The Richmond *Enquirer* (*right*) was "draped" in mourning "for the great and good man," whose funeral procession (*below right*) formed at V.M.I.

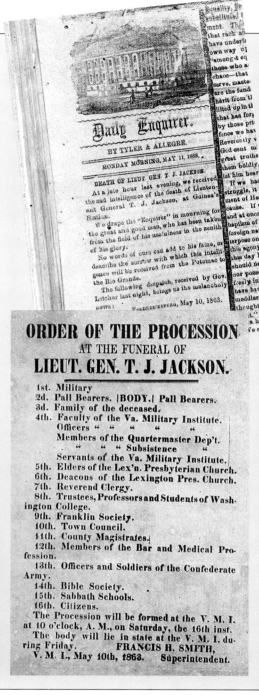

alive mingled with the piercing Rebel yell, the roar of the guns, and the rattle of musketry. Concerted Southern pressure began to force back the Federals who, in giving up the high ground of the Hazel Grove clearing at the head of the salient, made possible a devastating bombardment of their crumbling lines. Thirty-one Rebel guns were placed there, causing havoc in the Union positions. One round struck a pillar on the porch of the Chancellor House, which was Hooker's headquarters, bringing part of it down on the luckless general himself.

Hooker went to the rear, more badly injured than some perhaps thought at the time. He temporarily turned the command over to Major General Darius Couch of the II Corps, with orders to withdraw a mile to a new defense line formed across a bend in the Rappahannock and its Rapidan confluent, and covering US Ford. Couch had to move quickly, for Stuart and Lee had penetrated the salient and joined forces to drive the disjointed Union troops back toward the river.

As the Federals withdrew, Lee rode into the Chancellorsville clearing, where the Chancellor House was burning and the woods around were billowing smoke. There, he was greeted by prolonged cheers from his triumphant soldiers. It was not a time to savor victory, however. News arrived that Sedgwick had attacked Early at Fredericksburg and driven him off the fortified heights. This Union advance would, by mid-afternoon, be contested around Salem Church, six miles from Chancellorsville. Lee dispatched McLaws' division to assist Early, and closed up the rest of his tired army toward the Federals' new defense line.

May 4 passed without a resumption of the conflict north of Chancellorsville, and that day Lee himself went to Salem Church, along with more reinforcements, to help direct an attack on Sedgwick's

reinforced VI Corps. Although Hooker had forces at his disposal vastly superior to those of the Confederates in front of him, he made no move to help Sedgwick, who that night took his command back across the river.

Early returned to Fredericksburg on May 5, and Lee and his troops marched back to Chancellorsville, where he planned to assault the Union positions next day. It was not to be, however. Under cover of that dark and stormy night, Hooker decided to withdraw the Army of the Potomac to its quarters at Falmouth. Consequently, Lee decided to return to Fredericksburg with his army.

The aftermath

The Battle of Chancellorsville, which Hooker hoped would win a much-needed victory for the North, in fact ended in disaster. Hooker's excursion, which had begun so promisingly, cost 17,287 casualties—from an army of about 130,000 men.

Lee, whose daring conduct of the battle won admiration from military men the world over, suffered 12,463 casualties from a total of at least 60,000 effectives.

When news of Hooker's defeat and subsequent retreat reached President Lincoln, he was dumbfounded. "My God, my God, what will the country say?" he kept repeating.

The retreat of the Union forces after the Battle of Chancellorsville deprived Lee of a further opportunity to trade blows with the Army of the Potomac. So he took his triumphant soldiers back to Fredericksburg, harboring ambitious plans for another invasion of the North.

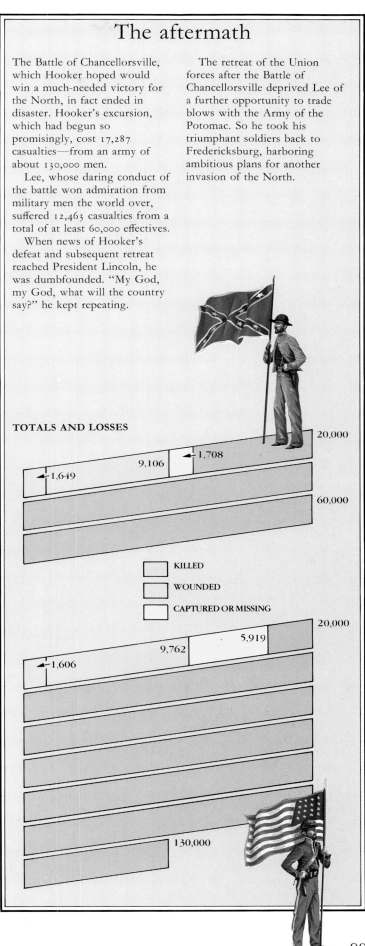

TOTALS AND LOSSES

9,106   ◄—1,708
◄—1,649   20,000

60,000

☐ KILLED

☐ WOUNDED

☐ CAPTURED OR MISSING

5,919   20,000
9,762
◄—1,606

130,000

Gettysburg

JULY 1–3, 1863

"The men and officers of your command have written the name of Virginia today as high as it has ever been written before."

GENERAL ROBERT E. LEE, CSA, to MAJOR GENERAL GEORGE PICKETT, CSA, after the failure of "Pickett's Charge"

THE PROTECTION OF RICHMOND was the major concern of the Army of Northern Virginia. But General Robert E. Lee reasoned that to hold on to the Southern capital he need not necessarily adopt a defensive posture.

After his victory at Chancellorsville at the beginning of May 1863, Lee decided not to wait to parry the renewed Union advances that were bound to occur some time in the future. Instead, he could just as easily guarantee the safety of Richmond and relieve pressure on the Confederacy by once more carrying the war into the North—Pennsylvania, this time—and compelling the Federal Army of the Potomac to follow him.

As Colonel A.L. Long, Lee's military secretary, recorded:

"In this plan he had a decided object.... There was in his mind no thought of reaching Philadelphia, as was subsequently feared in the North. Yet he was satisfied that the Federal army, if defeated in a pitched battle, would be seriously disorganized and forced to retreat across the Susquehanna—an event which would give him control of Maryland and Western Pennsylvania, and probably of West Virginia, while it would very likely cause the fall of Washington City and the flight of the Federal Government. Moreover, an important diversion would be made in favor of the Western department, where the affairs of the Confederacy were on the decline. These highly important results, which would in all probability follow a successful battle, fully warranted, in his opinion, the hazard of an invasion of the North."

There was another no less significant consideration too: food. Lee intended to subsist on the plentiful resources in Federal territory during the coming campaign so that Virginia could have some respite.

By the end of May, the high-spirited Army of Northern Virginia, increased in strength to some 77,000 men, had been reorganized into three corps: the I Corps under Lieutenant General James Longstreet; the II Corps under Lieutenant General Richard S. Ewell; and the III Corps under Lieutenant General Ambrose P. Hill. On June 3, the Confederates marched west from their fortified lines behind Fredericksburg, turned northward up the Shenandoah Valley, then crossed the Potomac River and entered Union territory.

It took Major General Joseph Hooker nine days to discover that most of the Army of Northern Virginia was no longer on the opposite side of the Rappahannock River. When he did, he made plans to strike against Richmond, which would have called Lee's bluff. But Lincoln's government intervened to remind Hooker that his immediate priorities were the protection of Washington and the pursuit and destruction of the Confederate army.

Hooker's problem was that he did not really know where Lee was—reports from his cavalry patrols varied. Nevertheless, he struck north, being careful to keep his 93,500-strong army between the capital and the Rebels' likely position.

From the west side of the Blue Ridge Mountains, Lee was also ignorant of the opposition's movements, because Major General J.E.B. Stuart's cavalry was out of touch with him. Until June 28, when a spy told him that the Union army was just 25 miles southeast, at Frederick, Maryland, Lee thought that Hooker was still south of the Potomac. Lee also learned from his intelligence sources that Hooker's request to be relieved of his command had been accepted after a disagreement with Washington. He had been replaced by Major General George G. Meade, a man whom Lee knew and respected.

This latest intelligence made Lee recast his plans. He issued orders for his three widely dispersed corps to concentrate at Cashtown, 35 miles southwest of Harrisburg, the Pennsylvania state capital. In the meantime, Meade had advanced his

GEORGE GORDON MEADE (1815–72)

Meade, a tough, hot-tempered soldier, commanded the Army of the Potomac at Gettysburg. Born in Spain of American parents—his father was US Naval Agent in Cadiz—he entered West Point aged 16, graduated in 1835, and served for a year as an artillery officer. He then resigned to pursue a career in civil engineering. Meade married in 1840, but, finding that he could not bring up a family on the income he was earning, he rejoined the US Army, as a second lieutenant.

Meade saw service in the Mexican War and afterward spent most of his time in military engineering. When the Civil War broke out, he obtained a brigadier generalship in the Pennsylvania Volunteers.

Initially, Meade was employed in the building of Fort Pennsylvania—a fort in the defenses around Washington. He did not see action until Major General McClellan's Peninsula Campaign of 1862, where he was wounded leading his brigade at Glendale. From then on, he made steady progress up the ranks, commanding a division at Antietam and Fredericksburg, and the V Corps at Chancellorsville in May, 1863.

By this time, Meade had established a reputation as a tenacious fighter, a fact which had not escaped President Lincoln's notice. And, when it came to choosing a new commander for the Army of the Potomac to replace Major General Joseph Hooker in June, 1863, Lincoln opted for Meade.

Meade's success in the forthcoming Battle of Gettysburg was tempered, however, with criticism over his decision not to pursue the retreating Rebels immediately after the battle. Nevertheless, Lincoln kept him in command of the Army of the Potomac until the end of the war. Thus, Meade became this army's longest-serving and most successful leader.

From early 1864 until the Confederate surrender in April, 1865, Meade, whose short temper was notorious, had to subordinate himself to Lieutenant General Ulysses S. Grant, the general in chief, who traveled with and directed the operations of the Army of the Potomac. It was a difficult situation for Meade, and Grant commended him for the way in which he handled it.

After the war, Meade's posts included being commander of the Division of the Atlantic. He died of pneumonia in 1872.

troops farther north and earmarked a good defensive position behind Pipe Creek in northern Maryland: his nearest corps to Lee was now at Emmitsburg, 12 miles south of Cashtown. The gap was closing fast.

Patrols of the two armies first sighted each other west of the small town of Gettysburg on the afternoon of June 30. Rebel infantrymen decided not to engage the Union cavalry, but returned next morning hoping to obtain footwear from a shoe factory there. The Rebel advance troops were seen by Lieutenant Marcellus E. Jones of the 8th Illinois Cavalry at about 5.30 a.m., as they moved up the Chambersburg Road toward his picket post east of Marsh Creek. He fired on the Confederates and attracted a fusillade of shots, the first fired in the Battle of Gettysburg.

Fortunately for the Union, the right man was in the right place when fighting broke out, namely Brigadier General John Buford, commander of the First Cavalry Division. He believed that once in the battle area, cavalry should dismount and deploy as infantry so that their breechloading carbines could be used to greatest effect. Although two brigades under strength, his men did just that on McPherson's Ridge, and managed to delay the Confederates until reinforcements arrived.

Both Lee and Meade were many miles away when the battle began and could exert no early influence on its course. Neither commander particularly wanted to fight at Gettysburg, which stood at the junction of ten roads, but now that strong elements of their forces had accidentally collided, they quickly poured troops into the area.

Although the Federals had a much stronger army than their opponents, they were farther away from Gettysburg. A.P. Hill's corps, attacking from the west, followed by R.S. Ewell's corps coming in from the north, brought overwhelming pressure to bear on the Union line. This line was held initially by the I Corps and the XI Corps (a USA corps was of lesser strength than a CSA corps). In the heavy fighting that ensued, the Federals lost their senior officer on the field, Major General John F. Reynolds, and were obliged to retire.

When Lee arrived on the scene in the afternoon, he found Ewell and Hill occupying commanding ground north and west of the town, and the Federals gathering on Cemetery Hill, an eminence to the south. Lee realized that the hill had to be taken before it could be fortified and

The changing face of field artillery

The Civil War marked a turning point for field artillery. Muzzle-loading smoothbore and rifled cannon, some with ranges little greater than that of a rifle-musket, dominated the battlefields. But, as the war progressed, more powerful breechloading rifled pieces were also beginning to appear, heralding a new era in gunnery.

As recommended by the US Ordnance Department, Northern field batteries avoided breechloaders in favor of two basic muzzle-loading types; the 12-pound smoothbore bronze Napoleon (named after its inventor, Emperor Napoleon III of France); and the 10-pound wrought-iron rifle. Both types fired solid projectiles, explosive shells, and a variety of case shot.

US batteries were generally equipped with six guns (though sometimes four, and occasionally eight) of the same kind, commanded by a captain. Two guns, under a lieutenant, constituted a section. A crew of seven served a gun which, along with its limber containing 50 rounds of mixed ammunition, was drawn by a team of six horses. Another six-horse team pulled the gun's caisson, which carried a further 150 rounds, a spare wheel, and other equip-

The 10-pound Parrott Rifle (*below left*) was a rifled muzzle-loader with a range of up to 3,500 yards. Made of cast iron, the gun had a wrought-iron "collar" encircling the touchhole. It was also cheap to manufacture.

ment. This one-gun unit—a platoon—was led by a sergeant, the chief of the piece.

The Federals calculated on having between two and three guns per 1,000 infantry, and concentrated their batteries in divisional groups, i.e. four to six batteries for 12,000 men. They also organized artillery reserves for their armies. These guns were kept under the commanding general's control, and proved particularly effective when massed fire was needed, because they could be deployed as one unit. The Army of the Potomac had more than 100 guns in its reserve.

A team of six horses drags a gun and its limber (*above*) at top speed in this sketch by Walter Taber. The limber, on which sit two Union soldiers, contained 50 rounds of mixed ammunition. Confederate gunners (*below*) fire a cannon from an embrasure in the Atlanta defenses in the struggle to stop Major General Sherman's troops from taking the city in the summer of 1864.

The Confederate field artillery was generally arranged in four-gun batteries, and, throughout the war, it was rare to find one battery with guns of all the same type. As a result, there were logistical problems of supplying ammunition for such a mixture of ordnance, but the situation was unavoidable. The South started out with a hodge-podge of artillery (a lot of which was obsolete), held by different states, and its capacity to manufacture modern guns was extremely limited. Captured weapons, therefore, played a large part in easing the Confederate shortage. In addition, some imported pieces managed to get through the US naval blockade.

Paradoxically, imported artillery—from Great Britain—represented the most up-to-date guns available: in particular, the Whitworth and Armstrong rifled breech-loaders offered exceptional power and accuracy. Although these superb guns were capable of firing more than three and a quarter miles, there was then no system of indirect fire control that could guide the shells onto a target not visible to the crew. Thus they were relegated to the same role as muzzle-loaders and used as direct support. Because horses were also in short supply in the South, Rebel guns were frequently pulled by only four-horse teams.

Confederate batteries were at first attached to brigades and used piecemeal in a fight. By the middle of the war, however, they had been reorganized into four-battery battalions, five of which were placed with a corps. This greatly increased their effectiveness on the battlefield.

July 3: Lee's last chance

Rebel Lieutenant General Richard Ewell's decision not to attempt to wrest Cemetery Hill from the Union forces gathering there on July 1, 1863, effectively cost the Confederates the invaluable high ground south of the town of Gettysburg.

So it was Federal Major General Winfield Hancock who formed a defensive line, shaped like an inverted fishhook, two and a half miles long, in this prime position. The Federal right lay on Culp's Hill, then the line curved through Cemetery Hill, extended down Cemetery Ridge and rested its left on two hills known as Little Round Top and Big Round Top.

At the end of the fighting on July 2, the Rebels gained a foothold on Culp's Hill, but lost it again prior to the main action on July 3. Having tried and failed to roll up the Union flanks, General Robert E. Lee opted to try to pierce the center of their line, just as the Army of the Potomac's commander Major General George Meade had predicted.

The Army of Northern Virginia occupied Seminary Ridge, roughly parallel with Cemetery Ridge, which lay about a mile to the east. It offered some tree cover, but was a less advantageous position for artillery than that which the Federals enjoyed. To soften up the Federal line before assaulting it, 150 Rebel guns on Seminary Ridge began, at 1 p.m., to blast away at the enemy. The Federals replied with their own cannonade, and, for two hours, the two sides pounded each other.

When the fire from Meade's batteries appeared to slacken, the men of Confederate Major General George Pickett (7), led by Brigadier Generals Lewis Armistead, Richard Garnett, and James Kemper, and the supporting divisions from Lieutenant General A.P. Hill's corps, began their charge on the Union center. The Rebel ranks headed toward the clump of trees (5) Lee had designated as the focus of their assault, compressing desperately as they were ravaged by renewed Union fire. From the front, the Rebels were hit by volleys from the 71st and 69th Pennsylvania Regiments (1, 4), and from the right by Vermont regiments (6) under Brigadier General George Stannard.

Armistead's momentary break (3) into the Union first line was the pinnacle of Pickett's Charge. However, without support, Armistead and 150 Rebels were soon killed or captured by the 72nd Pennsylvania (2).

The grand assault on the Union center had failed, with the loss of some 7,000 men. Lee broke off

the three-day battle and retreated to Virginia. His second invasion of the North was over.

During the late evening of the day before Pickett's heroic charge, Rebels under Major General Jubal Early assault, but cannot break, the Union line on Cemetery Hill.

garrisoned. He told General Ewell, now commanding the late Stonewall Jackson's men, to carry the high ground "if practicable," a dictum typical of the sort of discretionary order Lee regularly gave to Jackson, who would formulate his own plan to execute Lee's wishes. Ewell, however, interpreted the order literally, and decided that it was *not* practicable for his regiments to mount another attack,

---

An untimely civilian death

For all the fighting that took place around the town of Gettysburg in the huge three-day battle, only one civilian was killed: a 20-year-old woman named Jennie Wade.

Jennie and her mother were at her married sister's home in Baltimore Street, near Cemetery Hill, helping look after a baby that had just been born. The brick house was a little way out of the town, which was patrolled by Confederates, and just in front of the Union picket line. Shots were occasionally exchanged in the area, but that was all; the heavy fighting was elsewhere.

On the morning of July 3, while Jennie was busy making bread, a stray minié ball bored straight through two doors and smashed into her back, killing her at once.

A few days after Jennie was shot, news arrived that her fiancé, a corporal in the Union army, had died of wounds received in the Shenandoah Valley.

---

since they had already suffered heavy casualties.

Meanwhile, Federal reinforcements were arriving, and Major General Winfield S. Hancock, who had replaced Reynolds, was shaping a two-and-a-half mile defense line on the high ground south of the town. He placed his right on Culp's Hill, a wooded knoll northeast of Cemetery Hill, continued his fortifications through the latter height, then south along Cemetery Ridge, until he reached two other prominent hills, Little Round Top and Big Round Top, against which he rested his left. General Meade arrived at Gettysburg at midnight on July 1, and approved the choice of ground.

As Lee formulated his plans for the next day at his headquarters near Hill's position on Seminary Ridge, he was struggling against ill health. Despite a proposal by Longstreet to maneuver around Meade's left and give battle on ground of their own choosing, his instinct

---

A distinguished Union veteran

John L. Burns, the septuagenarian former constable of Gettysburg, was so angry when Confederate troops drove off his cows that he grabbed his musket and set out to get even with them.

A Union staff officer, Major E.P. Halstead, remembered encountering the old man, who was armed with an ancient musket and quaintly dressed in a white bell-crowned, broad-brimmed hat, a blue swallowtail coat with large brass buttons, and a yellow vest: "When near me he inquired, 'Which way are the rebels? Where are our troops?' I informed him that they were just in front, that he would soon overtake them. He then said with much enthusiasm, 'I know how to fight, I have fit before!'"

Indeed Burns had: he was a veteran of the War of 1812 and the Mexican War. He had even tried to volunteer for the Civil War but had been rejected because of his age.

On the firing line, Burns obtained a rifle-musket, though he declined the offer of a cartridge box from Sergeant George Eustice of the 7th Wisconsin Volunteers: "Slapping his pantaloons-pocket, he replied, 'I can get my hands in here quicker than in a box. I'm not used to them newfangled things,'" Sergeant Eustice later recalled.

Major General Abner Doubleday, commanding this part of the field on July 1, noted in his official report: "My thanks are specially due to a citizen of Gettysburg named John Burns, who, although over seventy years of age, shouldered his musket and offered his services to Colonel Wister, 150th Pennsylvania Volunteers. Colonel Wister advised him to fight in the woods, as there was more shelter there; but

he preferred to join our line of skirmishers in the open fields. When the troops retired, he fought with the Iron Brigade. He was wounded in three places."

Burns was captured by the Confederates, but was allowed to return to his home after the battle, where he recovered from his injuries. He soon became a national hero. The author and poet Bret Harte wrote verses about his exploits, and, when President Abraham Lincoln visited Gettysburg in November, 1863, he asked to be introduced to the old warrior.

John Burns died in February, 1872, and is permanently honored by a statue raised by the state of Pennsylvania in 1903 to mark the 40th anniversary of the Battle of Gettysburg.

---

told him that he had to fight at Gettysburg.

Lee's plan was as follows: early on July 2, Longstreet's fresh troops would assault from the southern end of Seminary Ridge, with their axis of advance northeast to a point beyond the Emmitsburg Road where Lee conjectured, wrongly, that the Union left flank was posted. In formulating his offensive, Lee anticipated that the weight of the oblique onslaught would be sufficient to roll up the entire Federal line along Cemetery Ridge.

As soon as Longstreet's attack began, Ewell's II Corps would demonstrate

against Meade's right flank, with permission to mount a full-scale assault if the chances for success looked promising. A.P. Hill was to create a diversion in the center, mainly by cannonading. With luck, the Federals would not be able to tell where the main blow was falling until it was too late.

Lee's plan hinged on close cooperation and coordination which, in the event, were not forthcoming. Things started to go awry when Longstreet, acting with even more slowness and deliberation than was his wont, delayed his attack until 4.30 p.m. Shortly before that time, Meade had

PICKETT'S IMMORTAL CHARGE

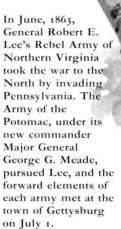

In June, 1863, General Robert E. Lee's Rebel Army of Northern Virginia took the war to the North by invading Pennsylvania. The Army of the Potomac, under its new commander Major General George G. Meade, pursued Lee, and the forward elements of each army met at the town of Gettysburg on July 1.

Neither commander was present at the start of the battle but each poured troops into the area, which was of strategic importance because no fewer than ten roads converged there. Lee lost an early chance to destroy the Federals on the 1st, and, on July 2, he suffered heavy losses.

On July 3, Lee decided to launch an all-out assault on the center of the Union line which stretched along Cemetery Ridge—roughly parallel with the Rebel positions a mile away on Seminary Ridge. A bombardment from the Rebel artillery ranged in front of Seminary Ridge would precede the assault. Then, with the Union positions "softened up," more than 12,000 Rebels under Major General George Pickett would try to smash their way through the Federal line.

At about 3 p.m. on July 3, when the huge artillery duel between Union and Confederate batteries tailed off, massed ranks of Rebels, in parade ground formation, began their advance. The focal point of their assault was the clump of trees (3) in the center of the Federal line.

But as they crossed the mile of open ground, the Rebels became increasingly exposed to Union fire. Once they had passed the Emmitsburg Road (4), their right flank was savaged by enfilading volleys from the Vermont regiments of Brigadier General George Stannard; and artillery on Little Round Top, Cemetery Ridge, and Cemetery Hill raked the Rebel ranks so that five tangled brigades bunched up 15 to 30 deep. As the Confederates approached the Union front line, their left flank was also exposed to enfilading infantry fire from the direction of Ziegler's Grove.

Despite the withering fire from the Union guns, the Rebels kept on coming, their battle yells mixing with the screams of the wounded, the rattle of rifle fire, and the boom of cannon. The high moment of the charge came when Brigadier General Lewis Armistead and about 150 men breached a low stone wall (5) marking the Federals' front line, which was defended by men of the 71st and 69th Pennsylvania (6, 2). Armistead soon fell, mortally wounded, and most of his men were killed, or captured by the 72nd Pennsylvania (1) who came rapidly to the support of their sister regiments.

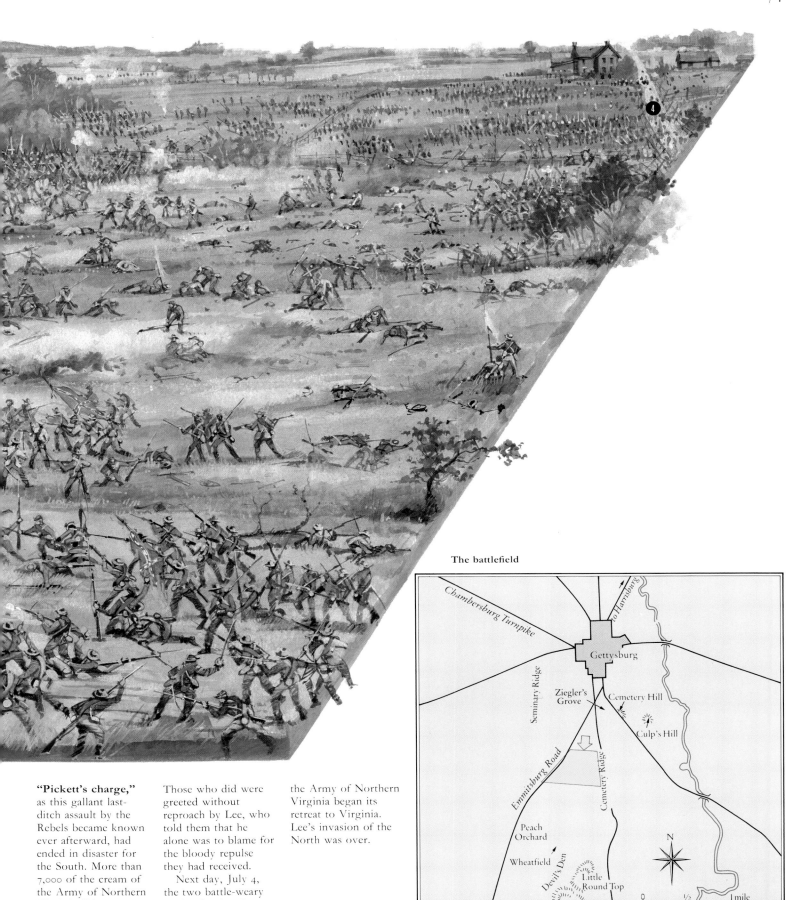

The battlefield

"Pickett's charge," as this gallant last-ditch assault by the Rebels became known ever afterward, had ended in disaster for the South. More than 7,000 of the cream of the Army of Northern Virginia did not return to the Confederate lines.

Those who did were greeted without reproach by Lee, who told them that he alone was to blame for the bloody repulse they had received.

Next day, July 4, the two battle-weary armies faced each other and licked their wounds. That night,

the Army of Northern Virginia began its retreat to Virginia. Lee's invasion of the North was over.

discovered to his horror that Major General Daniel Sickles, whose III Corps had been placed on the left flank covering the Round Tops and the south end of Cemetery Ridge, had advanced to what he considered to be a better line. The salient thus formed, in front of, and out of touch with the rest of the Union position, almost led to disaster.

Luckily for the Union, Meade's chief of engineers, Brigadier General Gouverneur K. Warren, was just then on Little Round Top, and had swiftly reached two conclusions: first, the undefended hill was a natural gun platform from which the whole Union position could be enfiladed; second, the enemy were concentrating in nearby woods in readiness to seize it.

Acting on his own initiative, Warren diverted to Little Round Top some infantry and artillery, which arrived on the crest just in time to beat back the Confederate advance. The critical area was then further strengthened, so removing the threat to the rest of the Union line.

Meanwhile, through the woods and fields west and northwest of Little Round Top, Longstreet was hammering home his belated attack. For four hours, some of the fiercest fighting of the war raged around such famous battlefield landmarks as Devil's Den, the Peach Orchard, and the Wheatfield. Sickles's salient was pushed back, but the Confederates failed to penetrate the Cemetery Ridge line. When he heard Longstreet's guns, Ewell opened an hour-long cannonade against the Union right flank, but did not send forward his infantry until late in the day.

Troops from Major General Edward Johnson's division succeeded in obtaining a lodgment around the base of Culp's Hill and two brigades of Major General Jubal Early's division pierced the Federal line on Cemetery Hill before being driven back in darkness by hastily summoned reinforcements. By the end of the second day's desperate fighting at Gettysburg, Lee, apparently unaware that he was outnumbered by some 20,000 men, still felt that success was within his grasp.

To hold fast in their positions was, indeed, the unanimous decision of a Union council of war held at Meade's headquarters, just east of Cemetery Ridge, late on July 2. As the meeting was breaking up, Meade correctly forecast that Brigadier General John Gibbon, in

The swollen bodies of dead soldiers create a macabre spectacle on the battlefield of Gettysburg, scene of the bloodiest clash of the war.

Embalming the dead

The majority of servicemen who died in the Civil War were hastily buried where they fell. They ended up in mass graves, or were later exhumed and reinterred in neat military cemeteries under headstones anonymously inscribed "A Confederate soldier" or "A Union soldier." Frequently, however, and particularly in the eastern theater, where communications were good, next of kin were rapidly informed of the deaths of soldiers at the front. This early news gave them a chance to claim the bodies for burial at home. But days could pass before arrangements for transportation could be made, and in such circumstances embalmers proved their usefulness.

These "embalming surgeons" set up shop behind the battle lines and did an excellent trade in preserving corpses. The photographer Mathew Brady, who took a picture of this grisly operation in process, noted in his lecture book: "The veins were pumped full of some liquid which possesses the power to arrest and prevent decay. Thus it was made possible to send to friends in the North the bodies of soldiers, which, but for the science of embalming, could not have been permitted a grave in their native soil."

Morticians, of whom there were many in battle areas, offered an alternative to families who could not afford to have their loved one embalmed—airtight metallic coffins. As their advertisements delicately put it: "Can be placed in the parlor without fear of any odor escaping therefrom."

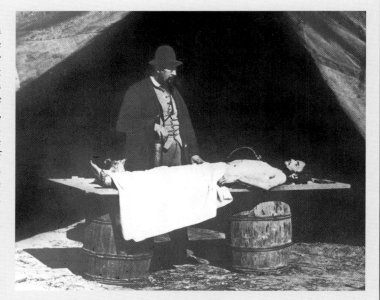

METALLIC COFFINS

for

Transportation of Bodies

To any part of the Country,

THIS SUPERIOR ARTICLE!

Warranted Air-Tight,

Can be placed in the Parlor without fear of any odor escaping therefrom. For Sale by

JOS. H. JEFFERIES,

AGENT,

GETTYSBURG.

"The veins were pumped full of some liquid which possesses the power to arrest and prevent decay."

So commented war photographer Mathew Brady after he had witnessed an embalmer, such as the one depicted (*above*), plying his trade.

For bereaved families unable to afford an embalmer, airtight metallic coffins as advertised (*left*) provided an alternative.

the center of the line, would bear the brunt of any further Rebel assault.

At 4.30 a.m., Federal artillery had begun a bombardment of Ewell's positions around Culp's Hill. This precipitated a general action in that quarter which lasted more than six hours, and ended in a Confederate withdrawal. Longstreet, who had been expected to resume the attack on the Federal left at an early hour, failed to do so. His reason was that the Federals were now in a position to threaten his rear when he advanced.

Thwarted on the flanks, Lee turned his attention to the apparently weak Union center. He devised a plan which would involve a massive artillery barrage, a mass charge spearheaded by fresh troops, and a move around the Federals' rear by the cavalry, which had finally arrived on the field late on July 2.

A reluctant Longstreet was given command of the operation and was ordered to assemble 150 pieces of artillery along Seminary Ridge. This was to cover a storming party made up of the fresh division of Major General George Pickett of his own corps, reinforced by divisions led by Major General Isaac Trimble and Brigadier General Johnston Pettigrew from A.P. Hill's corps. Longstreet claims to have told his superior:

"It is my opinion that no 15,000 men ever arrayed for battle can take that position."

Again there had been a misunderstanding. Lee had not designed this to be an isolated assault; it was meant to be supported by Longstreet's other two divisions and A.P. Hill's remaining division.

At 1 p.m., Longstreet's batteries began the bombardment of Cemetery Ridge to

H.C.Bispham
1865

"soften" the way for the infantry. At once the Federals replied with 80 guns, and, for the next 90 minutes, Gettysburg reverberated to the sound of the largest cannonade the world had then known. It was noisy, and impressive, but not effective.

As the Confederates ran out of long-range ammunition and Union batteries were seen to withdraw from Cemetery Hill, Major General Pickett, the senior officer of the three Confederate divisions, led his men out of the cover of the trees on Seminary Ridge. They began to cross a mile of open, gently sloping farmland toward a clump of trees on Cemetery Ridge, which Lee had selected as the axis of their advance.

In the Union center, artillerymen and thousands of infantrymen watched the Confederates approach, appearing as if they were taking part in a review. The order to fire was given and the long gray ranks were raked by shot, shell, and a hail of minié balls. But the Southerners pressed on relentlessly, the Rebel yell rising high above the din of battle. Double charges of canister from the guns immediately in front of them and enfilading fire from infantry and artillery on their flanks now plowed into them as well; nevertheless, about 150 men, gallantly led by Brigadier General Lewis Armistead, got inside the Union lines. Longstreet made no attempt to support the assault, and so Pickett's Charge, as it became known, lost its momentum and the survivors found themselves isolated nearly a mile from their own lines. They fell back under fire, leaving behind 7,000 men.

"All this has been my fault," General Lee told the returning men, whom he exhorted to form a line on Seminary

Savage hand-to-hand fighting marked the clash between Major General J.E.B. Stuart's Rebel troopers and Federal cavalry from the divisions of Brigadier

Generals Judson Kilpatrick and David Gregg on July 3. The Federals managed to stop Stuart's men from breaking through the Union line.

Ridge to meet a possible counter-attack.

Thus ended the biggest and most bloody battle ever fought on American soil. All through the next day—July 4, Independence Day—the weary armies faced each other without seeking combat. That afternoon the good weather broke, just as Lee's 17-mile-long wagon train, laden with casualties, set off in the direction of the Potomac and Virginia. At night, when he was certain that the Union army would not attack, Lee also started moving his troops toward the south.

The immortal words of the Gettysburg Address, as it became known afterward, were delivered by President Abraham Lincoln on November 19, 1863, at the dedication ceremony of the National Cemetery at Gettysburg.

The aftermath

The Battle of Gettysburg proved to be the bloodiest battle ever fought on American soil. Lee's Army of Northern Virginia suffered losses of more than 28,000 out of some 77,000 men. The Army of the Potomac lost more than 25,000 men from a total of 93,500.

Lee felt his defeat keenly, though he never exhibited the slightest disappointment in front of his troops. He shepherded his depleted army back to Virginia, and, by August 1, had established it in a strong position behind the Rapidan River. He then offered his resignation to the Confederate government. President Davis would not accept it, assuring Lee that his confidence in him was unshaken, despite the setback at Gettysburg.

The South, therefore, still had its greatest general, and he would go on to demonstrate most forcibly that the Army of Northern Virginia still had a lot of fight left in it.

TOTALS AND LOSSES

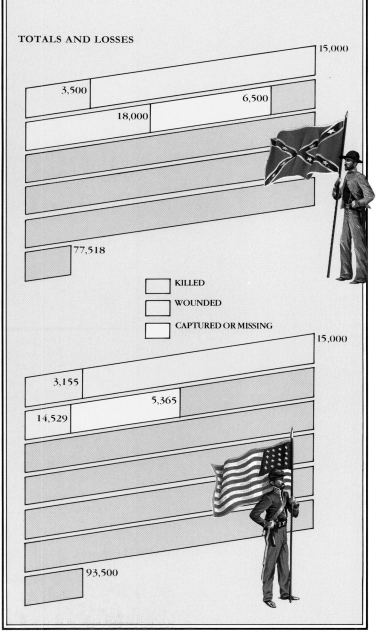

15,000

3,500

6,500

18,000

77,518

KILLED

WOUNDED

CAPTURED OR MISSING

15,000

3,155

5,365

14,529

93,500

Chickamauga

*"You and your noble army now have the chance to give the
finishing blow to the rebellion. Will you neglect the chance?"*

US SECRETARY OF WAR EDWIN M. STANTON to MAJOR GENERAL WILLIAM S. ROSECRANS, USA, before the battle

THE FIRST WEEK of July 1863 was disastrous for the Confederacy. Between the 1st and the 3rd, at Gettysburg, Pennsylvania, General Robert E. Lee's invasion of the North was bloodily repulsed. On the 4th, Vicksburg, the key to the control of the Mississippi River, was surrendered by Lieutenant General John C. Pemberton after a long siege, allowing the Union to isolate the Southern states west of the river. And, from middle Tennessee, also on the 4th, came news of a bloodless victory for Major General William S. Rosecrans: he had succeeded in maneuvering Confederate General Braxton Bragg out of his fortifications covering Tullahoma, Manchester, and Shelbyville, forcing him to retire south to Chattanooga.

In addition to being a crucial railroad center, Chattanooga was also the gateway to the Deep South; rapid possession of it would put intolerable pressure on the apparently crumbling Confederacy.

As it turned out, Rosecrans missed this great chance. While Washington seethed with impatience, Rosecrans gave a display of deliberation worthy of General McClellan. Although Rosecrans' Army of the Cumberland had had six months to recover from the Battle of Stones River, and had forced Bragg to retreat from Tullahoma without a fight, Rosecrans felt it necessary to halt his advance while reinforcements and more supplies were brought up. Six weeks passed before he moved again. This respite, coupled with a lull on other fronts, gave the Confederacy time to review its forces and start transferring regiments to help Bragg, something it had been unable to do during that critical first week of July.

On August 21, elements of Rosecrans' army appeared across the Tennessee River from Chattanooga, and began shelling the town. Rosecrans bluffed Bragg into thinking that he would try to force a crossing upriver; then, in a virtual carbon copy of his successful maneuver at Shelbyville, Manchester, and Tullahoma, he sent Major General Alexander McCook's XX Corps and Major General George H. Thomas's XIV Corps on a wide right-flanking movement.

By September 4, McCook and Thomas were over the Tennessee about 35 miles below Chattanooga. They then advanced slowly across the mountainous country to threaten the Confederate army's vulnerable line of communication with Atlanta, Georgia. Later that week Major General Thomas L. Crittenden followed them over the river with his XXI Corps, but with orders to keep a close watch on Chattanooga.

Once again Rosecrans' maneuverings had the desired effect. On September 8,

Bragg judged his position at Chattanooga to be untenable and, despite the misgivings of some of his senior officers, decided to abandon this important town to the Federals: the Confederates would fall back over the state line into Georgia to protect their communications and give themselves room to maneuver.

The Confederates moved out on the 8th and Crittenden occupied Chattanooga the next day. It was then that Rosecrans made his first big mistake of the campaign. He became convinced that Bragg and his Army of Tennessee were in retreat, probably toward Rome. So, keeping his Reserve Corps back and leaving just a brigade to hold the town's defenses, Rosecrans let his other three corps push on after Bragg, out of touch with each other, and across a 50-mile-wide front.

Not everyone on the Union side shared Rosecrans' conviction. Bragg's army had disappeared behind a succession of ridges which the Union cavalry had been unable to penetrate. Without firm information of the Rebels' retreat, there was a danger that the Federals were being led into a trap which, if sprung, would insure that the widely dispersed Union corps would be defeated in detail. Even Washington was beginning to get edgy about the likelihood of such a scenario. Consequently, Assistant Secretary of War Charles Dana was sent to report on the situation.

In fact, far from fleeing in haste, Bragg had made an orderly withdrawal to the vicinity of Lafayette, some 20 miles to the south. There he was concentrating his growing forces. Indeed, on the 11th, Bragg learned that General James Longstreet, with two divisions, was being sent to him from Virginia to supplement the reinforcements he had already received from Mississippi. He was well on the way

GEORGE HENRY THOMAS (1816–70)

JAMES LONGSTREET (1821–1904)

Solid, dependable, and a tenacious fighter, "Pap" Thomas was among the most capable and loyal of the Union's commanders. At Chickamauga, his resolute stand on the Federal left earned him the nickname "The Rock of Chickamauga." Though a Virginian, Thomas remained loyal to the Union in the Civil War. He was a graduate of West Point, at which he later became an instructor of cavalry and artillery.

A veteran of the Second Seminole and Mexican Wars, Thomas won the first real victory of the Civil War for the Union in January, 1862, when he routed Brigadier General George Crittenden's army at Mill Springs (Logan's Cross Roads), Kentucky. He was later a divisional commander in the Army of the Cumberland, at the Battle of Stones River, and, in September, 1863, led the XIV Corps at Chickamauga. He superseded Major General William S. Rosecrans as commander of the Army of the Cumberland, leading it to victory at Missionary Ridge in December, 1863, and during Major General Sherman's Atlanta campaign the next year.

Thomas was then sent back to Tennessee by Sherman in the fall of 1864 to defend the state against Rebel General John B. Hood's invasion. In December, 1864, Thomas eventually struck Hood's Army of Tennessee so hard at Nashville that it ceased to be an effective force. For this victory, he was promoted to the rank of major general in the Regular Army.

Longstreet, a capable but cautious soldier, whom Robert E. Lee once called "My old warhorse," led the Rebel assault at Chickamauga which annihilated the Union right. Born in South Carolina, Longstreet graduated from West Point in 1842, and went into the infantry.

A brigadier general at the start of the Civil War, Longstreet became major general in October, 1861, and commanded a division in the Virginia Peninsula against Major General McClellan. General Robert E. Lee gave him operational command of more than half of the Army of Northern Virginia, and in this capacity he fought in the actions at Second Bull Run and Antietam. Just before the Battle of Fredericksburg in December, 1862, Lee formed his army into two corps, giving Longstreet command of the I Corps. However, in July of 1863, during the Gettysburg campaign, Longstreet was much criticized for his apparent procrastination.

Two months after Gettysburg, he was sent west with two divisions of his corps to reinforce General Braxton Bragg's Army of Tennessee, in time for the Battle of Chickamauga. Later, in the spring of 1864, he was back in Virginia with Lee, and was accidentally wounded by his own men at the Battle of the Wilderness on May 6. He did not return to active service until the following October, when he was given command of troops at Bermuda Hundred and north of the James River.

to outnumbering the Federals and would, eventually, have more than 66,000 men present for duty, compared with 56,965 in the Army of the Cumberland. Bragg could now think about going on the offensive.

Realizing that there were isolated Union corps for the taking, Bragg twice dispatched troops to trap them, but with-out success. He proposed an attack on Thomas, while the latter's command was vulnerably deployed near the entrance of a mountain-ringed blind canyon called McLemore's Cove, and one also on Crittenden, who was lying at Lee and Gordon's Mills on Chickamauga Creek, some ten miles farther north. However, for reasons that are not entirely clear, the attacks did not materialize.

While Bragg, disappointed that his chance to destroy Rosecrans had not been exploited, was drawing his forces back to Lafayette and pondering his next move, there was feverish activity in the Union ranks. As long as the three corps remained strung out, Thomas was convinced that "nothing but stupendous blunders

on the part of Bragg can save our army from total defeat."

This fear had at last communicated itself to Rosecrans who, on the 13th, issued urgent instructions for his forces to concentrate on Crittenden's position along the west side of Chickamauga Creek, about 12 miles south of Chattanooga. It was easier said than done, however, for Rosecrans' right-hand corps, McCook's, was by then a circuitous 57-mile march away.

However, after making exhausting forced marches, McCook did manage to come in on Thomas's right flank on the 17th, and a northward movement was continued to join with Crittenden, still in the area of Lee and Gordon's Mills. Next day, Rosecrans had a line six miles long running southwest from the mills to Pond Springs. He then decided to make further changes in his position to cover the two main southern routes into Chattanooga from Chickamauga Creek Valley: these were the Dry Valley Road, which cut westward through Missionary Ridge, and the Lafayette Road that ran north–south, parallel to the creek.

Bragg, meanwhile, had been laying his own plans, and was moving cautiously

Rebel infantry from Major General Patrick Cleburne's command advance through woods to attack Major General George Thomas's Federals at twilight on September 19, the first day of the battle. The Rebels succeeded in pushing back the Union line, but were unable to break it.

The Irish-born Cleburne was one of the South's toughest and most aggressive fighters. He was killed later on in the war at the Battle of Franklin, in November, 1864, during Rebel General John B. Hood's invasion of Tennessee.

The distinctive green regimental flag of the 1st Arkansas displays the names of the engagements in which it was involved— including Chickamauga. At this battle, the 1st Arkansas fought under Major General Patrick Cleburne's command of Lieutenant General D.H. Hill's corps.

The regiment contributed to the intense pressure brought upon Federal Major General Thomas's front on September 20.

because he was unsure about the exact positions of all the Federal forces. Because he assumed that Crittenden was on the left flank of Rosecrans' army, Bragg decided that his best option was to march north from Lafayette, cross Chickamauga Creek, and place himself between Crittenden and Chattanooga. He could then start pushing southward, rolling up the Union line as he went. Bragg started out on the 16th, intending to launch his attack early on the 18th. Progress, however, was slow, and, after 48 hours, he had succeeded only in securing the necessary fords and bridges over Chickamauga Creek and crossing about 8,500 men.

Rosecrans, on the other hand, had done remarkably well, considering the plight in which he had found himself. He had leapfrogged Thomas's large corps well beyond Crittenden to create a new and stronger left at Kelly's Farm; he had ordered Crittenden to close on Thomas's

Reporting the news from the front

The war was big news, and droves of reporters and artists, both American and foreign, followed the armies. These correspondents had no official status and were tolerated—or not, as the case may be—by the senior officers of the commands to which they attached themselves.

Transatlantic communications were slow, so the dispatches of overseas journalists, such as *The Times* of London's great war reporter, William Howard Russell, took a long time to get into print. The same drawback did not hamper the American pressmen. Rivalry was intense—especially among the big New York City newspapers—to be first on the streets with the latest from the combat zones.

The newspaper industry in the North flourished during the war, its revenue inflated by increased advertising and burgeoning circulation. In the South, however, publishing contracted as the war dragged on and the blockade of Confederate ports bit deeper.

The one thing that remained constant was the public's undiminishing thirst for news. While civilians bought newspapers to read about the war, the soldiers on both sides looked forward to them because they kept them in touch with what was happening at home.

The troops had various ways of obtaining newspapers: through the mail by subscription (at a ruinous ten cents a time, a cost usually shared among several men); direct from vendors coming into the camps; or sent to them by their families.

Although photography was common-place by the 1860s, the technique for reproducing monochrome pictures in newspapers had not yet been developed. Line drawings produced from woodcuts were the only means of illustration, so specialist artists such as Alfred R. Waud (*above*) were retained to sketch scenes from the front. The North's two big picture journals were *Harper's Weekly*, a reissue of which is shown (*above*)—for which Waud worked from 1862 to the war's end—and *Frank Leslie's Illustrated Newspaper*. These conveyed the only images of war that a large proportion of the population ever saw. The South had no comparable publications.

right, and instructed McCook to come up and occupy Crittenden's old position at Lee and Gordon's Mills. When this redeployment was complete, it would give Rosecrans a reasonably manageable six-mile-long battle line. He placed his Reserve Corps, under Major General Gordon Granger, four miles north of his left flank, astride the main road to Chattanooga, with orders to keep that route open at all costs.

Next morning, Thomas, who had been erroneously informed that only one Confederate brigade was across the Chickamauga, sent out reconnaissances in force toward the two principal bridges over the creek near his front. Around 7.30 a.m., Colonel John T. Croxton's Union brigade ran straight into Brigadier General Nathan Bedford Forrest's cavalry and two Rebel infantry brigades, and battle was joined. As the rattle of musketry grew in crescendo, indicating serious fighting, Bragg expressed surprise that the Union left was so far north and did the only thing he could do in the circumstances: he sent in more troops to support those already engaged.

Time after time that morning, Thomas was assailed by furious Confederate attacks, some of which resulted in grave indentations in his line. But somehow he managed to avoid giving way. Around midday, Major General A.P. Stewart's Confederate "Little Giant" division went in against Major General J.M. Palmer's division of Crittenden's corps, pushed it back, then encountered Brigadier General Horatio P. Van Cleve's division and sent it reeling, too.

Stewart was followed in by the divisions of Major General John B. Hood (of Longstreet's corps from Virginia) and Brigadier General Bushrod Johnson, and, for a time, they had the Union right-center driven west of the Lafayette Road. After hard fighting, however, they met four fresh Federal divisions hurried to this critical point in the line, and were in turn hurled back by them.

While the fighting was drawing to a close in the center, Bragg decided to have another go at Thomas. He therefore ordered Major General Pat Cleburne's division to move from the left and attack Thomas with the support of Major General B.F. Cheatham's division, which had already been in action. It took Cleburne some time to march from one end of the Confederate line to the other and dusk was falling before he and Cheatham fell upon Thomas: a sharp but inconsequential fight ensued until darkness brought a halt to the firing.

Thomas weathers the storm

The Federal army at Chickamauga faced complete disaster on the morning of September 20, after Brigadier General Thomas J. Wood had pulled his division out of line on the Federal center to reinforce the left.

Wood's departure left a large gap which was immediately exploited by Rebel Lieutenant General James Longstreet, who drove his men into it. Soon, the Union center and right was in full rout; only Major General George H. Thomas and his strong left wing remained to prevent a total catastrophe.

With Major General Rosecrans fleeing the field (7) toward Chattanooga, and half the Union army in tatters, Longstreet's jubilant troops (6) began to wheel to their right to attack Thomas's Federals, positioned in a horseshoe shape on and around Snodgrass Hill (2). Union troops under Wood and Brannan (5) repulsed wave after wave of Rebel assaults. Then, as Confederates under Hindman began to outflank Brannan's right, the Union line was extended just in time by brigades from Major General Gordon Granger's Reserve Corps (1), which had marched from a point some three miles north of the battlefield.

For the whole of the afternoon, Thomas, whose presence seemed to inspire those around him, fought off relentless Rebel assaults. While

Longstreet's men continued to press from the south, Polk's troops (3, 4) attacked the Federals from the east and north.

With the coming of nightfall, the Federals, whose brave and determined line had remained unbroken, began a skillful withdrawal to Chattanooga. Thomas, who had been reported to Rosecrans as "standing like a rock," was soon to be christened by the North "The Rock of Chickamauga."

Among the trees of the Chickamauga battlefield, a determined Rebel battle line pours a volley into the Federals.

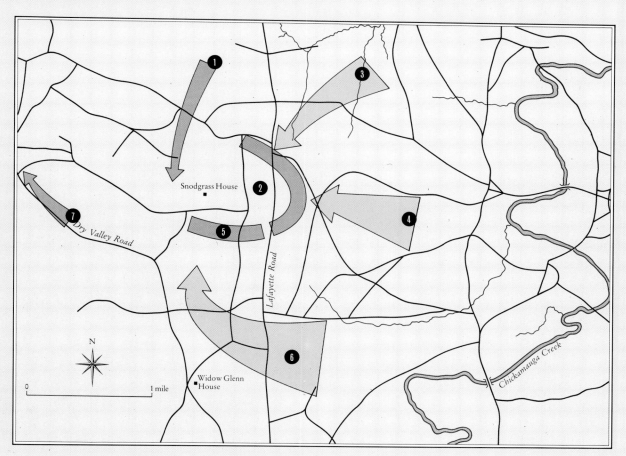

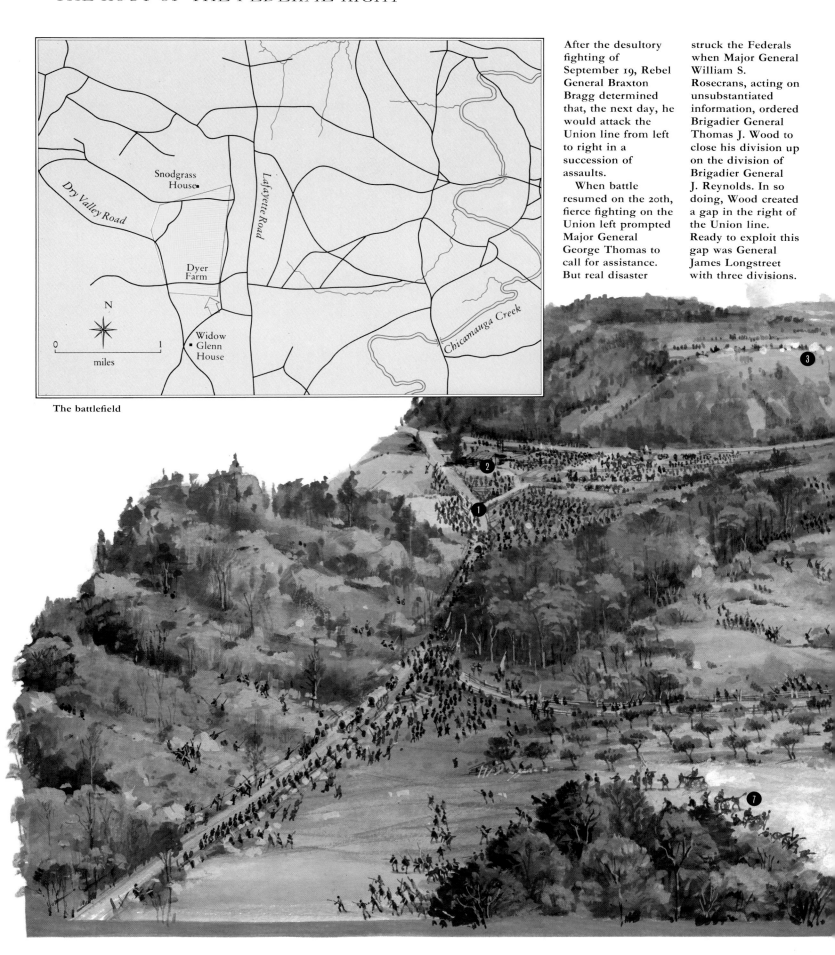

The battlefield

After the desultory fighting of September 19, Rebel General Braxton Bragg determined that, the next day, he would attack the Union line from left to right in a succession of assaults.

When battle resumed on the 20th, fierce fighting on the Union left prompted Major General George Thomas to call for assistance. But real disaster struck the Federals when Major General William S. Rosecrans, acting on unsubstantiated information, ordered Brigadier General Thomas J. Wood to close his division up on the division of Brigadier General J. Reynolds. In so doing, Wood created a gap in the right of the Union line. Ready to exploit this gap was General James Longstreet with three divisions.

At about noon on the 20th, a hot, sunny day, Longstreet, commanding the Rebel left wing, spotted the gap created in the right of the Union line. This was held by Major Alexander McCook's XX Corps, with Major General Thomas Crittenden's XXI Corps in reserve. Longstreet immediately sent three divisions—some 23,000 men—

storming into this gap. The Rebels charged across the Lafayette Road, over fields, and drove McCook's troops before them.

Soon, the massed ranks of Confederates **(5)**, under Brigadier General Bushrod Johnson, swept from the woodland to the east of the Dyer House **(6)**. Johnson himself described the advance: ". . . the rush of our heavy

columns sweeping out from the shadow and gloom of the forest into the open fields flooded with sunlight, the glitter of arms . . . the shouts of hosts of our army, the dust, smoke, the noise of fire-arms . . . made up a battle scene of unsurpassed grandeur."

The Federals were driven by the irresistible Confederate onslaught into a full retreat toward the Dry Valley Road **(1)**. This escape route, which ran past the Vidito House **(2)**, was soon jammed with soldiers, wagons, and other army impedimenta.

To try to stem the tide of the jubilant Rebels and buy time for their comrades, Federal gunners **(4, 7)** worked their cannon before being overrun.

With the Union right routed and in headlong retreat, Longstreet gave the order for his troops to wheel to the right in an attempt to get behind the Federal center and left. By this time, Rosecrans, along with McCook and Crittenden, was on his way to Chattanooga, leaving the remaining Union forces in the hands of Thomas.

Longstreet's men soon began to assault the Federal positions on Horseshoe Ridge **(3)** and, later, Snodgrass Hill, which lay 200 yards in the rear. However, Federal troops of Wood's and Brigadier General Brannan's commands, later reinforced by General Granger's Reserve Corps, prevented a Rebel breakthrough.

When nightfall brought an end to the day's fighting, the Army of the Cumberland had been soundly thrashed; but, thanks in particular to the efforts of Thomas—"The Rock of Chickamauga"—it had not been destroyed.

Feeding the soldiers

The Civil War soldier's daily ration comprised, in theory, $1\frac{1}{4}$ pounds of meat, 1 pound of bread or hardtack biscuits, and a few ounces of vegetables, coffee, sugar, and salt.

Although the North was able to provide enough food for its troops, poor

Sutlers—civilians who sold a more luxurious merchandise to the soldiers—pose among crates of their supplies.

Mountainous supplies (*top*) at a Federal commissary depot epitomize the North's ability to fe its troops adequately

The first day's battle was later summed up by Rebel Lieutenant General D.H. Hill:

"It was desultory fighting from right to left, without concert, and at inopportune times. It was the sparring of the amateur boxer, and not the crushing blows of the trained pugilist."

That night, Longstreet himself arrived with another division and, after a council of war, Bragg decided to split his army into two wings. He gave the left to Lee's experienced lieutenant, and the right to his own senior corps commander, Lieutenant General Leonidas Polk. As far as

Bragg was concerned, there would be a resumption of successive attacks from left to right on the Union line, starting at daybreak on Sunday, September 20.

Meanwhile, at his headquarters in the Widow Glenn House near the Dry Valley Road behind the Union right, Rosecrans was making his plans for the next day. He would shorten his line and pay particular attention to the left, where he placed Thomas with six divisions. McCook was to hold the right with two divisions and Crittenden would command two reserve divisions. Thomas, who was expecting trouble, began to throw up breastworks during the night on the curved line he

occupied around and east of Kelly's Farm. Inspecting his lines in the early hours of the morning, he concluded that he still did not have enough men to protect his left, and so he sent to Rosecrans for another division.

Such was Rosecrans' faith in Thomas's judgment that he immediately gave orders for Brigadier General J.S. Negley's division to be transferred from the Union right to be replaced by Brigadier General T.J. Wood's division from Crittenden. In fact, Wood failed to relieve Negley promptly, and only one of Negley's three brigades reached the extreme Union left in time to meet the Rebel onslaught. It

organization often directed troops' rations to the wrong place on their line of march, obliging them to forage for subsistence. Also, bad management rendered some supplies either unappetizing or inedible. Soldiers did not call their hardtack "worm castles" for nothing.

Throughout the war, the US Commissary Department was always on the lookout for ways of preserving large quantities of food. In one instance, canneries in Chicago were contracted to supply the army with tinned meat, which the men immediately dubbed "embalmed beef." Another commissary preoccupation was reducing the weight of food a soldier had to carry, and this gave birth to "instant" coffee—a paste of sugar, milk, and coffee which dissolved in boiling water.

The South had the greatest difficulty in procuring rations for its fighting men; as often as not, its commissariat could not cope with the demands made on it. A little bacon, flour, and peanut "coffee" was the best a Confederate soldier could ever expect—and certainly not every day. Often, he made do with roasted ears of corn.

The monotony of army fare, particularly in Union camps, was relieved by the presence of sutlers, civilian merchants who sold "extras" to the troops, frequently at inflated prices. Cans of condensed milk and preserved peaches were popular, but the best-selling line was molasses cookies. However, a private, earning, for much of the war, 13 dollars a month, could not make his money go very far at the sutler's when a can of condensed milk cost a dollar, and six cookies a quarter.

Hungry and weary Rebel soldiers (*left*), on the retreat from Petersburg in April, 1865, find time to grind some corn.

Federal soldiers (*left below*) are shown roasting a pig —the result of a successful forage—in this sketch by A.R. Waud.

the bivouac feast. a successful forage in the enemies country, after the occupation of Munson's Hill —

was this incident that sowed the seeds of Union disaster.

When day dawned on the 20th, Bragg's planned attack did not begin. Confusion in Polk's right wing meant that troops were out of alignment and unprepared for battle. It was not until 9.30 a.m. that the difficulties were resolved and the delayed assault was launched. Intense fighting developed along, and to the left of, Thomas's breastworks, and, as Confederate attacks began to extend around his left toward his rear, Negley's other two brigades were sorely missed. Holding on as best he could, Thomas sent repeated appeals to Rosecrans for reinforcements.

Wheeler and Forrest: riding for the Confederacy

Rebel cavalry in the western theater was dominated by two men—Lieutenant Generals Joseph Wheeler (*below*) and Nathan Bedford Forrest (*below right*). Wheeler, a West Pointer and chief of cavalry in the west, incurred the anger of Forrest in February, 1863, because the latter's command was badly shot up in Wheeler's unsuccessful attack on Fort Donelson. Forrest vowed that he would never again serve under Wheeler, and, for the remainder of the war, the two generals each led their own cavalry corps, operating independently.

Joe Wheeler's command was run on traditional cavalry lines, though few sabers were to be seen, let alone used. His men were primarily horse soldiers who per-

formed valiant service protecting the army's flanks in pitched battles, and in scouting and raiding behind enemy lines. The Union's Major General William T. Sherman was so impressed with the performance of Wheeler that he wrote after the Civil War: "In the event of war with a foreign country, Joe Wheeler is the man to command the cavalry of our army."

Long after the demise of the Confederacy, Wheeler did serve the United States against a hostile power: he was a major general in the Spanish-American War in 1898.

Nathan Bedford Forrest, whose formula for winning battles was to "get there first with the most," had been a successful

businessman before the war, with no military training. However, he displayed, early on, an intuitive talent for soldiering which would bring him great acclaim. His men used only firearms, and were just as adept fighting on foot as they were from horseback. In a statement which left purists aghast, Forrest said he thought the finest weapon for a cavalryman was a shotgun.

After the war, this hot-tempered, self-made cavalry general served briefly as Grand Wizard of the feared Ku Klux Klan.

Rebel troopers of Lieutenant General Joe Wheeler's command attack a Federal wagon train on October 3, 1863, as it attempts to bring much-needed supplies to those besieged at Chattanooga.

One of Thomas's staff officers on his way to Army Headquarters with a call for assistance sparked a move which proved to be Rosecrans' undoing. He reported a gap between the divisions of Brigadier General Thomas J. Reynolds and Brigadier General T.J. Wood, which he had noticed while riding along behind the lines. Had Rosecrans or anyone else at headquarters bothered to check, they

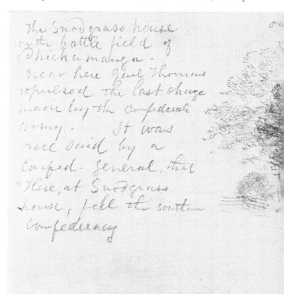

The Snodgrass house on the battle field of Chickamauga. near here genl Thomas repulsed the last charge made by the confederate army. It was once said by a Confed. general, that "Here, at Snodgrass house, fell the southern confederacy

The aftermath

The Battle of Chickamauga was long and particularly bloody. Rosecrans' Army of the Cumberland lost a total of 16,170 out of 56,965 men. The Confederates suffered more casualties—18,454 from an army of about 66,000 men.

Bragg did not realize until the morning of the 21st that he had won the battle, and did not pursue the Federals. He seemed content with an empty victory and gave orders for the day to be spent burying the dead and gathering up equipment. It was

the breathing space that Rosecrans needed—"the panic among the [Union] troops subsided," wrote Confederate General D.H. Hill, "and Chattanooga—the objective point of the campaign—was held."

☐ KILLED

☐ WOUNDED

☐ CAPTURED OR MISSING

TOTALS AND LOSSES

11,000

2,312

14,674 1,468

ABOUT 66,000

11,000

1,657

4,757

9,756

56,965

would have discovered that Brigadier General John M. Brannan's division was in the "gap," positioned in trees out of the staff officer's line of sight. Instead, an order was dashed off to Wood to close immediately on Reynolds, thus creating a gap which had not been there before.

Such a break would not have mattered much had the full weight of the Confederate army been ranged against Thomas; but it was not, as a quick reconnaissance would have revealed.

Longstreet was nearby with three divisions (eight brigades) arrayed in a column of attack, four brigades deep, across a half-mile front, and, at about noon, just as the opening appeared in Rosecrans' ranks, he sent this formidable force roaring straight into it. The effect was shattering. Two Union divisions, with

Snodgrass House was sited on top of the hill of the same name where the Federal left, under Major General George Thomas, valiantly fought off Rebel assaults until nightfall.

According to the author of this sketch, which was drawn on different colored paper, a Confederate general said after the battle that "Here, at Snodgrass House, fell the southern Confederacy."

artillery and all their impedimenta, were swept from the field, dragging with them Rosecrans and two corps commanders, McCook and Crittenden.

But the battle was not over yet. Thomas, reinforced on his right by Wood's and Brannan's divisions and, later, by two brigades brought by Major General Granger of the Reserve Corps, now occupied a strong position on the rising ground of Snodgrass Hill; the angle in his line rested on the right flank of the breastworks he had defended since the battle began. Constantly pressed by Longstreet from the south and by Polk from the east, Thomas encouraged his infantry and artillery to stand fast, and, in so doing, won himself the name of "The Rock of Chickamauga."

As evening drew on and ammunition began to dwindle, Thomas began to think about executing an earlier order to withdraw that had come through from Rosecrans, now at Chattanooga. Shortly after 6 p.m., Thomas began a fighting retreat to Chattanooga that carried on into darkness, and extricated the remains of his divisions through a narrow gap still left between the encircling wings of Polk and Longstreet: the Federal army had escaped absolute disaster by a hair's breadth.

Chattanooga

NOVEMBER 23–25, 1863

"A panic which I had never before witnessed seemed to have seized upon officers and men, and each seemed struggling for his personal safety. . . ."

GENERAL BRAXTON BRAGG, CSA, after the storming of Missionary Ridge

AFTER THE DEFEAT of the US Army of the Cumberland at the Battle of Chickamauga on September 19–20, 1863, Major General William S. Rosecrans regrouped his forces at strategically important Chattanooga. There he immediately had his men strengthen and extend the city's defenses, for he believed that a full-scale Confederate attack was imminent.

Soon, Chattanooga, which is situated on the south bank of the winding Tennessee River, was protected on its landward side by a crescent of fortifications three miles long. However, as it turned out, this hastily constructed line was never needed.

Confederate General Braxton Bragg, who, for reasons that are not clear, had not ordered a swift pursuit of the retreating Federals on September 21, arrived in force before the city two days later, and laid siege to it. His Army of Tennessee occupied both Missionary Ridge, rising to 800 feet and dominating the Union left and center, and the 2,200 foot heights of Lookout Mountain, commanding Rosecrans' right and, even more importantly, his principal supply line.

The sustenance of some 40,000 Federal soldiers and several thousand horses and mules now rested on a difficult 60-mile-long wagon track looping northward over the Cumberland Mountains to the nearest railhead, at Bridgeport, Alabama. This fragile supply line was subject to raids by Confederate cavalry, and Bragg knew that when the fall rains came, it would become impassable. All he had to do was wait: the Army of the Cumberland would be starved into submission.

Washington, alarmed at the turn of events, began taking steps to raise the siege. Two corps under Major General Joseph Hooker were sent west from the Army of the Potomac in Virginia, and, by early October, they were concentrated at Bridgeport. Major General Ulysses S. Grant, the victor of the siege of Vicksburg, was asked to send reinforcements from his Army of the Tennessee. Then, on October 17, Grant was promoted to command the newly constituted Military Division of the Mississippi. The responsibility of relieving Chattanooga now fell on Grant.

Rosecrans, having lost the confidence of the administration, was replaced by Major General George H. Thomas, the "Rock of Chickamauga." Thomas was ordered by Grant to hold the beleaguered city "at all hazards."

Grant himself arrived in Chattanooga on October 23, and he was appalled at the conditions there. He saw that the first priority was to open a proper supply line, and gave his approval to a plan worked out by Brigadier General William F. Smith, the chief engineer of the Army of the Cumberland. Smith proposed to seize control of the river, which was easily navigable to a point eight miles below Chattanooga, by having Hooker cross at Bridgeport, march up to Lookout Valley, north of the Confederate positions on Lookout Mountain, and then entrench.

Meanwhile, in a separate night operation, troops from Thomas would take Brown's Ferry, a crossing three miles north of Lookout Mountain and just a mile from the city across the neck of a large bend in the river. There he would lay a pontoon bridge. Since Chattanooga was already connected to the north bank by a bridge, this would insure an uninterrupted road for wagons; it would also be outside the range of Rebel artillery. By October 27, Smith's scheme had been executed faultlessly, and to Grant's immense satisfaction, supplies began getting through to Chattanooga.

Grant also had to consider the plight of Major General Ambrose E. Burnside, and 25,000 men around Knoxville, east Tennessee, about 150 miles northeast of Chattanooga. Confederate troops were making threatening moves toward Burnside's force, which was dangling at the end of a 100-mile-long wagon route stretched out over mountainous country: if Burnside was to be helped, it was imperative for Grant to break Bragg's stranglehold on Chattanooga.

Anxiety over Burnside increased on November 4 when it was discovered that General James Longstreet with 15,000 infantry, together with Major General Joseph Wheeler and 5,000 cavalry, had left Bragg and started toward Knoxville. Luckily for Grant, Longstreet took a long time getting there, and the town was not under direct siege until the 18th. This breathing space more or less coincided

WILLIAM FARRAR SMITH (1824–1903)

Smith, the man who saved the Union forces from starvation in the siege of Chattanooga, was a native of Vermont, who graduated from West Point in 1845. He entered the Corps of Engineers, and his service between then and the start of the Civil War encompassed survey work, teaching mathematics at the US Military Academy, and engineering duties in Florida, where he caught malaria.

Captain Smith, nicknamed "Baldy" at West Point for his thinning hair, became a colonel in the US Volunteers in July, 1861, taking command of the 3rd Vermont Infantry Regiment. He fought at First Bull Run as a staff officer that same month, rose to brigadier general in August, and led a brigade until October. He was then made a divisional commander and, in the spring and summer of 1862, fought in most of the battles in Major General McClellan's abortive Peninsula Campaign.

Smith, who was promoted to major general in July, 1862, saw further action with the Army of the Potomac at South Mountain and Antietam in September. Two months later, he was given command of the VI Corps, which he led at Fredericksburg in December.

As a result of his outspoken criticism of Major General Ambrose E. Burnside's leadership in the Fredericksburg campaign, which upset Congress, Smith's appointment as major general was allowed to expire in March, 1863. Smith, now a brigadier general again, had to give up his corps and revert to being a divisional commander.

In September, 1863, Smith was transferred to the western theater, becoming chief engineer of the Military Division of the Mississippi. It was in the former role that he distinguished himself, laying out the defenses of besieged Chattanooga, then planning and executing a daring operation to open a supply line—the "cracker line"—to the starving garrison.

Smith, on Lieutenant General Ulysses S. Grant's recommendation, was reappointed a major general of Volunteers in March, 1864, and returned to field command at the head of the XVIII Corps—but not for long. His handling of troops in operations at Petersburg in the middle of June left so much to be desired that Grant had him removed. Smith, whose sharply critical manner made him unpopular with army colleagues, stayed on in the regular army after the war, resigning in 1867.

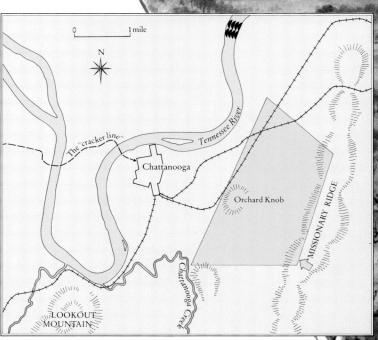

When Major General Ulysses S. Grant, now in overall command of Federal forces in the western theater, arrived at Chattanooga on October 23, 1863, he

The battlefield

found the situation there desperate. With Rebel General Braxton Bragg's Army of Tennessee securely positioned on Missionary Ridge and Lookout Mountain, the besieged Federals were in danger of being starved into submission.

However, with Grant's arrival, Federal fortunes began to change. First, a supply route—the "cracker line"—was opened up on the 28th. Then Major General Joe Hooker arrived with his corps of about 16,000 men; and Major General William T. Sherman would soon be there with his 20,000-strong Army of the Tennessee.

Once all his forces were present, Grant set about raising the

siege. Prior to a major assault by Sherman on the Rebel right, Grant ordered Major General George Thomas to seize Orchard Knob, a small, lightly defended eminence between Chattanooga and Missionary Ridge.

Thomas took it on November 23, and, next day, Hooker ousted the Confederates from Lookout Mountain. However, when Sherman attacked the Rebel right on November 25, he met stiff resistance from Major General Pat Cleburne's division. To take the pressure off Sherman, Grant ordered Thomas's Army of the Cumberland to capture the Rebel rifle pits at the base of Missionary Ridge.

From Orchard Knob (2), just east of Chattanooga (1), more than 20,000 men from the Army of the Cumberland prepared to advance against the Rebel line at the base of the ridge. At about 3.30 p.m., the signal was given, and Thomas's men, still smarting from their humiliating defeat at

Chickamauga, charged the rebel positions with a new-found determination. Such was the vigor of the Federal assault that the Rebels soon broke and fled up the slopes—to what they supposed would be the safety of their line on top of the ridge.

Then, much to the consternation of Grant

and his fellow officers, who were watching the spectacle from Orchard Knob, the Federals, in direct contradiction to their orders, stormed after the Rebels in hot pursuit.

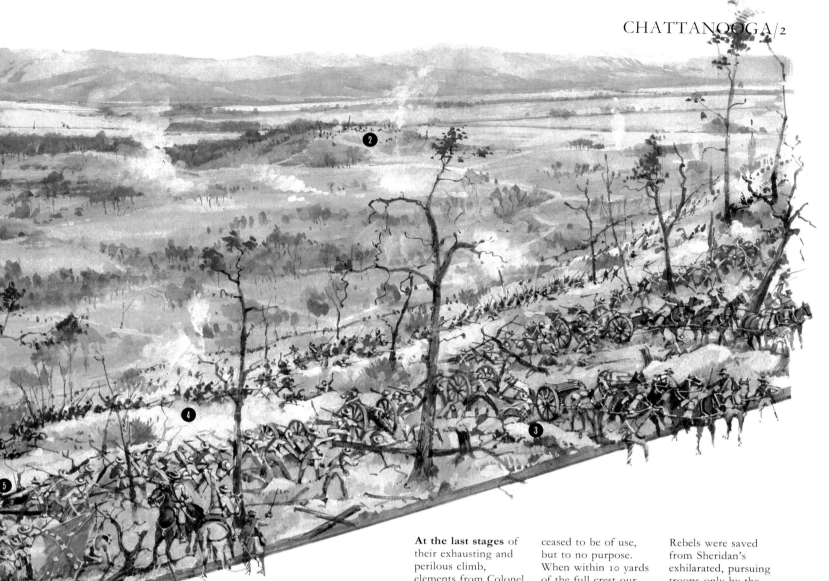

As their anxious generals looked on, the Federals clambered over rocks and through bushes, taking advantage of the numerous tree trunks, boulders, and small depressions to shelter from Confederate fire. Because the slopes of Missionary Ridge consist of a series of small ridges crisscrossed by dirt tracks and numerous undulations, it was impossible for the Federals to maintain a regular formation.

During the ascent, Colonel Charles Harker, of Major General Philip H.

Sheridan's division, reported that his men were "exposed to the most galling fire of musketry and under a ceaseless storm of grape, canister, and other deadly missiles. The brave officers and men pushed forward with a determination which nothing could daunt . . . taking advantage of every depression in the ground—or tree, or stump—to rest for an instant, reload, and then move forward; thus foot by foot and pace by pace, the crest was being reached to the admiration of all who witnessed it. . . ."

At the top of the ridge, the still unfinished Confederate breastworks **(5)** of stones and logs had been laid out incorrectly. Instead of being on the slope's military crest, that is, in a position where the Rebel guns would have commanded the greatest possible area, the works were sited on the highest elevation. Thus, as the streams of blue lines began to approach the summit, the Rebel gunners **(6)** were not able to depress their cannon low enough to find their targets. Nor could the Rebel infantrymen fire their muskets without unduly exposing themselves to Federal fire.

At the last stages of their exhausting and perilous climb, elements from Colonel Harker's right and Colonel Francis T. Sherman's left combined before the last push to the top. As Francis T. Sherman reported:

"Slowly and surely we pressed up the hill, overcoming all obstacles, defying the enemy in his efforts to check our determined advance. Officers and men alike vied with each other in deeds of gallantry and bravery, cheering one another on to the goal for which we were contending. In this manner we gradually worked our way to the summit, over the rugged sides of the ridge, every foot being contested by the enemy. Rocks were thrown upon our men when the musket

ceased to be of use, but to no purpose. When within 10 yards of the full crest our men seemed to be thrown forward as if by some powerful engine, and the old flag was planted firmly and surely on the last line of works. . . ."

With the irresistible Union infantry (4) surging toward them, the seasoned veterans of the Army of Tennessee panicked and began to break formation. Some artillery pieces **(3)** were limbered up before they could be captured. Many, however, fell into Federal hands.

In just an hour after the advance from Orchard Knob, the Federals had driven the enemy from Missionary Ridge. In headlong retreat, the

Rebels were saved from Sheridan's exhilarated, pursuing troops only by the descent of darkness.

General Braxton Bragg wrote in his report on the battle: "No satisfactory excuse can possibly be given for the shameful conduct of our troops on the left in allowing their line to be penetrated. The position was one which ought to have been held by a line of skirmishers. . . ." On December 2, Bragg asked to be relieved of his command.

The Army of the Cumberland's revenge

Although the opening of a supply route—"the cracker line"—had helped the plight of the Federals trapped in Chattanooga, Major General Ulysees S. Grant still had to deal with the besieging Rebels.

To clear the way for a major assault on the enemy positions on Missionary Ridge, Grant ordered Major General George Thomas's men (7) to seize forward Rebel positions at Orchard Knob. On November 23, the Federals accomplished their mission, and the knob was taken.

The next day, Grant sent troops under Major General Joe Hooker (1) to knock out a small band of Confederates under Major General Stevenson (8), on Lookout Mountain. In what became known as "The Battle Above the Clouds," the Federals succeeded in forcing the Rebels to withdraw to Missionary Ridge.

The moment was now ripe for a major assault on the Rebel right by Major General William Sherman: the Federals (2) had previously negotiated the Tennessee with a pontoon bridge; then, at dawn on November 25, they advanced against a veteran Rebel division (3) on the northern end of Missionary Ridge: despite a superiority in numbers, Sherman was unable to dislodge the determined Rebels.

To take the pressure off Sherman, Grant ordered four divisions from the Army of the Cumberland, still smarting from their defeat at Chickamauga, to assault the Rebel line (5) at the base of the ridge. As it turned out, the Federals (6) not only drove back the first Rebel resistance, but then stormed up the slope, causing panic and confusion in the main Confederate line (4) on the crest: Bragg's men were routed.

Crucial to supplying the besieged Federals once the "cracker line" had been opened up, was the hastily built steamboat *Chattanooga*, shown here unloading its cargo.

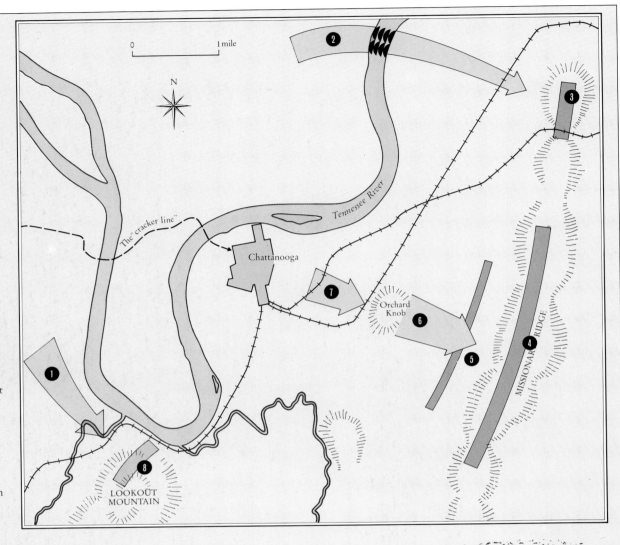

with the delay in bringing up four divisions of Grant's old Army of the Tennessee, now commanded by Major General William T. Sherman. The latter's presence was crucial if the Federals were to take offensive action against Bragg's strong positions.

Sherman and leading elements of his 25,000-strong army reached Brown's Ferry on November 20. Grant was keen to organize an assault the next day, but torrential rain intervened to upset his plans. Continuing bad weather also canceled out any thought of action on the 22nd.

That day, however, a Confederate deserter came into the Union lines with news that Bragg had sent another division to Knoxville and was preparing to withdraw his army from Chattanooga. The last thing Grant wanted at this critical juncture was to lose contact with the Confederates: the relief of Burnside depended upon Grant meeting and beating the Rebels where they were. Disregarding the weather, therefore, Grant ordered a probing attack for early the next day, directed at an outpost line well in advance of Missionary Ridge.

The assault, by two divisions from the Army of the Cumberland, was a success. In full view of the Confederates, they formed on flat ground in front of their breastworks as if on dress parade, then surprised the unsuspecting Rebel spectators by making a sudden dash upon their positions. About 1,000 men on both sides were lost in this action, which took the Union center a mile closer to the base of Missionary Ridge.

But Bragg was still there with two corps, and, on November 24, Grant resolved to attack him in earnest. The main blow was to be delivered by Sherman, who now had three of his four divisions with him. He was to fall upon the Confederate right at the north end of Missionary Ridge, but first he had to negotiate the Tennessee River.

On the night of the 23rd, 116 Federal pontoon boats, each carrying 30 men, were steered to the south bank of the Tennessee near the point chosen for the assault. The Confederate pickets were driven in, a bridgehead established and work begun on building a pontoon bridge.

By 1 p.m. on the 24th, Sherman had three divisions of infantry across the river and was deploying to attack Lieutenant

General William Hardee's corps. His cavalry followed a little later and set off on a circling ride to threaten the Rebel lines of communication. Some high ground was gained, but not on Missionary Ridge itself, and all efforts by the Federals to eject the Confederates from this menacing position were defeated.

Meanwhile, Bragg's left flank, on Lookout Mountain, had also been under attack by Hooker with three divisions. The Union troops advanced with difficulty up the steep, wooded slopes and were soon lost to view in a thick mist which enveloped the peak. Volley after volley of musketry, interspersed with the booming of cannon, were clearly heard in what was picturesquely called "The Battle Above the Clouds." Hooker's troops succeeded in carrying most of the Confederate positions. A rearguard covered the withdrawal of Bragg's left across the Chattanooga Valley to Missionary Ridge and, on the night of the 24th and early hours of the 25th, the Rebels evacuated the mountain.

Grant's plan for the 25th called for Sherman to renew his attack on Bragg's right and oblige him to reinforce heavily. Meanwhile, Hooker would strike across

The aftermath

The Battle of Chattanooga added yet another victory to Ulysses S. Grant's growing string of successes. It also earned him more gratitude from the Lincoln administration.

The Federals, who numbered some 56,000, lost a total of 5,824 men. Although estimates vary, General Braxton Bragg's Army of Tennessee probably had about 30,000 men, excluding Longstreet's troops detached to capture Knoxville, and suffered nearly 7,000 casualties.

For the North, Chattanooga was held, and Burnside was promptly relieved at Knoxville by Sherman. Also, the Federals now had a springboard from which to launch an offensive aimed at the destruction of Bragg's army and against Atlanta, the South's important manufacturing center.

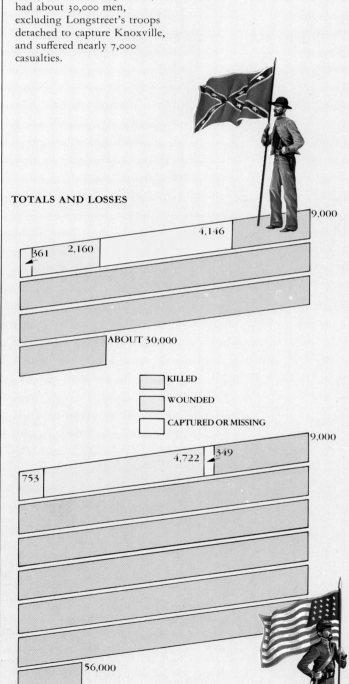

TOTALS AND LOSSES

361 | 2,160 | 4,146 | 9,000

ABOUT 30,000

☐ KILLED

☐ WOUNDED

☐ CAPTURED OR MISSING

753 | 4,722 | 349 | 9,000

56,000

the Chattanooga Valley to turn the Rebel left and draw supports to that flank. Thomas would then drive at the weakened Rebel center.

Throughout the morning and afternoon, Sherman launched several vigorous assaults. The fighting was fierce and often hand-to-hand, but each Union charge was ultimately turned back by the steadily strengthening Confederate right.

By mid-afternoon, Hooker should have been falling upon Bragg's left, but he had been seriously delayed in getting his troops across the Chattanooga Creek in Chattanooga Valley. Grant realized that if pressure was to be taken off Sherman, it could only be done by advancing Thomas's force in the center.

The divisions of Major General Philip H. Sheridan and Brigadier General T. J. Wood, supported by the divisions of Brigadier Generals A. Baird and R.W. Johnson, were detailed to attack the Confederate fortifications at the foot of Missionary Ridge. Once they had taken them, the Federals were to stop there and re-form.

The extraordinary events which followed may be explained by the fact that the lead divisions of the Army of the Cumberland still felt their defeat at Chickamauga keenly and were anxious to redeem themselves. They broke from their positions, rushed several hundred yards across open ground swept by the fire of 60 Rebel guns and concentrated

Federal troops of Major General George Thomas's corps of the Army of the Cumberland occupy defenses at Chattanooga, besieged by the Rebel Army of Tennessee. Lookout Mountain rises majestically in the background.

The strongly fortified Fort Grose is in the foreground manned by men of the 24th Ohio and 36th Indiana Regiments, to the left and right of the fort respectively. The 1st Ohio Battery takes its position to the extreme left and center.

When the besieged Federals went on the offensive, troops from the Army of the Cumberland redeemed their humiliating defeat at Chickamauga by storming Missionary Ridge and routing the Rebels.

Keeping the troops posted

Civil War soldiers—who were, more often than not, highly literate—went off to war with writing materials (*below right*) tucked into their knapsacks. Many men wrote home regularly. For the soldier serving on some distant battlefront, however, it was the arrival of mail from home which was most eagerly anticipated. These letters, sometimes written on colorful writing paper, were often sent in envelopes emblazoned with patriotic slogans and topical cartoons (*left*).

The North, with its much better network of communications, was able to move mail faster than the postal services in the South. In fact, the Federal Army of the Potomac, operating in the more populous eastern theater and closer to the capital, enjoyed the fastest collection and delivery of mail of all.

Alexander Gardner, the war photographer, recorded just how good the postal service to Grant's army was in 1864: "...a letter which left Boston on the morning of

the first of the month, reaching Washington on the night of the second, would generally be delivered to the private soldier in the trenches at Petersburg on the night of the fourth."

As the war progressed, the US Government decided to let soldiers send their letters free, provided the words "Soldier's Letter" were written in a corner on the front of the envelope. The US Christian Commission came to the rescue of Federal servicemen who were apt to forget this by supplying them with printed envelopes free of charge.

musketry, and overran the line at the bottom of the ridge. Then, without stopping—and contrary to orders—they stormed on up the steep, rocky face.

Grant and his senior officers, observing the operation from a nearby knoll, were astounded and Grant muttered that "it would be all right if it turned out all right." In fact, it did turn out all right. Out of formation and out of breath, the Union troops scrambled up the ridge, driving the Rebels out of a second line of rifle pits half-way up, and pushing on until they reached the crest. Then, suddenly, the whole Confederate line began to crumble, and soon it was in full retreat with Sheridan's division in pursuit.

Bragg had lost control of his army. Only the intervention of darkness saved his disordered troops from an even more crushing defeat. Afterward, no acceptable excuse could be offered for these veteran Confederate regiments and batteries in defense of a supposedly impregnable position; and their general, upset by their uncharacteristic behavior, asked to be relieved of his command.

The Wilderness

MAY 5–6, 1864

"The appalling rattle of the musketry, the yells of the enemy, and the cheers of our own men were constantly in our ears."

BREVET MAJOR GENERAL ALEXANDER STEWART WEBB, USA, after the war

WHEN ULYSSES S. GRANT was promoted to lieutenant general and given command of all the land forces of the United States on March 9, 1864, the Civil War drama entered its last long and bloody act. The new general had won a series of significant victories in the western theater. He now proposed to use all the considerable might of the Union in a carefully orchestrated campaign which would crush the rebellion once and for all. Grant's stated aim was

"to hammer continuously against the armed force of the enemy and his resources until by mere attrition, if by nothing else, there should be nothing left for him but an equal submission with the loyal section of our common country to the Constitution and the laws."

There were two major Confederate armies in the field: General Robert E. Lee and the Army of Northern Virginia in the east, and General Joseph E. Johnston and the Army of Tennessee in the west. Grant planned to subject them to simultaneous pressure, hoping they would crack under the strain.

In the coming spring offensive, Major General William T. Sherman, now filling Grant's former post as head of the huge Military Division of the Mississippi, was to lead a drive into Georgia against Johnston. Meanwhile, the new supreme commander stayed with Major General George G. Meade's Army of the Potomac to direct operations against Lee in Virginia.

After due consideration of the Rebel army's strong winter position along the south bank of the Rapidan River, Grant decided to move around its right flank and head straight for the Confederate capital at Richmond. Then Lee would be compelled to leave his fortifications to pursue him. Once the fighting started, he would not let it stop until the enemy was beaten, no matter what the cost.

On May 4, Grant started the Army of the Potomac across the Rapidan at Germanna and Ely's Fords. He was, however, completely unaware that Lee had predicted his move at least 36 hours in advance of its being made, and had laid plans to take advantage of the situation.

But the Army of the Potomac, which Lee had beaten so many times before, had never been stronger. There were three big infantry corps: the II commanded by Major General W.S. Hancock, the V under Major General G.K. Warren, and the VI under Major General John Sedgwick. There was also a newly constituted cavalry corps under Major General Philip H. Sheridan, 318 pieces of artillery, and a massive train of more than 4,000 wagons that occupied 65 miles of road space. The IX Corps of Major General Ambrose Burnside reported directly to Grant because Burnside outranked Meade. The 118,000 Federal troops were well-fed, well-clothed, well-equipped, and in good heart as they passed over the pontoon bridges on the road to Richmond.

The Confederate soldiers were also in good spirits, but that is all they had in common with their opponents. Lee had not been able to swell his ranks much over the winter, so he started the 1864 campaigning season with just 61,953 men of all arms. Desertions had further sapped the strength of the Confederates, and many officers had been lost in the campaigns of 1863. Because rations were scarce, the Army of Northern Virginia was almost perpetually hungry, and it presented a tattered, run-down appearance for want of replacement clothing and accouterments. Only its weapons were in good order, but the Rebel artillery was reduced to just 224 guns.

However, the great disparity between the two armies would not matter too much for what Lee had in mind. Grant's ponderous columns were going to have to negotiate the Wilderness, a large jungle-like area of mostly second-growth timber. Only a year before the Confederate commander had skillfully deployed a small

ULYSSES SIMPSON GRANT (1822–85)

By the end of the Civil War, Grant was the North's most celebrated commander. Born Hiram Ulysses Grant, the son of an Ohio tanner, Grant was in overall control of the Army of the Potomac at the Wilderness.

Grant's name was inexplicably changed to Ulysses Simpson by his Congressman when the latter was registering him as a replacement for a local West Point cadet who had not stayed the course. At West Point, his colleagues facetiously decided that Grant's initials stood for "Uncle Sam," and throughout the army he was known as Sam Grant. Grant graduated from the academy in 1843, coming 21st out of a class of 39. Although a superb horseman, he was sent to the infantry, in which he served for the next 11 years, distinguishing himself in the Mexican War, and rising to the rank of captain.

The boredom of a posting to the Pacific coast, which involved a painful separation from his wife and children, lead Grant into heavy drinking, and, in 1854, he felt obliged to resign when threatened with a court-martial.

With the coming of the Civil War, he helped raise a volunteer unit in Galena, Illinois, and the state governor made him colonel of the 21st Illinois Regiment. Grant spent half of the war in the western theater, first coming to national attention when he captured the Confederate stronghold of Fort Donelson in the early part of 1862. The terms he offered the beleaguered Rebels gained him yet another name: "Unconditional Surrender" Grant.

Although he was criticized for his conduct of Union forces at Shiloh, Grant soon restored his reputation, particularly after his capture of Vicksburg in 1863. In October of the same year, he was given overall command of Union forces in the western theater; then, five months later, he was called east by an admiring President Lincoln, promoted to lieutenant general, and given supreme control over all US armies.

In the spring of 1864, Grant embarked on a campaign of attrition against General Robert E. Lee's Army of Northern Virginia: it lasted a year and was punctuated by several bloody battles, notably at Spotsylvania and Cold Harbor. Sheer weight of numbers ground down the Confederates, who surrendered in April, 1865.

After the war, Grant became, in 1868, president of the United States, and served two terms. He died of throat cancer in 1885.

force through this difficult terrain to defeat Major General Joseph Hooker's far larger army at the Battle of Chancellorsville. Artillery and cavalry were virtually useless in this sort of fighting, and superiority of numbers counted for nothing in the tangled undergrowth. What he had done once, he would try to do again.

At midday on May 4, while the Army of the Potomac was congratulating itself on conducting an unopposed crossing of the Rapidan, Lee was setting his troops on a collision course with Grant's right flank. From his headquarters near Orange Court House, Lee ordered Lieutenant General Richard S. Ewell's II Corps to march east along the Orange Turnpike, which cut straight through the middle of

the Wilderness, and Lieutenant General A.P. Hill's III Corps to advance by way of the Orange Plank Road, which ran parallel to it a mile or so to the south. Lieutenant General James Longstreet, whose I Corps was at Gordonsville, 20 miles to the west, was urged to close on the Wilderness as quickly as possible.

By nightfall on the 4th, Grant was pleased with his progress. While Burnside's corps remained north of the Rapidan to guard the line of communication, the cavalry corps, three infantry corps, the artillery, and most of the wagon train had crossed the river. Warren's corps, followed by Sedgwick's, had gone over Germanna Ford. The former was bivouacked along the Germanna Plank Road, while the latter was on the south

The dense woodland of the Wilderness was responsible for the inability of both armies to maneuver effectively. Winslow Homer's painting shows how easily the battle could become— as one soldier put it— "bushwhacking on a grand scale."

bank of the Rapidan. Hancock's corps had moved by Ely's Ford, about seven miles downstream, and was now camped around the Chancellorsville crossroads. Here, a liberal scattering of bleached bones served as grisly reminders of the fierce battle fought in these same woods in May, 1863. An early start the next day would soon have the army in open country and lying squarely between Lee and Richmond.

Lee knew that his army had to surprise

Music for the troops

The Civil War produced an abundance of popular songs, many of which are familiar to this day. Each side freely adapted the other's music, altering the lyrics to suit their cause. "Dixie," for example, the most famous song of the war, began life in 1859 as "I Wish I Was in Dixie's Land," having been written by a Northerner, Daniel D. Emmett of Ohio, for Bryant's Minstrels in New York. The song did not attain mass popularity until 1861, when it was adopted by the South, and given new lyrics by Albert Pike, a Confederate general. Not to be outdone, the North countered with its own versions of the song, notably the one by John Savage, which began: "Oh, the Starry Flag is the flag for me. . . ."

The songs the soldiers sang were usually patriotic, inspirational, or nostalgic. Other famous tunes from both camps included: "The Battle Hymn of the Repub-

The patriotic covers of Northern music sheets include a song and a "Grand March" in honor of Union generals William T. Sherman (*right*) and George B. McClellan (*below*) respectively.

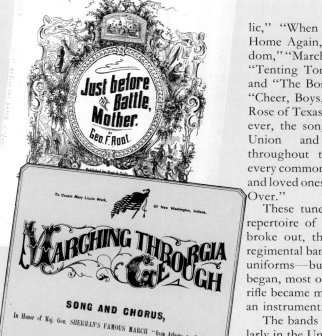

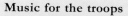

lic," "When Johnny Comes Marching Home Again," "The Battle Cry of Freedom," "Marching Through Georgia," and "Tenting Tonight," sung by the North; and "The Bonnie Blue Flag," "Lorena," "Cheer, Boys, Cheer," and "The Yellow Rose of Texas," sung by the South. However, the song most heard around both Union and Confederate campfires throughout the long conflict reflected every common soldier's yearning for home and loved ones—"When This Cruel War is Over."

These tunes also formed part of the repertoire of military bands. When war broke out, there was a proliferation of regimental bands—often clad in gorgeous uniforms—but when real campaigning began, most of them disappeared: firing a rifle became more important than playing an instrument.

The bands that were retained, particularly in the Union army, were to be found attached to brigades, or larger formations. During fighting, the bandsmen came under the surgeon's orders, and generally served as stretcher-bearers; but there are instances on record when their musical talent was called upon to inspire their comrades at the front.

A musical "contest" took place on the eve of the Battle of Stones River at the end of 1862, when opposing bands tried to outplay each other, attracting much partisan encouragement from the troops. Also, on the second day of the great Battle of Gettysburg in July, 1863, Lieutenant Colonel Arthur Freemantle, a British observer with the Rebels, noted: "When the cannonade was at its height, a Confederate band of music between the cemetery and ourselves, began to play polkas and waltzes, which sounded very curious, accompanied by the hissing and bursting of the shells."

the Federals by meeting them as soon as they crossed the river, so the Confederates marched early on the 5th. At around 6 a.m., Major General Edward Johnson's division of Ewell's corps, advancing on the Orange Turnpike, was first to see the enemy as they moved southward from Germanna Ford. Ewell quickly sent word to Lee, who was down on the Plank Road with A.P. Hill, that he had made contact with the Federals, and formed a line of battle across the turnpike. The Union troops, from Warren's corps, halted,

The Federal push toward Richmond

The savage fighting of the Battle of the Wilderness came about when the Army of the Potomac's southward advance toward the Confederate capital in May, 1864, was intercepted by General Robert E. Lee's Army of Northern Virginia.

The large area of thick woods south of the Rapidan River was difficult battlefield terrain; and the handful of primitive roads that crisscrossed it became all-important arteries for troop movements.

Lieutenant General Ulysses S. Grant would have preferred to have met Lee on more open ground, where Federal superiority in artillery would have made a decisive impact. However, Lee, aware of the advantage that these same dense woods had afforded his weaker army at the Battle of Chancellorsville the year before, sought to repeat that success against the might of Grant.

Lee knew by the morning of May 5 that the Federal push south had started. From the northwest, Major General G.K. Warren's corps (8) advanced down the Germanna Plank Road (9); to Warren's left, Major General W.S. Hancock's corps (1), having crossed the Rapidan at Ely's Ford, headed for the Brock Road (2), the crucial route south.

Lee, meanwhile, ordered his troops east on roughly parallel roads that intersected the Brock Road. Lieutenant General Richard Ewell's II

Corps (6) advanced along the most northerly, the Orange Turnpike (7); Lieutenant General A.P. Hill's III Corps (5) took the Orange Plank Road (4), just over a mile south. Lieutenant General

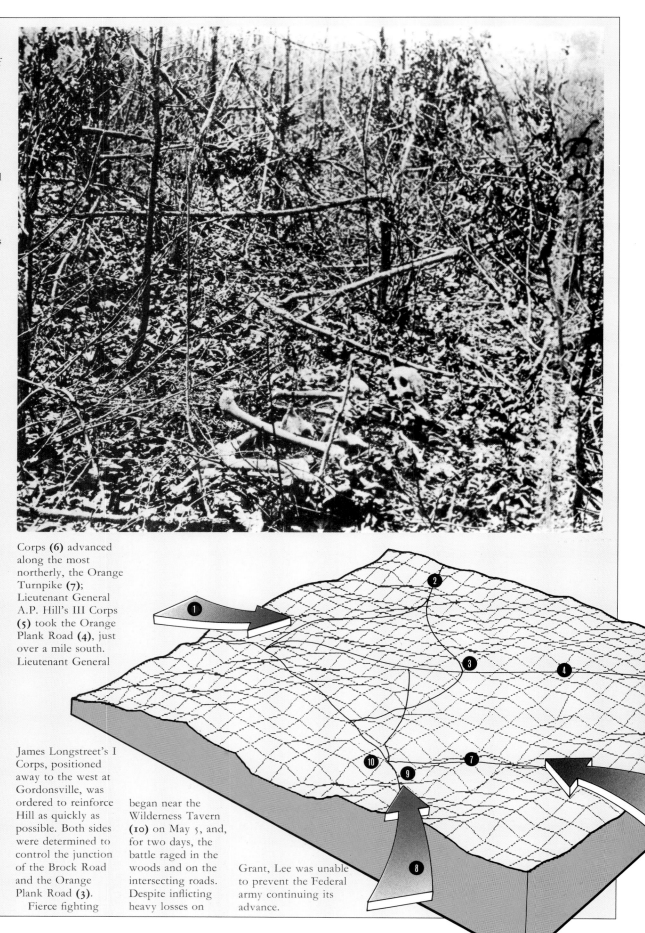

James Longstreet's I Corps, positioned away to the west at Gordonsville, was ordered to reinforce Hill as quickly as possible. Both sides were determined to control the junction of the Brock Road and the Orange Plank Road (3).

Fierce fighting

began near the Wilderness Tavern (10) on May 5, and, for two days, the battle raged in the woods and on the intersecting roads. Despite inflicting heavy losses on

Grant, Lee was unable to prevent the Federal army continuing its advance.

Skeletons of men (*left*) killed in May, 1863, at Chancellorsville greeted the combatants in the Wilderness.

Federal soldiers unload boxes of ammunition from a wagon for distribution to Major General Gouverneur K. Warren's V Corps during the fighting on May 6. In the background, smoke billows out of the Wilderness, where fires incinerated many of the wounded.

faced right and did likewise.

When General Meade learned that Rebel infantry had appeared on the right flank of the line of march, he at first dismissed it as no more than a divisional-strength force positioned to cover the withdrawal of the main Confederate body in face of the approaching might of the Army of the Potomac. It was not long before he changed his mind. As a fierce fight developed between elements of Warren's and Ewell's Corps, a Union cavalry skirmish line thrown out on the Orange Plank Road near Parker's Store engaged the head of A.P. Hill's column. The fighting was desperate. A Zouave who met the Rebel onslaught wrote:

"Closing with the enemy, we fought them with bayonet as well as bullet. Up through the trees rolled dense clouds of battle smoke, circling about the green of the pines and mingling with the white of the flowering dogwoods. Underneath, men ran to and fro, firing, shouting, stabbing with bayonets, beating each other with the butts of their guns. Each man fought on his own resources, grimly and desperately."

Realizing the danger he was in, Meade—with Grant's approval—began deploying to protect the north-south route running through the Wilderness Tavern crossroads: the Germanna Plank Road and the Brock Road. Warren's V Corps was already formed west of the intersection and fighting in the woods on both sides of the Orange Turnpike. Briga-

dier General George Getty's division of Sedgwick's command was ordered to pass behind Warren and come in on his left and hold the intersection of the Orange Plank and Brock Roads to help stave off the threat from A.P. Hill, along the Orange Plank Road. The rest of the VI Corps was to close as fast as it could on Warren's right. Meanwhile, Hancock, whose II Corps had started to move southwest and had reached Todd's Tavern, was told to return post haste, form the Union left and—when ready—drive the enemy back along the Orange Plank Road.

The left and right wings of both the Rebel and Federal armies were out of touch that day. Therefore, two separate battles developed: Ewell pinned down Warren and Sedgwick along and on either side of the Orange Turnpike, while A.P. Hill grappled with Hancock and Getty's IV Corps division in the area of the Orange Plank Road.

Between bouts of close combat in the disorienting gloom of the Wilderness, some of them prolonged and intense,

THE ASSAULT ON THE BURNING BREASTWORKS

In May, 1864, Lieutenant General Ulysses S. Grant, two months after his appointment as supreme commander of all Union land forces, was ready to move south with the Army of the Potomac against General Robert E. Lee's Army of Northern Virginia in a bid to crush it once and for all.

As the spring offensive loomed, the opposing armies, based north and south of the Rapidan River, were in good heart. Grant's intention was to cross the river, go around Lee's right flank, and head toward Richmond. Lee, duty-bound to defend the Confederate capital, would thus be pried from his Wilderness fortifications, and Grant's plan to bleed the South dry by a war of attrition would begin to take its inexorable course.

A fierce clash initiated by Lee's men on May 5, the day after the Federals crossed the Rapidan, resulted in heavy casualties but with no clear advantage to either side. When fighting resumed on the 6th, troops of Lieutenant General A.P. Hill's corps, forming the Rebel right, were driven back in full retreat—before the timely arrival of Lieutenant General James Longstreet's I Corps restored the situation and made a strong counterattack which sent the Union left reeling.

As Longstreet sought to consolidate his gains, he was accidentally shot by his men. The wound was serious and he had to be replaced.

The delay caused by this incident cost the South crucial momentum, especially since Union reserves were beginning to come up. At 4 p.m. on May 6, the Rebels finally resumed their offensive, storming the Federals' log breastworks—which soon caught fire—along the Brock Road.

Meanwhile, on the Rebel left, just before sundown, Brigadier General John Gordon launched an attack on the Federal right flank, captured part of the enemy line and 600 prisoners. Darkness, however, brought the assault to a close before the Rebels were able to press their advantage.

All told, the Army of the Potomac had been badly hurt, but it held its ground; and Grant, unlike his predecessors, was adamant about not turning back. After a day's pause, he moved south toward Spotsylvania, hoping to get around Lee's right flank. But the wily Rebel general was too quick for him.

The disarray in the left of the Union line which Longstreet had intended to exploit no longer existed by the time his replacement, Major General R.H. Anderson, sent his Confederate troops out of the woods, through the Federal abatis (5) and onward to the Union defenses on the Brock Road. Waiting for the Rebels behind stout breastworks was Brigadier General Gersham Mott's brigade, supported by artillery.

The forest at first gave valuable cover to the Confederates, but soon sparks from exploding shells set fire to large patches of the tinder-dry woods (6) trapping the wounded soldiers, many of whom were burned alive. Fires then spread to the Union's log and brush breastworks so both sides shot blindly through the dense smoke and leaping flames.

The wind blowing west to east drove smoke and flames directly into the faces of Mott's Federals (2). But the fire also handicapped the charging Rebels and ruled out an organized Confederate advance. The Rebel high point came when Anderson's men, among them Colonel John Henagan's South Carolinians, planted their flags (3) atop the burning earthworks of Mott's front.

The triumph was short-lived, however, because the Army of Northern Virginia lacked adequate reserves, whereas the Federals were reinforced by the brigades of Colonel Samuel Carroll (1) and Brigadier General John Brooke (4). Within an hour, Union troops drove off the Rebels and secured the Brock Road.

The battlefield

139

Communicating by telegraph

The electric telegraph, which, unlike other means of military signaling, was not limited by distance or visibility, played an important role in sending orders and receiving reports during the Civil War. Both the Union and Confederacy made full use of the existing civilian telegraph networks at the start of hostilities and developed and extended them as the conflict grew.

The industrialized North capitalized on the telegraph more than the agricultural South, and, between 1861 and 1865, laid an astonishing 15,000 extra miles of wire.

This branch of the Federal signal service, although known as the US Military Telegraph Corps, was manned by civilians who reported to the Secretary of War, Edwin M. Stanton, a former director of the Atlantic and Ohio Telegraph Company. It was an uneasy arrangement, and inevitably led to clashes with the military high command, who were using the system extensively but who had no jurisdiction over it.

Federal soldiers make use of their bayonets to attach the insulated wire that carried their telegraph messages. This sketch was made by Walter Taber after the war.

Battery wagons, such as this one, photographed in 1864, supplied the necessary power for the Federal field telegraph operators to send their messages.

On both sides, messages were transmitted in Morse code, the most important ones being enciphered. Only a handful of operators were entrusted with coding and decoding. Union telegraphers claimed to have broken the Confederate ciphers, but it seems that the Federal ones remained inviolate.

Lieutenant General Ulysses S. Grant made the most extensive use of the telegraph during his campaign in Virginia in 1864–5. Using insulated wire, specially developed to withstand being accidentally run over by cannon or wagon wheels, his Telegraph Construction Corps laid and maintained a network of lines connecting all Grant's senior commanders to headquarters. The latter was in turn linked to Washington. This gave Grant unprecedented control over the operations of widely dispersed units, and soon became the norm in the world's armies.

Both sides tapped each other's wires in an attempt to glean military intelligence, with varying success. The acknowledged longest and most fruitful wire tap was carried out by the Confederate C.A. Gaston, General Robert E. Lee's telegraph operator. He entered the Union lines during the siege of Petersburg, connected himself to the Union telegraph, and, for six weeks, intercepted all messages. He could only read those sent unciphered, but still collected a lot of useful information.

troops on both sides hurriedly constructed log and earth breastworks. By nightfall, when the musketry at last died down, partially fortified lines stretched for five miles through the woods west of the Germanna and Brock Roads. In some cases, the Federal front line was backed by a second, or even a third, line of entrenchments.

As the opposing forces settled down to sleep on their weapons, thousands of dead and wounded still lay in the brushy no-man's-land. It would be a long time before the injured were attended and the bodies brought in for burial; some would never be found.

Late that evening, Lee sent a message to Longstreet ordering him to make a night march to insure that his command reached the field by morning. For Lee was certain that the fighting would resume then.

Longstreet started out at 1 a.m., but did not arrive before three of Hancock's divisions—now supported by Getty's IV Corps division and Wadsworth's V Corps division—launched a powerful attack on A.P. Hill's position. The Union battle line curved round the Confederate flanks north and south of the Orange Plank Road and began to roll it up. Lee, who was nearby, saw Hill's troops disintegrat-

ing and, fearing the worst, sent orders for the supply train to get ready to retreat. An aide was sent galloping off to Longstreet with an appeal to him to hurry. Then the Confederate commander tried to rally the disordered regiments and make a stand until reinforcements arrived.

In the nick of time, the head of Longstreet's two divisions appeared, moving along the Orange Plank Road in two files at the double-quick. Brigadier General Joseph Kershaw's division, on the right side of the road, wheeled south and drove the Federals beyond their front-line entrenchments.

The leading unit of Major General Charles Field's division on the left side of the road—Brigadier General John Gregg's 800-strong Texas-Arkansas brigade—swung north across a clearing on the edge of the Wilderness and flung itself into the path of a heavy enemy force. They suffered 50 percent casualties but checked the Union threat. Lee himself had attempted to lead Gregg's men in their valiant charge, only to be told by them: "We won't go on unless you go back." This was the start of a series of bloody attacks and counterattacks in this area, which went on for most of the day.

Now that the immediate crisis facing the Confederates was over, Lee and Long-

Federal soldiers carry a wounded comrade in a blanket suspended from rifles away from fires that broke out during the battle.

A.R. Waud, who drew this sketch, wrote that the fires were "caused by the explosion of shells, and the fires made for cooking. . . . The fire advanced on all sides through the tall grass, and, taking the dry pines, raged up to their top."

street reconnoitered the enemy lines and discovered that Grant's left flank seemed to be in the air and would be easy to turn. By late morning Longstreet had four brigades in position to strike the left and rear of Hancock's reinforced corps, while the rest of his command attacked it frontally. As the Union infantry broke

Signaling by flag and torch

For relatively short-range signaling in operational areas, both the North and the South relied on a system using flags in daytime, and torches or colored lights at night. The Confederate army was the first to institute a Signal Corps. The Union forces soon followed suit.

The signalers worked from hilltops, high buildings, or specially constructed towers, often 100 feet high. Their messages could be read easily with a telescope from ten miles away during the day, and at about eight miles in darkness. Important messages were sent in cipher.

The most commonly used flags were six feet square. They were usually white with a two-foot red square in the middle; but, if there was snow on the ground, black flags with a white square in the center were used.

The signal system, whether with flags or torches, was based on the numerals 1, 2, and 3. Combinations of 1 and 2 made up the

signal alphabet—11 = A, 1221 = B, 212 = C, and so on. The numeral 3 was used to indicate the end of a word; 33 the end of a sentence; and 333, the end of the message. Starting with his flag in the upright position, the signaler waved it to the left for 1, to the right for 2, and dipped it to the front for 3.

In addition to the more commonly used torches, 20 combinations of colored lights, called Coston signals, each of which had a prearranged meaning, were available for nighttime signaling.

Union signalers (*top*) are photographed at their signal tower overlooking the battlefield of Antietam in September, 1862.

At night, flags were replaced with torches. The signaler (*above*) sends out a message into the darkness while an officer mans a telescope in readiness for a reply. Twenty combinations of colored lights—

Coston signals—each of which had a prearranged meaning, also existed for signaling at night.

Giant towers, such as the one photographed (*right*), were specially built for signaling. Rising to 100 feet or more, they were conspicuous— and important— enough to attract enemy fire.

and ran, it seemed that the Rebels were about to repeat the success of Stonewall Jackson's great flanking attack at the Battle of Chancellorsville. Then cruel fate took a hand.

In the same area where Jackson had been mortally wounded by his own men, and almost a year to the day since that tragic accident, a Confederate volley rang out as Longstreet and a party of mounted officers rode through the woods. The commander of the I Corps received a serious wound which would keep him out of the war for six months. But the gallant Brigadier General Micah Jenkins, whose troops Longstreet had been directing into position for a fresh assault, was killed.

The momentum of the offensive was quickly dissipated. Lee sent for Major General Richard H. Anderson, a senior divisional commander in the III Corps, to take over from Longstreet, then hurried to the scene himself to try to get the attack moving again. It took a long time, however, to reorganize, and when the Confederate battle line next rolled forward at about 4 p.m., the Federals were re-grouped, reinforced and ready for the attack. In the fierce fighting which ensued, the undergrowth caught fire and spread to the logs in the Union breastworks, obliging attackers and defenders to back away.

By early evening, the opposing forces in this charred and blood-soaked sector had fought each other to a virtual standstill. Up on the Confederate left, however, where Ewell had been continuing to keep the combined weight of Warren and Sedgwick in check all day, plans were being finalized to try to turn the Union right at sundown. Major General John B. Gordon led two brigades in an attack which captured part of the Federal line and 600 prisoners, but it was a case of too little, too late. Darkness halted Gordon's operations and brought to an end the vicious two-day Battle of the Wilderness.

Next day, the two exhausted armies lay watching each other, knowing that nothing was to be gained by either side attacking. As a result of this stalemate, most of the Federal soldiers expected Grant to go back the way he had come, repeating a routine so familiar to the Army of the Potomac: advance, get a bloody nose, and then retreat. But the US commander in chief was made of sterner stuff. On the night of May 7, he ordered his surprised and delighted men to continue their march south, while reinforcements were ordered up: there was to be no going back this time.

The aftermath

The Battle of the Wilderness marked the first direct confrontation between Lieutenant General Ulysses S. Grant and General Robert E. Lee. Grant had never yet fought against an opponent of such daring and flexibility; while Lee, for the first time, was confronted with a soldier of great nerve and determination.

Such was the confusion of this sprawling fight that accurate casualty figures were never compiled. The best estimate of the Union losses is 17,666 out of an army of 118,000 men. Lee's Army of Northern Virginia lost in the region of 8,000 men out of about 61,000.

Although the Rebels had had the better of the fighting, they had not stopped Grant from continuing the advance on Richmond. However, they would soon have another chance at Spotsylvania, a few miles to the south.

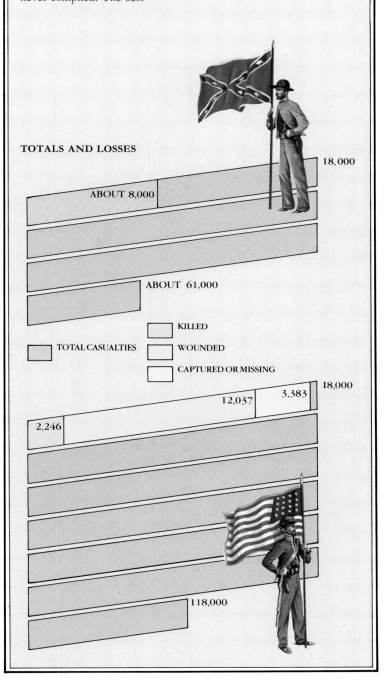

TOTALS AND LOSSES

ABOUT 8,000

18,000

ABOUT 61,000

KILLED
WOUNDED
CAPTURED OR MISSING

TOTAL CASUALTIES

2,246   12,037   3,383   18,000

118,000

Spotsylvania

MAY 8–19, 1864

"It was a life or death contest. . . . The stars and stripes and the stars and bars nearly touched each other. . . ."

BREVET MAJOR GENERAL ROBERT McALLISTER, USV, after the war

THE TWO-DAY STRUGGLE against odds of two to one which General Lee initiated in the Wilderness on May 5, 1864, showed the world that the Army of Northern Virginia was still capable of taking on the North's larger battalions and coming out best from the fight. This time, however, the Army of the Potomac would not be deflected from its march toward Richmond; General Grant's determination would see to that.

On May 7, Grant ordered a southeasterly move to try to get around the Confederate right flank. And, when it came to another confrontation, he would rely on sheer weight of numbers and abundance of war materiel to wear down his numerically weak and inadequately supplied opponent. From then on, it was to be Lee's brains against Grant's brawn and—miracles excepted—there could be only one outcome: Federal victory. It was just a matter of time.

That Lee prayed for miracles is evident from a conversation he had with Brigadier General John B. Gordon the day after the Battle of the Wilderness. In a discussion about the Confederacy's obvious weakness, compared with the Union's strength, Gordon relates:

"He [Lee], however, hoped—perhaps I may say he was almost convinced—that if he could keep the Confederate army between General Grant and Richmond, checking him for a few months longer, as we had in the past two days, some crisis in public affairs or change in public opinion in the North might induce the authorities in Washington to let the Southern States go, rather than force their retention in the Union at so heavy a cost."

When Lee learned from Major General J.E.B. Stuart's cavalry of Grant's re-sumed advance, he set his army in motion to head off the Federals at Spotsylvania Court House, 15 miles southeast of the Wilderness. Several roads converged on this courthouse village, making it strategically important.

Throughout the night of May 7, Stuart harried the Federals, slowing their progress as much as possible. Meanwhile, Major General Richard H. Anderson, who now commanded Longstreet's corps after the latter had been wounded by his own men in the Battle of the Wilderness, was leading the Rebel dash for Spotsylvania, and making excellent time.

By daybreak, Stuart's tireless troopers were dismounted and covering the much desired crossroads against a spirited attack by Major General Philip H. Sheridan's cavalry. Then, Major General Gouverneur K. Warren's V Corps, unrested and unfed, came up and slowly began to form a line of battle.

Alarmed at this development, Stuart sent an urgent appeal for help to Anderson who, fortunately for the Rebels, was breakfasting close by with his troops after their hard march. At 8 a.m., the refreshed Confederate infantry arrived and drove off Warren and Sheridan without difficulty. Lee had won the race to Spotsylvania Court House.

As more and more troops poured into the vicinity, the Confederate position manned by General Anderson's men on Laurel Hill, about two miles northwest of the court house, became the target in the afternoon for a head-on assault by the corps of Warren and Major General John Sedgwick. Luckily for Anderson, Lieutenant General Richard S. Ewell's corps joined him just in time to send the Union attack reeling.

By the 9th, both armies had reached the field in their entirety, and the day was spent entrenching and extending their respective lines. Lee's position encompassed Spotsylvania Court House in a wide crescent facing northeast. His line made full use of rising ground and had both flanks anchored on the Po River, flowing southeast behind the village. In front, trees and dense undergrowth provided a screen, so that much of the Confederate position was hidden from the Federals.

WINFIELD SCOTT HANCOCK (1824–86)

RICHARD STODDERT EWELL (1817–72)

A fastidious man, who was renowned for always appearing in immaculate white shirts, even while campaigning, Hancock led the powerful Federal charge by the II Corps against the Rebels' "Mule Shoe" salient at Spotsylvania.

The son of a Pennsylvania lawyer, Hancock joined the infantry after graduating from West Point in 1840. He fought in the Mexican and the Third Seminole Wars, and served on the frontier.

At the outbreak of the Civil War, Hancock was in California as chief quartermaster of the Southern District. It was not until September, 1861, that he became a brigadier general of US Volunteers. He subsequently saw action as a brigade commander in Major General McClellan's Peninsula Campaign and at Antietam, and as a division commander at Fredericksburg, and also at Chancellorsville.

Promoted to major general in November, 1862, Hancock took command of the II Corps of the Army of the Potomac in May, 1863, and led it at Gettysburg, where he was badly wounded.

He was back at the head of II Corps for the start of Grant's offensive in the spring of 1864, and was involved in a great deal of fighting on the march from the Wilderness to Petersburg. In November of the same year, Hancock took on the job of organizing the I Corps of Veterans; then, from February to June, 1865, he headed the Department of West Virginia and the Middle Military Division.

With his squeaky voice and lisp, "Old Bald Head," as Ewell was known in the Confederate army, was one of the oddest of the Southern generals. During the Battle of Spotsylvania, he commanded the II Corps which bore the brunt of the Federal assault on the "Mule Shoe" salient.

A native of the District of Columbia, Ewell was a West Pointer in the class of 1840. Afterward, he joined the dragoons and fought both in the Mexican War and against Indians on the frontier. After the outbreak of the Civil War, Ewell was promoted to brigadier general and led a brigade at the Battle of First Bull Run.

Ewell had a leg amputated after being wounded at Groveton on the eve of Second Bull Run, and was on convalescent leave until May, 1863. He returned to active service as a lieutenant general commanding the II Corps in General Robert E. Lee's Army of Northern Virginia. In July, 1863, he fought at Gettysburg where he attracted considerable censure for his hesitancy.

Ewell, strapped in his saddle, helped to blunt the Union offensive in the spring of 1864; but soon after a serious fall at Spotsylvania, broken in health, he turned over the command of his corps to Lieutenant General Jubal A. Early. At the end of the war, he commanded the Richmond defenses, and was captured by the Federals on April 6, 1865, at Sayler's Creek.

The first black troops

From the outbreak of war, free blacks in the North had been anxious to play their part in defending the Union. At first, the Federal government was reluctant to tap this source of volunteers, fearing that it would alienate the border slave states which had remained loyal. However, Northern sentiment slowly turned in favor of making use of blacks; and the Militia Act of July, 1862, made provision for them to be recruited into the army, albeit as laborers, rather than as fighting soldiers.

As the rate of white volunteers for the US Army fell during the unsuccessful summer of 1862, blacks were only a short step away from being armed and sent to the front. That fall, the Lincoln administration authorized the experimental raising of a black regiment. It was mustered from freed slaves on the Union-occupied islands off the South Carolina coast, and was known as the 1st South Carolina Volunteers. The experiment was considered as a success, and the US Colored Troops swiftly came into being. Before the war's end, a total of 178,975 blacks served in the army, which had 140 black regiments. Of that number, some 37,000 were killed or died in service.

The blacks were generally treated as second-class soldiers, often receiving inferior arms and equipment, and doing most of the dirty work. And for nearly two years the privates were paid only half the monthly wage of a white serviceman: $7 compared with $13. It was not until June, 1864, that the US Congress voted to give black fighting men full pay.

The North's arming of the blacks outraged the Confederacy. Southern soldiers took grim delight in pouring fire into black regiments on the battlefield, and frequently treated black prisoners of war with considerable harshness. The worst excess of Rebel feeling against black soldiers manifested itself in the western theater in the April of 1864. This was when Major General Nathan Bedford Forrest's cavalrymen massacred black troops after they had surrendered at Fort Pillow.

However, just before the end of the war, the Confederate government, desperately short of white recruits, seriously considered allowing blacks to enlist. A Negro Soldier Law was signed by President Davis in February, 1865, and a handful of black companies was raised. But, by this time, it was too late, and no black infantryman was ever required to fire a shot for the South.

Members of the 4th US Colored Infantry (*right*) pose for the camera at Fort Lincoln, Washington, D.C. More than 178,000 blacks served in the US Army before the war ended. Some 37,000 were killed.

One battle in which blacks played a part was Nashville. The 1st Tennessee Colored Battery (*below*) survey part of the railroad depot at Johnsonville before going on to Nashville.

Anderson held the left, and Lieutenant General A.P. Hill's Corps, temporarily led by Major General Jubal Early while its commander was sick, was on the right. The center, occupied by Ewell, formed a salient projecting toward the Union lines, three quarters of a mile deep and half a mile across at its base.

Because of its shape, the salient was called the "Mule Shoe" by the soldiers. By itself, the defending infantry was vulnerable there, but 22 cannon had been hauled up to make sure that this hilly area was not taken by the Federals and used as a convenient gun platform from which to bombard the Confederate rear. However, as a precaution, a reserve line was being prepared at the base of the salient.

Within a remarkably short time—and to the astonishment of the Union observers—Lee's engineers had laid out and constructed strong defenses. These comprised deep trench systems with traverses to protect against enfilade fire, gun emplacements, and abatis (a tangle of felled trees, the forerunner of barbed wire entanglements) to obstruct the enemy's approach to their front line. Grant, whose troops were massed behind breastworks of a less formidable nature, contemplated the Confederate line and wondered where best to try to force his way through.

Grant's problems were not helped by the loss, on the 9th, of one of his most able and popular officers, Major General "Uncle John" Sedgwick, the VI Corps commander, who was killed by a sharpshooter. His place was taken by Major General Horatio G. Wright. That day, too, Grant gave permission for Sheridan to "break loose" from the army and take his Cavalry Corps off on a ride around the enemy toward Richmond. This excursion, of course, compelled Stuart to give chase. Two days later, that gallant officer was mortally wounded when the two sides clashed at Yellow Tavern. Like Stonewall Jackson, Stuart was considered irreplaceable: his death was yet another body-blow to Southern hopes.

On May 10, Grant started probing Lee's position in earnest. He first tried to move around the Confederate left flank, but that move was intercepted and turned back. Then, three consecutive attacks were made on Anderson's left wing, each of which was beaten back with serious loss.

Another determined assault was tried, this time against Ewell's left center by Colonel Emory Upton with 12 regiments, and for a while it looked quite promising. Upton believed that an attack could be most successful if his initial thrust was made by a concentrated force advancing on a narrow front. Once this formation

Amid the mud, smoke, and carnage which typified the Battle of Spotsylvania, Union officers (*foreground right*) discuss their next move while their men take shelter as best they can behind earthworks.

In what war artist A.R. Waud termed the "toughest fight yet" in his caption to this sketch, the earthworks, part of the Confederate Mule Shoe defenses, were the scene for some of the most brutal hand-to-hand fighting of the war. Isolated hats elevated above the top of the earthworks are intended to draw the enemy's fire.

The assault on the "Mule Shoe" salient

In winning the race to the Spotsylvania crossroads, General Robert E. Lee's Rebel army was able to construct its entrenchments on ground of its own choosing. These were roughly arc shaped and swept northeast in front of Spotsylvania Court House and the Po River. The line was screened by dense woodland in front, and further protected by a substantial abatis of pine and oak as well as a deep ditch. The trench system, constructed in record time by the Confederates, followed the rolling topography so cunningly that it was scarcely visible from the Federal side.

Protruding from the Rebel line was the controversial "Mule Shoe" salient (2)—the jagged center of their front. The salient, a rough inverted V-shape, was three-quarters of a mile deep, with a half-mile-wide base.

The salient had a mixed reception from Lee's men. In favor were Lieutenant General Richard Ewell and Major General Edward Johnson, whose division occupied the apex. They were confident the Mule Shoe would be secure with adequate artillery. Others were worried that should the salient be broken, the Army of Northern Virginia would be cut in half and vulnerable to defeat in detail.

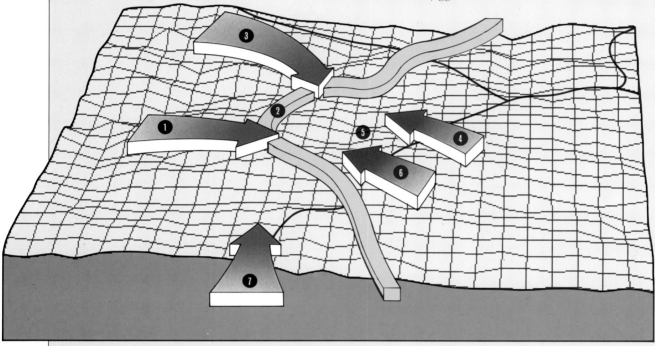

Spotsylvania Court House was situated near crossroads whose strategic importance made the race for the control of this intersection crucial to both Lee and Grant. The Rebels arrived there first, and dug in before the Federal onslaught began.

As Lieutenant General Grant's men maneuvered around this tempting target on May 11, Lee misinterpreted his opponent's intentions, and assumed the Union army was on the move toward Richmond. In making a commander's agonizing decision between security and mobility, Lee ordered most of the Rebel guns out of the Mule Shoe. Thus, it became most vulnerable at the very moment that it was most threatened.

In the battle that developed in the early hours of May 12, Federal Major General Winfield Hancock's II Corps drove in from the north in a major assault on the salient. Leading the first wave of the assault at about 4.30 a.m. was the division (3) of Brigadier General Francis Barlow, who had Major General David Birney's division (1) on his right. The Federals soon broke through the Rebel defenses.

A determined counterattack by Brigadier General John G. Gordon with three brigades (4), supported on his left by troops (6) under Major General Robert E. Rodes, advanced past the McCoull House (5), and stemmed the Union tide. As desperate fighting developed, more Federals (7) from Major General Horatio Wright's VI Corps assaulted the Rebel line where it kinked. This spot became the scene of horrific carnage and was afterward called "the Bloody Angle."

The savage fighting continued all day with the Confederates desperately holding on while a second defensive line was completed at the base of the salient. Only in the early hours of the 13th were Lee's battered veterans able to retire behind this new line—and wait for the next onslaught.

148

had penetrated the enemy's front line, a second wave would push through the gap. This plan almost worked: the first line of Rebels was carried and 300 prisoners taken, but then Confederate reinforcements arrived and drove the Federals away in disorder. Grasping the significance of what Upton's unsupported troops had achieved, Grant remarked:

"A brigade today, we'll try a corps tomorrow."

But heavy rain fell on the 11th, bringing a welcome respite in the fighting. There was considerable movement of troops within the Union lines, however, and the Confederates wrongly supposed that Grant was preparing to attempt another flanking march. Lee, ever-anxious to be one step ahead of his powerful adversary, ordered that all artillery in the salient which had been difficult to maneuver into position should be withdrawn, so it could be moved quickly by road that

Battle-seasoned Federals of Major General Gouverneur K. Warren's V Corps, whose badge is displayed behind

them, were among those who, on May 10, assaulted the Rebel line under Major General R.H. Anderson.

night if necessary. The action turned out to be one of Lee's worst errors of judgment.

Most of the cannon, deemed so necessary for the protection of the salient, were removed at a time when Grant was, in fact, planning to launch a hammer blow at that very point. During the night, Major General Edward Johnson, whose division was holding the apex of the salient, formed the opinion that he was about to be attacked and called for the return of the guns. But it was too late.

At dawn, Major General Winfield S. Hancock's II Corps issued from the woods half a mile in front of the "Mule

Shoe." According to General Johnson, they advanced through the mist and rain "in great disorder, with a narrow front, but extending back as far as I could see." In a matter of minutes, the Confederate line was overrun by the 18,000-strong Union tide. Johnson and some 2,800 men were captured along with 20 guns which had just arrived back in the salient; most of the guns were not even in position.

Brigadier General Gordon's division, lying in reserve, sprang to counterattack. For the second time in a week, Lee tried to lead his men into battle during a crisis, and once again he was dissuaded from risking his life. "General Lee to the rear," the soldiers shouted as Gordon forcefully reminded his superior:

"These men behind you are Georgians, Virginians, and Carolinians. They have never failed you on any field. They will not fail you here."

Nor did they.

Scarcely pausing after the Battle of the Wilderness, Lieutenant General U.S. Grant forged onward around General Robert E. Lee's right flank toward the strategically important crossroads at Spotsylvania Court House—the next objective in the Federal advance on Richmond. The Confederate cavalry quickly informed Lee of his opponent's course. The Rebel commander, therefore, ordered Major General Jeb Stuart and his horsemen to hold Spotsylvania pending the arrival of the I Corps, under Major General Richard Anderson, who would make a night march to join them as quickly as possible. Anderson and his men made excellent time and were on hand to relieve Stuart's hard-pressed cavalry from a Union assault which, had it been successful, would have opened the way to Richmond.

As it was, on May 8 and 9, Lee's men constructed entrenchments of such quality, making ideal use of the high ground they had gained, that they were later able to fend off concerted attacks by large numbers of the enemy.

On May 10, Federal troops under Colonel Emery Upton made an experimental attack on the Rebels' "Mule Shoe" (as both sides termed the salient in the Confederate center, on account of its shape). Although the assault was eventually repulsed, Grant thought the method of attack might succeed with greater numbers.

At dawn on May 12, therefore, a powerful Union assault of 18,000 men took just minutes to pierce the Confederate line. However, the Rebels then counterattacked and, by about 5.30 a.m., an hour later, the Federal advance was checked.

The vast inverted V-shape in the Rebels' first line of defense—the "Mule Shoe" salient—had its apex jutting north, making it an obvious point for an assault by the Army of the Potomac.

Streaming out of the thick fog that blanketed the entire battle area, the men of Major General W.S. Hancock's II Corps (1, 2) penetrated the salient soon after 4.30 a.m., and proceeded to take thousands of Rebel prisoners, including Major General Edward Johnson and 26 pieces of artillery.

The momentum of the Union attack, which had broken through the Confederates' first line, carried the Federals into the salient, then they began to flounder. As they struggled with their prisoners and captured cannon in the mud and mist, their units became intermingled. Confusion and discouragement quickly set in, stopping the thrust of the assaults.

With the Army of Northern Virginia in real danger of being overwhelmed, General Lee himself sought to lead his men into the fray, but was persuaded to go to the rear by Brigadier General John B. Gordon, who took charge of the counterattack. Gordon swiftly brought up three brigades, deployed them in a textbook line of battle (3), and advanced in steady formation against the Federals whose dozen different brigades in the area were now an unmanageable jumble.

Gordon's division was aided on its left by brigades (5) from Major General Robert E. Rodes' division, and other Confederate commands; but there was a dangerous gap between these forces which was spotted by General Robert E. Lee, and plugged before it could be exploited by the Federals.

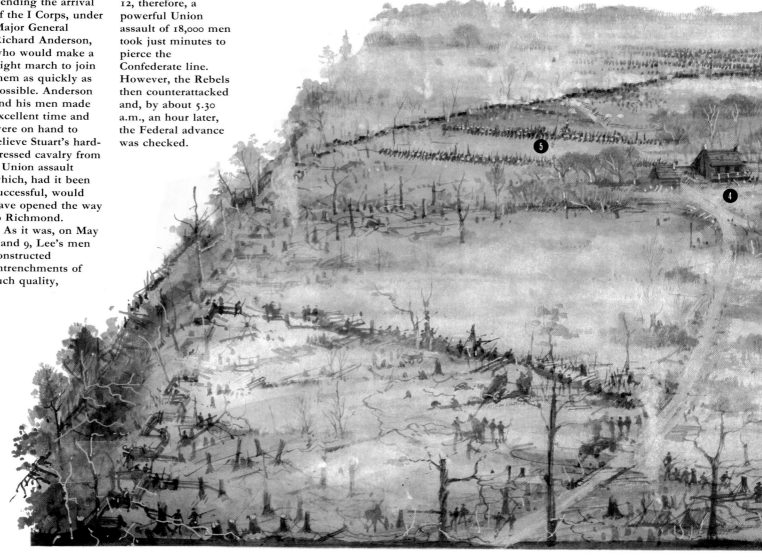

Gordon and Rodes advanced to each side of the McCoull House **(4)** and effectively halted any further penetration by the disorganized Federals of the Mule Shoe defenses.

But this repulse was to be merely the prelude to the most desperate and savage fighting seen in the 12-day conflict at Spotsylvania. Both commanders—Grant with victory in mind, and Lee trying to buy enough time for a new defense line to be constructed across the base of the Mule Shoe—continued to feed troops into the cramped area of the salient.

Fighting was particularly savage in a northwest section of the salient where the Rebel defensive line kinked, known ever after as "the Bloody Angle." The slaughter here was made more horrific by the hand-to-hand combat— "skulls were crushed with clubbed muskets." Even when the Federals were forced back, they clung to the parapets and kept fighting. After some 18 hours of continuous blood-letting, a stalemate was reached.

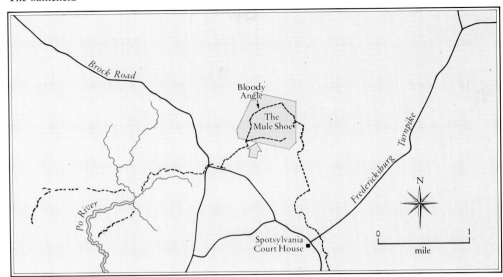

The battlefield

The Battle of Spotsylvania dragged on for a further six days. Grant threw his men at the new defense line Lee had created while the fighting in "the Bloody Angle" was under way, but could not break the Confederates in any head-on attack. Both sides suffered enormous casualties— the Federals about double the number of the Rebels, although, in proportion, the losses were about equal.

Lee was feeling the bite of Grant's war of attrition more keenly than ever. From now on he could envisage only defensive battles as the Union leader once more side-stepped east and south toward Richmond.

The art of entrenching

At the outset of the war, soldiers on both sides were contemptuous of digging in. Their first taste of action, however, soon convinced them that a "heap of earth" could help them to survive.

Federal Captain O.E. Hunt thus described the construction of these hasty entrenchments: "The men, deployed in a line of skirmishers, would dig, individually, shallow trenches about four or five feet by two, with their longest dimension toward the foe, and throw up the earth in a little mound of a foot or 15 inches in height, on the side toward the opponent. This would result in a line of such excavations and mounds, each individually constructed and without any communication with its neighbors. Then the neighbors would dig out the ground between them and throw it to the front, thus forming a continuous line of earthen parapet; but, if their antagonists were firing, or danger was near, it was preferable to deepen the trenches and throw up a larger earth protection before joining the individual trenches. In the rear of such hasty works, heavier lines often were constructed by large forces working with spades."

It was the Confederate army, however, that was first to appreciate the enormous

Part of the Rebel fortifications (*below*) around Atlanta show how sophisticated entrenchments had become in the latter part of the war. The formidable chevaux-de-frise were the forerunners of barbed wire.

Federals hastily construct breastworks of logs and earth at Cold Harbor, the next clash between Lee and Grant following Spotsylvania, in June, 1864. The soldiers are digging with bayonets, tin plates, and their bare hands.

advantages of fighting from behind carefully prepared field fortifications. The defenders could oppose a force three times their own size and inflict enormous casualties on their attackers at little cost to themselves. General Robert E. Lee was probably the greatest exponent of this economical method of fighting.

As the war progressed, troops on both sides habitually built defenses whenever they halted, whether the enemy was in the vicinity or not—just as a precaution. But the Confederates seem to have been quicker and more efficient at this than the Federals. As a Union staff officer recalled: "It is a rule that when the Rebels halt, the first day gives them a good rifle pit; the second a regular infantry parapet with artillery in position; and the third a parapet with abatis in front and entrenched batter-

ies behind. Sometimes they put this three days' work into the first 24 hours."

By the time Lee and Grant stood each other off in the lines around Richmond and Petersburg in 1864–5, field entrenchment and fortification had been elevated to a high art. Parallel works, sometimes just yards apart, stretched for nearly 40 miles. Federals and Confederates lived in bomb-proof dugouts and manned intricate networks of rifle-pits and gun emplacements commanding cleared fields of fire. Approaches were protected by rows of chevaux-de-frise—logs spiked with sharpened wooden stakes.

Gordon's division and brigades from Major General Robert E. Rodes' and other divisions stemmed the Union assault, but could not drive the enemy out of the salient. Both sides then began piling men and guns into the disputed area. By 10 a.m., Lee had committed all the troops he could spare to the defense of his threatened center. The Confederates would *have to* hold on, or the Army of Northern Virginia would fight its last battle of the war at Spotsylvania.

For the rest of the day, and far into the night, fighting of hitherto unimaginable ferocity took place. The bitter struggle reached a crescendo at a point on the northwest side of the salient, where the line kinked. Ever after, this spot would be known as "the Bloody Angle."

Colonel Horace Porter, one of Grant's staff officers, described the prolonged battle for the salient, which was unrelieved by both Union and Rebel attempts to create diversions elsewhere:

"It was chiefly a savage hand-to-hand fight across the breastworks. Rank after rank was riddled by shot and shell and bayonet thrusts, and finally sank, a mass of torn and mutilated corpses; then fresh troops rushed madly forward to replace the dead; and so the murderous work went on. Guns were run up close to the parapet, and double charges of canister played their part in the bloody work. The fence-rails and logs in the breastworks were shattered into splinters, and trees over a

The aftermath

The Battle of Spotsylvania, which turned into a grim slogging match of brutal hand-to-hand fighting, ended in a tactical draw, though the Confederates inflicted heavier losses on their opponents.

The Army of the Potomac, which had been forced to assault an enemy making the most of their entrenchments, lost 18,399 men out of a total of about 100,000. The Confederates never made an accurate return of their casualties. Estimates put the Army of Northern Virginia's total losses at approximately 10,000 out of about 50,000 men. But, unlike their powerful enemy, the Rebels could not afford to lose such high numbers.

General Lee had succeeded in checking Grant's thrust toward Richmond for the second time in almost two weeks. But Lee knew that unless he destroyed the Federal army outright, the campaign would probably end in a siege of the Rebel capital—and an inevitable Union victory.

TOTALS AND LOSSES

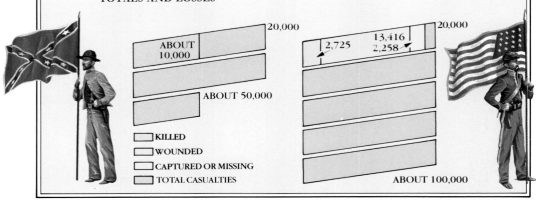

ABOUT 10,000

20,000

ABOUT 50,000

2,725   13,416   2,258

20,000

☐ KILLED
☐ WOUNDED
☐ CAPTURED OR MISSING
☐ TOTAL CASUALTIES

ABOUT 100,000

---

foot and a half in diameter were cut completetly in two. . . . The opposing flags were in places thrust against each other, and muskets were fired with muzzle against muzzle. Skulls were crushed with clubbed muskets and men stabbed to death with swords and bayonets thrust between the logs in the parapet which separated the combatants. Wild cheers, savage yells, and frantic shrieks rose above the sighing of the wind and the pattering of the rain, and formed a demoniacal accompaniment to the booming of the guns."

While the battle was raging, the Confederates were hastening to complete a fortified line across the base of the salient. At 3 a.m., on the morning of the 13th, the exhausted Southerners were finally able to break off the fight and retire behind these newly finished works. From then until the 16th, a steady downpour of rain bogged down the armies and prevented serious clashes.

The ground began to dry out on the 17th, and, next day, Grant returned to the offensive, sending Hancock's and Wright's battered II Corps against the new enemy line at the base of the salient. It was repulsed with heavy losses, and Grant finally accepted that nothing was to be gained by repeatedly storming Lee's entrenchments before Spotsylvania. So he proposed once more to sidestep to his left.

Lee sensed that another Federal flank march was in the offing and sent Ewell on a reconnaissance in force around Grant's right to ascertain whether this was so. Heavy fighting developed and lasted until nightfall.

Next day Grant began pulling out to loop round the Confederate right. But Lee once more was able to prevent him from getting between the Army of Northern Virginia and Richmond, though the fighting was drawing ever closer to the South's capital.

Lee knew the difficulties facing him. Talking to General Jubal Early after Spotsylvania, he remarked:

"We must destroy this army of Grant's before he gets to the James River. If he gets there it will become a siege, and then it will be a mere question of time."

How right he was.

The death of the South's great cavalier
Lieutenant General James Ewell Brown "Jeb" Stuart, who led the Army of Northern Virginia's cavalry with such dash and courage, was mortally wounded on May 11, 1864. While the armies of Lee and Grant slugged it out around Spotsylvania Court House, Stuart went in chase of Major General Philip H. Sheridan's Cavalry Corps, which had reportedly left to raid toward Richmond.

Stuart, with 4,500 troopers, intercepted Sheridan's 10,000-strong command at Yellow Tavern, six miles from the Confederate capital. In the unequal fight that followed, one of the South's greatest cavalry leaders received a pistol shot through the liver. He was carried from the field and died the next day, May 12. A deeply religious man, Stuart's last words were: "I am going fast now. I am resigned; God's will be done."

Stuart's death stunned the Confederacy,

The loss of Jeb Stuart, shown waving his ostrich-plumed hat (*below left*), was a tragedy for the South. Stuart had begun the war with the famous 1st Virginia Cavalry (*left* and *below right*), known as the "Black Horse Cavalry." Long hair and beards and slouch hats contributed to the regiment's "cavalier" style.

which had always been thrilled by his daring exploits. General Robert E. Lee was distraught when he heard the news. "I can scarcely think of him without weeping," he told an aide. Stuart, who had begun the war with the famous Black Horse Cavalry of Virginia, was responsible for building up, training, and inspiring Lee's excellent Cavalry Corps.

Atlanta

"I was not so much pained by the fall of Atlanta as by the recurrence of retreat. . . ."

GENERAL JOHN B. HOOD, CSA, after the war

IN EARLY 1864, BOTH the Confederate and Union troops in the western theater found themselves with new commanding generals. Also, the fighting in this theater was about to enter a phase of prolonged campaigning which would have a significant impact on the ultimate outcome of the war.

After the Confederate Army of Tennessee was defeated at Chattanooga in November, 1863, General Braxton Bragg was replaced by General Joseph E. Johnston. This was a popular choice with the military, but not with President Jefferson Davis, who had never gotten along with him.

Johnston faced a formidable task. His new command, which was in winter quarters at Dalton, Georgia, 30 miles southeast of Chattanooga, was demoralized, poorly fed and equipped, and rife with desertion. He had to transform it into a strong fighting force in time for the start of the campaigning season in the spring. That he largely succeeded in doing so was a credit to his ability as an organizer and administrator.

On the Federal side, Major General William T. Sherman had succeeded Lieutenant General Ulysses S. Grant (who had now become commander of all Union land forces) as head of the huge Military Division of the Mississippi.

Grant was eager for the troops in the west to act in concert with those in the east, which he now directed personally. When the Armies of the Potomac and James moved against the Confederate capital of Richmond, Sherman was to lead a powerful force comprising 60,773 men of the Army of the Cumberland, under Major General George H. Thomas; 24,467 men of the Army of the Tennessee, under Major General James B. McPherson; and 13,559 men of the Army of the

Ohio, under Major General John M. Schofield, into northwest Georgia.

Sherman's objective was the destruction of Johnston's army and the capture of Atlanta, a large manufacturing city and important railroad junction. It was situated at the heart of the South's most prosperous cotton state, and was a principal arsenal and supply depot. If Atlanta could be captured, Grant reasoned, the downfall of the ailing Confederacy would be considerably hastened.

On May 7—three days after Grant crossed the Rapidan River in Virginia to begin his offensive against General Robert E. Lee—Sherman moved from his forward base at Ringgold, Georgia, 15 miles south of Chattanooga, keeping close to the Western & Atlantic Railroad. This single track, which led to Atlanta, 120 miles away, was also the Federals'

lifeline; along it passed all the supplies for 100,000 men and 23,000 animals. Because the railroad was in hostile territory, it needed to be heavily protected from Confederate raiding parties; and the farther Sherman penetrated into Georgia, the more men he would have to detach to guard this all-important supply line. However, this handicap was not so critical because Sherman's troops outnumbered the Confederates by almost two to one.

Skirmishing between the two sides began almost as soon as the Union armies marched; but the first significant test of strength came on May 8, near the Confederate positions around Dalton. There, the railroad passed through the 1,500-foot-high Rocky Face Ridge at Buzzard Roost Gap, and Sherman found the narrow gorge too strongly held to be carried by frontal assault. He therefore sent McPherson's Army of the Tennessee on a right-flanking march to threaten the Rebel rail supply line at Resaca, 18 miles farther south.

McPherson's troops passed through the undefended Snake Creek Gap and advanced toward Resaca. However they then encountered a body of about 4,000 Rebel reinforcements blocking their path to the town. McPherson overestimated the Rebels' strength and so retreated to the gap.

Sherman then moved the rest of his force to support McPherson and, in so doing, obliged Johnston to fall back on Resaca, where the latter was reinforced by Lieutenant General Leonidas Polk and his corps. The Confederates hurriedly constructed a fortified line three miles long, which came under heavy attack on May 13, 14, and 15. By sheer weight of numbers, the Federals succeeded in turning Johnston's left flank so that once

WILLIAM TECUMSEH SHERMAN (1820–91)

A tall, lean, dynamic man, who became one of the Union's most respected generals, Sherman led the Federal forces advancing on Atlanta. A native of Ohio, Sherman graduated from West Point in 1840, and joined the artillery. He served for 13 years, but missed the Mexican War because he was on garrison duty in California.

At the outbreak of the Civil War, Sherman entered the conflict as colonel of the 13th Infantry, and commanded a brigade at First Bull Run. He became a brigadier general of US Volunteers in August and was sent west, eventually taking over the Fifth Division of the Army of the Tennessee in early 1862. Sherman fought well at Shiloh, in April, 1862, and soon after was made a major general, USV.

In 1864, when Ulysses S. Grant went east to take command of all US army troops, Sherman was appointed to run much of the war in the western theater. In the spring of 1864, he began a campaign to capture Atlanta, which fell in September. Two months later, he led an army of 60,000 veterans in a destructive march from Atlanta to the sea. He then turned north and drove up into the Carolinas, coming within 100 miles of linking up with Grant's army in Virginia when the war ended.

Sherman remained in the army after the war, rising to the rank of full general. Within four years, he succeeded Grant as commander in chief of the US Army in March, 1869.

JOHN BELL HOOD (1831–79)

Hood became commander of the Rebel Army of Tennessee during the final struggle to prevent Major General William T. Sherman's Federal troops reaching Atlanta in July, 1864. Thus, at the age of 33, he became the youngest army commander of either side during the war.

A Kentuckian, Hood graduated from West Point in 1853, and joined the infantry. A first lieutenant when the Civil War started, Hood sided with the South and went on to become a brigadier general with command of the Texas Brigade in March, 1862. Always a hard fighter, he led his troops successfully in the Seven Days Battles, at Second Bull Run, and at Antietam where he led a division.

In October, 1862, Hood was promoted to major general and again handled his men well at Fredericksburg and Gettysburg, where a shot crippled his left arm. However, he recovered quickly from this wound, and was sent to the western theater to command a corps at Chickamauga in September, 1863. There he lost his right leg.

Promoted to lieutenant general, he was back leading a corps in General Joe Johnston's Army of Tennessee in the spring of 1864. In July, Johnston was replaced by Hood, who was instructed to go on the offensive. His efforts failed and Atlanta fell. Hood then invaded middle Tennessee, but was defeated at Nashville, in December, 1864. A month later, he requested to be relieved of his post.

157

again the Confederate commander had no choice but to abandon his position and retreat south across the Oostanaula River in search of a stronger one.

Three days later, in the vicinity of Cassville, Johnston thought he had discovered the ideal place to hit the head of Sherman's force in front and flank. On the 18th, Lieutenant General John B. Hood was ordered to make the flank attack.

Inexplicably, Hood failed to carry out the directive, and the opportunity was lost.

That evening, another disappointment awaited Johnston at Cassville, where his army was strung out on a ridge south of the town. Although he judged the position to be a strong one, two of his three corps commanders told him that they did not think they could hold it if the Federals brought enfilading artillery fire to bear on

them. Faced with this half-hearted response, Johnston reluctantly ordered a further withdrawal. On May 19, the Army of Tennessee crossed the Etowah River, the second of three natural barriers in front of Atlanta, which now lay only 50 miles away.

Sherman negotiated the Etowah on May 23 and, boldly forsaking the railroad, struck south across country to Dallas.

The Federals' deadly firearms

Reliable breechloading and magazine rifles and carbines were much prized during the Civil War, and most of them were in the hands of Union troops. Of the many types produced, three gained widespread acclaim—the Sharps, the Spencer, and the Henry. All were manufactured by Northern gunmakers.

Christian Sharps, a former employee of the Federal arsenal at Harpers Ferry, Virginia, developed a single-shot, breechloading weapon in .52 caliber, which enjoyed enormous success both during the war and afterward as a buffalo gun on the Western plains. It came in two versions: the carbine (1), $37\frac{1}{2}$ inches long and weighing 8 pounds; and the rifle, 47 inches long and weighing $8\frac{3}{4}$ pounds.

Christopher Spencer, a young Connecticut industrialist, perfected a .52 caliber repeater. An underlever action fed metallic rimfire cartridges into the breech from a seven-shot tubular magazine concealed in the butt. The carbine version (2) was 39 inches long and weighed $8\frac{1}{4}$ pounds, while the rifle was 47 inches long and weighed 10 pounds.

The Henry, however, was also a popular weapon. Developed by B. Tyler Henry, the manager of the New Haven Arms Company, Connecticut, it was a .44 caliber, underlever-action repeater, carrying 15 rimfire cartridges in the carbine version (3) and 16 in the rifle. The ammunition was stored in a tubular magazine underneath

the barrel. The Henry rifle, which weighed $9\frac{3}{4}$ pounds, was an expensive weapon, costing up to $50 (compared to $13 for a Springfield rifle-musket), but there was no lack of customers.

Many soldiers bought Spencers and Henrys out of their own pockets, looking on them as a life-preserving investment. Southerners disliked encountering the Spencer, a weapon they called "that

1

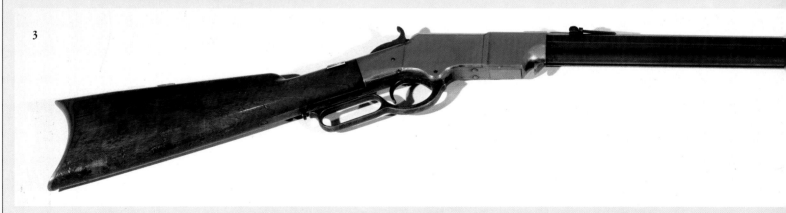

2

3

Alerted to this move by his cavalry, Johnston was waiting in entrenchments at New Hope Church, north of Dallas, when the Federals arrived on May 25. Major General Alexander Stewart's division of Hood's corps, supported by four batteries of artillery, bore the brunt of a two-hour assault by Major General Joseph Hooker's XX Corps from the Army of the Cumberland. Severe casualties were inflicted on the Federals, who called the muddy shot-swept field "The Hell Hole."

Sporadic fighting, sometimes quite intense, continued in this area for several days, without much result. By the first week of June, Sherman was back on the railroad, and Johnston, now reinforced to a strength of about 62,000, was attempting to defend a ten-mile line at Marietta. Here, Johnston had Brush Mountain on his right, Pine Mountain in his center, and Lost Mountain on his left. It was at this time that the South lost another prominent officer: General Leonidas Polk. Polk, who had been a classmate of Jefferson Davis at West Point, and went on to become a bishop in the Episcopal Church, was killed by an artillery shell while visiting a strong point on Pine Mountain.

On June 19, the Rebels contracted

damned Yankee rifle that can be loaded on Sunday and fired all week."

In 1866, the New Haven Arms Company's proprietor, Oliver Winchester, renamed his firm the Winchester Repeat-ing Arms Company, and began producing an advancement on the wartime Henry known as the Winchester Model 1866. It was the first of one of the most famous lines of rifles ever made.

Federal troopers (*below*) of Brigadier General John Buford's command defend a ridge at Gettysburg with their carbines.

Color bearers (*bottom*) of the 7th Illinois display their Henry repeating rifles—one of the most coveted of weapons.

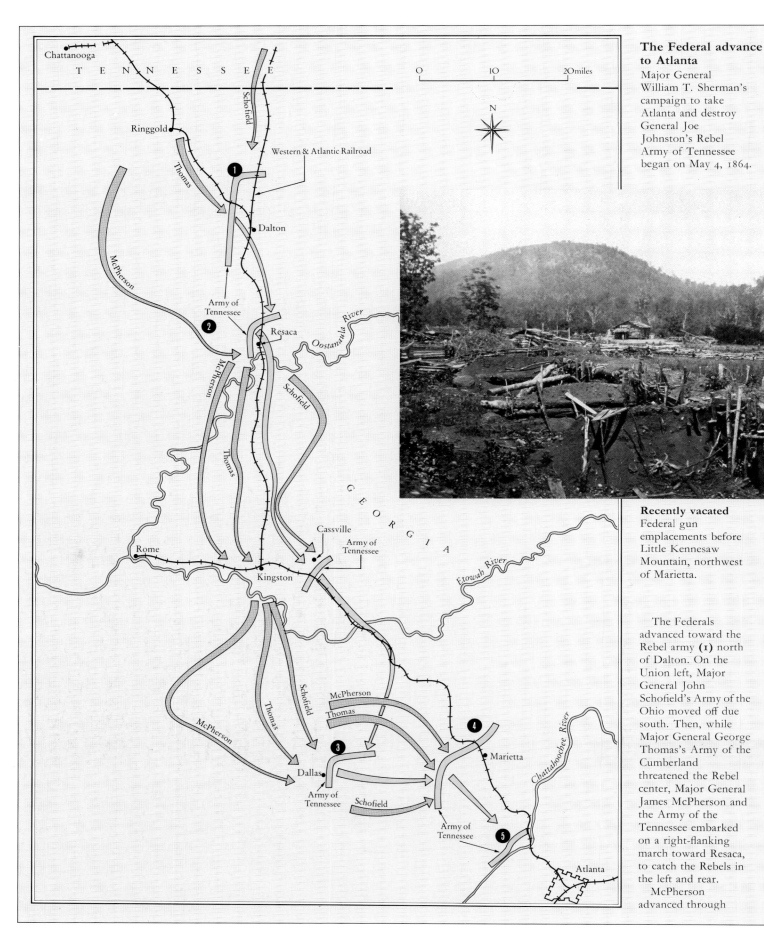

The Federal advance to Atlanta

Major General William T. Sherman's campaign to take Atlanta and destroy General Joe Johnston's Rebel Army of Tennessee began on May 4, 1864.

Chattanooga

T E N N E S S E E

Ringgold

Schofield

0   10   20miles

N

Western & Atlantic Railroad

❶

Thomas

Dalton

McPherson

Army of Tennessee

❷

Resaca

Oostanaula River

McPherson

Schofield

Thomas

G E O R G I A

Rome

Cassville

Army of Tennessee

Kingston

Etowah River

McPherson

Thomas

Schofield

McPherson

Thomas

❸

Dallas

Army of Tennessee

Schofield

❹

Marietta

Chattahoochee River

Army of Tennessee

❺

Atlanta

Recently vacated
Federal gun emplacements before Little Kennesaw Mountain, northwest of Marietta.

The Federals advanced toward the Rebel army (1) north of Dalton. On the Union left, Major General John Schofield's Army of the Ohio moved off due south. Then, while Major General George Thomas's Army of the Cumberland threatened the Rebel center, Major General James McPherson and the Army of the Tennessee embarked on a right-flanking march toward Resaca, to catch the Rebels in the left and rear.

McPherson advanced through

Snake Creek Gap **(2)**, but was then stymied by Rebels lately arrived at Resaca. Overestimating their numbers, McPherson retreated to the gap. But his presence there compelled Johnston to retreat to Resaca, where, from May 13 to 15, he fought stubbornly against the Federal armies.

Gaining no advantage, Sherman continued his advance over the Oostanaula River, forcing Johnston to retreat to Cassville. Here, the Rebel generals advocated a further withdrawal, to which Johnston grudgingly assented. The Federal armies pursued, and the two forces clashed in a series of battles. These included, on May 25, New Hope Church **(3)**, near the town of Dallas.

From the resultant stalemate, Sherman moved eastward, and Johnston followed suit, making a new line centered on Kennesaw Mountain **(4)**, northwest of Marietta. The Federals attacked and lost 3,000 men, and failed to shift the Rebels. So Sherman once more began a right-flanking move, forcing Johnston to retreat **(5)** to the Chattahoochee River.

Sherman was now dangerously close to the city, but still blocked by Johnston, who had conducted a skillful retreat. The Richmond government, however, felt that by allowing Sherman to get so far, Johnston had put Atlanta in jeopardy: on July 17, Johnston was ordered to hand over his command to General John B. Hood.

their position, anchoring their right on Big and Little Kennesaw and their left on Olley's Creek, because they did not have enough resources to man such a long front. Although slowed by heavy rain, Sherman eventually closed up with Johnston, and heavy skirmishing, interrupted by the Battle of Kolb's Farm on June 23, took place until the 27th, when Sherman ordered a full-scale attack. After a bombardment by 140 guns, his battle line advanced at 9 a.m., under a hot sun, and was met by devastating fire from the well-entrenched Confederates. By 11.30 a.m., Sherman accepted that the assault, which cost him more than 2,000 casualties, had failed.

Once more the Union commander reverted to a right-flanking maneuver, and again Johnston had to yield his position to cover the approach to Atlanta. By July 5, the Army of Tennessee was occupying formidable earthworks on the north bank of the Chattahoochee River, only ten miles from the city.

Instead of committing his troops to another costly frontal attack on fortifications, Sherman created a diversion downstream on the Confederate left; then, while the Rebels were concentrating on that, he, on July 8, pushed a strong force across the river 15 miles upstream and secured a bridgehead. Johnston had to move quickly across the bridges behind

him in order to place his army between the Federals and the outer defenses of Atlanta at Peach Tree Creek.

However, the Richmond government, which had been closely following Johnston's skillful withdrawal in the face of a more powerful foe, became convinced disaster was imminent: not only was the Federal force intact—it was also at the gates of Atlanta. President Davis, therefore, sent his military adviser, General Braxton Bragg—the man who had lost Chattanooga and the confidence of the Army of Tennessee—to supply him with a first-hand assessment of the situation. Bragg recommended a change in command, and suggested that General John B. Hood was the best candidate for the job.

On July 17, therefore, Johnston was ordered to hand over to Hood, a 33-year-old who had lost his right leg and the use of his left arm in previous battles. Sherman, who had a healthy respect for Johnston's generalship, was delighted when he heard the news. He knew of Hood's reputation as an adherent of the "see-the-enemy-and-charge" school, and hoped that at long last the Confederates would fight him in the open.

Hood did not disappoint him. Feeling that constant defensive fighting from the cover of breastworks dulled soldiers' combative spirit, he immediately laid

Confederate troops, under Brigadier General Arthur M. Manigault, storm over Federal breastworks to capture four 20-pound Parrotts during the fighting east of Atlanta on July 22, 1864.

Manigault's Alabamians were unable to move the guns because the battery's horses had been killed. The Rebels' moment of triumph was short-lived, however: Union reinforcements counterattacked, and troops under Colonel August Mersy recaptured the Parrotts—much to the joy of Federal artillery Captain Francis De Gress.

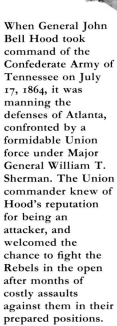

When General John Bell Hood took command of the Confederate Army of Tennessee on July 17, 1864, it was manning the defenses of Atlanta, confronted by a formidable Union force under Major General William T. Sherman. The Union commander knew of Hood's reputation for being an attacker, and welcomed the chance to fight the Rebels in the open after months of costly assaults against them in their prepared positions.

Hood obliged his opponent by planning an assault on a perceived gap in the Federal line: on July 20, he ordered an assault against Major General George Thomas's forces in the Battle of Peach Tree Creek, but was unable to break the Federal line.

Undeterred by the costly failure of his debut attack, Hood decided to carry out what was intended to be a combined flank and frontal assault on Federals to the east of the city on July 22.

However, the two assaults were poorly coordinated and the Federals were able to launch a successful counterattack. Between 4 and 4.30 p.m., in the blazing July heat, Union troops stormed back to recapture their frontline earthworks next to the Georgia Railroad.

Hood's planned double assault on the Federal line might have worked if the two attacks, each of which enjoyed temporary success, had been carried out simultaneously. As it was, the charge on the Union flank made by Lieutenant General William Hardee's men had been repulsed by the time Major General Benjamin Cheatham's corps was sent to hit the Federal front just east of Atlanta by the Georgia Railroad (4).

A Confederate brigade of Alabamians led by Brigadier General Arthur N. Manigault managed briefly to overrun the Union front. They took earthworks of Major General John Logan's XV Corps and fought to hold them from behind a makeshift barricade (3) of cotton bales and logs erected in sight of the as yet unfinished Troup Hurt plantation house (5). However, their triumph was cut short by the swiftness and power of the Federal counterattack.

Union troops of the XV Corps under Major General Logan, who was also in temporary command of the Army of the Tennessee after General McPherson's death, rallied to repair their broken line. To reinforce them, a brigade (2) from the XVI Corps under Colonel August Mersy swept up the slope shouting at the tops of their voices. Two more XV Corps brigades (1) of Brigadier General Charles A. Woods' division poured downhill to overtake the Confederates' left flank (7).

During their initial burst through the Union front line, Manigault's Rebels captured four 20-pound Parrotts (6) of Battery A, 1st Illinois Artillery, but were unable to get them out because the guns' horses had fallen in the crossfire.

When the guns were eventually recovered by Mersy's men, Captain Francis De Gress, who commanded the battery, was overjoyed, and the weapons were soon turned on the retreating Rebels.

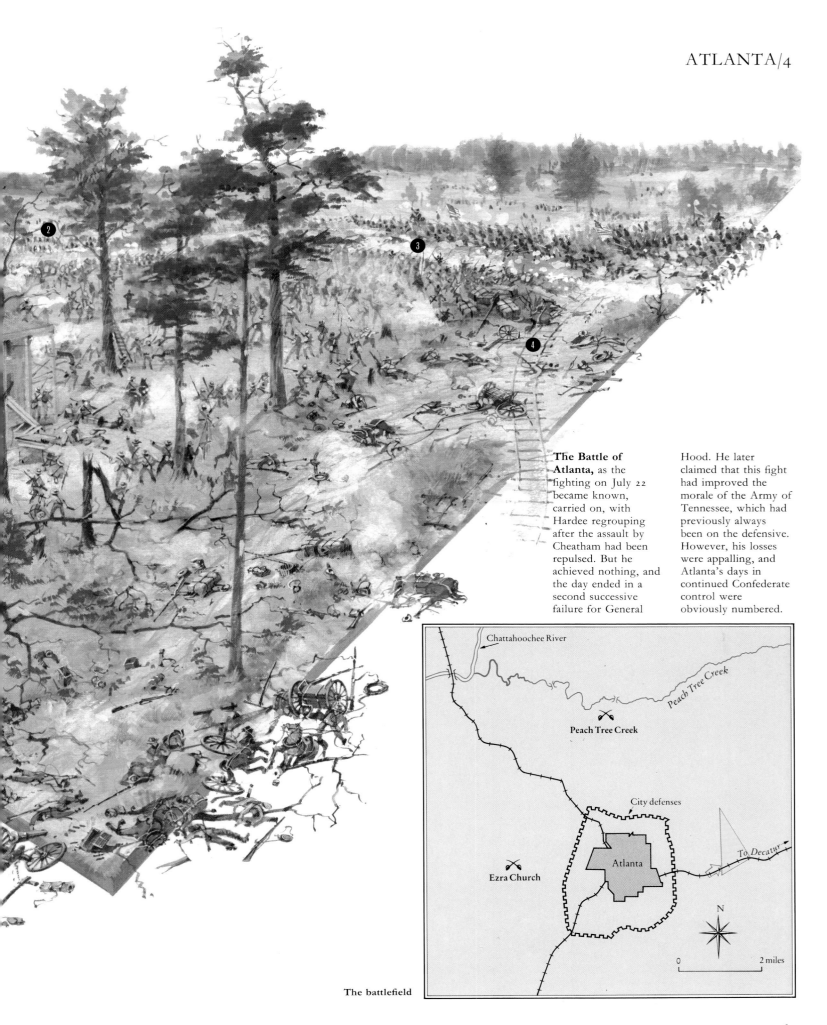

The Battle of Atlanta, as the fighting on July 22 became known, carried on, with Hardee regrouping after the assault by Cheatham had been repulsed. But he achieved nothing, and the day ended in a second successive failure for General Hood. He later claimed that this fight had improved the morale of the Army of Tennessee, which had previously always been on the defensive. However, his losses were appalling, and Atlanta's days in continued Confederate control were obviously numbered.

The battlefield

Chattahoochee River

Peach Tree Creek

Peach Tree Creek

City defenses

Ezra Church

Atlanta

To Decatur

N

0   2 miles

plans for an offensive against Major General George Thomas's Army of the Cumberland at Peach Tree Creek. He would try to smash it before it could be joined by the Armies of the Ohio and the Tennessee, which were away trying to cut Atlanta's rail links with the east.

The corps of Lieutenant Generals William J. Hardee and A.P. Stewart (formerly Polk's) were to launch the assault at 1 p.m. on July 20. That hour came and went while Hardee struggled to get his troops into position, and, at 4 p.m., an exasperated Stewart took it upon himself to attack on his own. At first, his leading division managed to exploit a gap in the Federal line, but this advantage was lost when Thomas hurried up reinforcements to meet the threat. Elsewhere, Stewart's onslaught was slowed, then beaten back, some units suffering fearfully from concentrated Union musketry. A half-hearted attempt by Hardee to turn the Federal left flank was disrupted by artillery fire, and soon the whole Southern offensive spluttered out.

The Confederates returned to the shelter of Atlanta's outer defenses, having lost 4,800 men compared with about 1,775 in Thomas's army.

Undismayed by this reverse, Hood decided to return to the attack on July 22. His plan, if executed properly, would, he believed, produce an effect similar to that of the late Stonewall Jackson's great flanking assault at the Battle of Chancellorsville.

Hood learned from his cavalry commander, Major General Joseph Wheeler (who had been trying to delay Schofield and McPherson in their advance on Atlanta from the east), that McPherson's left

The once-proud city of Atlanta suffered the ravages of total war during the summer of 1864. Factories and other buildings deemed useful to the enemy were destroyed by General Hood before he evacuated the city on September 2; and even more property was later destroyed by occupying Federals.

With the fall of their city to Federal forces under Major General William T. Sherman becoming inevitable, citizens of Atlanta pack themselves and their belongings into the last train to leave town.

wing was "in the air." Hood resolved to send Hardee's corps on a long and circuitous night march to come in on the rear of the Army of the Tennessee at dawn on the 22nd, while Wheeler's troopers rode even farther east to destroy the Union supply trains at Decatur. As the Union left collapsed, Hood intended that his remaining forces should take up a general assault all along the line. But all did not go according to plan.

Hardee was late setting out, some of his troops lost their way in the dark, and it was noon before he was ready to attack. Even then, according to Hood, he was not in the correct position; he had not gone far enough to turn McPherson's left flank and was blocked by Major General Grenville M. Dodge's XVI Corps.

Savage fighting developed and the crash of musketry sent McPherson, who had been lunching with Sherman, hurrying back to his command. But, while out on a reconnaissance, this popular officer accidentally rode into the Confederate lines and was killed. This tragedy for the Federals meant that Major General J.A. Logan of the XV Corps was given temporary command of the Army of the Tennessee, with orders to hold his line at all hazards—and he did.

Hardee had some local successes but, by mid-afternoon, it seemed to Hood that he was about to come under a concentrated counterattack. To relieve pressure on Hardee, therefore, Hood ordered forward his old corps, now commanded by Major General B.F. Cheatham. With great fighting spirit, the Confederates stormed and captured the Federal earthworks to their front. They were not there long, however, before well-directed enfilading artillery fire drove them out. Major General G.W. Smith, who had led his Georgia state troops in support of Cheatham's left, was also compelled to retire because the Federals were too strong.

By nightfall, Hood had called off the first pitched battle of the Atlanta campaign. In an engagement that was disappointing for the South, he had lost some 8,000 men to Sherman's 3,700, but had satisfied himself that it had

"demonstrated to the foe our determination to abandon no more territory without at least a manful effort to retain it."

On July 28, the Confederates again sortied from their earthworks and attacked the Army of Tennessee west of Atlanta at Ezra Church. Once again, they were turned back with heavy losses.

The Confederate infantry now manned Atlanta's 12-mile-long defensive perimeter, while the cavalry continued to operate in the Georgia countryside.

Sherman at first tried to use his own cavalry to sever the city's remaining rail links, but these efforts were thwarted by Rebel troopers. He then settled down to extend his own fortifications around the east, north, and west and lay partial siege to Atlanta.

On August 9, after Hood had shown no inclination either to abandon his position or come out and fight, the Union commander ordered a continuous bombardment of the city, regardless of the fact that it was still full of civilians. He saw it as a legitimate military target and rained shot and shell on it for 17 days; but he could not batter it into submission.

Sherman then realized that the two railroads still feeding into Atlanta from the south were the key to the city's capitulation; so he decided to leave his prepared positions and move his forces south to cut these vital lines and enter the city by its own "back door."

Hood tried to intercept this deadly maneuver at Jonesboro on August 31 and September 1, but he did not have the strength to oppose it successfully and was obliged to evacuate Atlanta on the night of September 1. The city surrendered the following day, sparking great rejoicing in the Union. After four months of hard campaigning, Sherman had at least reached his goal. He then set about evacuating more than half the civilian population, and turned the city into a military base.

Prisoners of war and their fate

Because neither the Union nor the Confederacy expected hostilities to last long, no preparations were made for the detention of large numbers of prisoners of war. A great many men died needlessly as a result.

Both governments, whose main efforts were directed toward winning the war, improvised as they went along, utilizing forts, civilian jails, large commercial buildings, hutted and tented camps, and—in the case of the South only—open stockades.

Around 150 military prisons sprang up between 1861 and 1865, and catered for a total of more than 400,000 captive soldiers—194,000 Federals and 214,000 Confederates. Early in the war, the conditions in some of these places were tolerable. But, as the numbers of inmates increased, the situation got out of hand. Overcrowding, poor sanitation, inadequate water and fuel supplies, a monotonous and scanty diet,

and a lack of proper medical attention combined to make life much more miserable than it needed to be for those captured.

In all, some 30,000 Union soldiers died in Southern prisons, and about 26,000 Confederates in Northern prisons. Many thousands more on both sides had their health ruined for life. To the Federals goes the record of the highest mortality rate in a month of any prisoner-of-war compound—387 men out of 3,884 detained at Camp Douglas, Chicago, in February, 1863.

But the most infamous prison of the war was undoubtedly the South's Camp Sumter in Georgia, better known as Andersonville. Opened in February, 1864, it was designed to hold between 8,000 and 10,000 prisoners. Plans to build barrack huts had to be abandoned for lack of materials, and the captives were obliged to make their own shelters from whatever

In Camp Douglas, Chicago (*right*), painted here by a Union private, 387 Rebels died in one month from the appalling conditions.

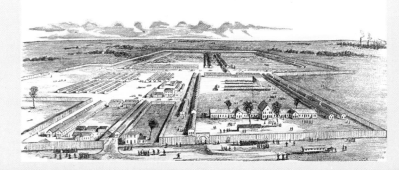

came to hand—blankets, oilcloth or just burrows in the ground. By August, 1864, 33,000 men were confined within a 27-acre stockade, a large area of which was a swamp. Food, which was scarce in the Confederate army, was even scarcer for prisoners. Within 11 months, more than 12,000 Federals died.

Andersonville, Georgia, was the most infamous prison of the war. By August, 1864, 33,000 starving Federals were rotting away in the summer heat. After the war,

the camp commandant, Captain Henry Wirz, was executed on November 10, 1865, for "murder in violation of the laws and customs of war."

The notorious Libby Prison in Richmond (*left* and *above*) was a converted warehouse. Union officers were its only inmates.

In 1864, 109 Federals escaped from the prison via a tunnel. Fifty-nine men avoided recapture.

The aftermath

General John B. Hood's fight to prevent Major General William T. Sherman's Federal force from capturing Atlanta was the climax of a campaign that lasted four months. The casualty figures over this period are difficult to calculate, but the Federals probably lost in the region of 30,000 men out of a total of about 100,000 at the start of the campaign. The Army of Tennessee started the struggle with about 53,000 men (though it received reinforcements later on) and suffered estimated casualties of more than 30,000.

On September 2, 1864, Sherman entered Atlanta and immediately evacuated more than half the civilian population. He turned the city into a military base where his troops could rest after their exertions of the previous four months. However, with Hood and some 40,000 Confederate troops at large in the Georgia countryside, there still remained a lot to do to crush the rebellion in the west.

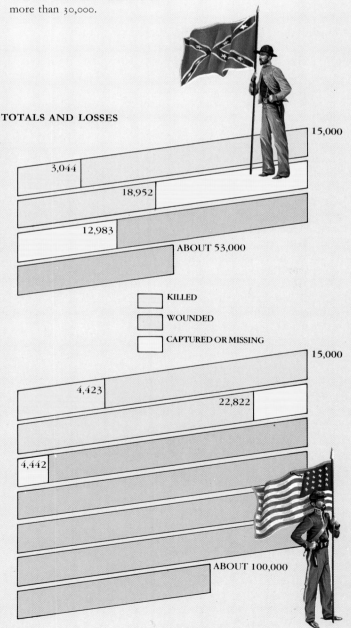

TOTALS AND LOSSES

3,044
18,952
12,983
ABOUT 53,000

KILLED
WOUNDED
CAPTURED OR MISSING

15,000
4,423
22,822
4,442
ABOUT 100,000

15,000

Nashville

DECEMBER 15—16, 1864

"Didn't I tell you we could lick 'em?"

MAJOR GENERAL GEORGE H. THOMAS, USA, to
MAJOR GENERAL JAMES H. WILSON, USA, on the night of December 16

WITH THE SURRENDER of Atlanta to Federal Major General William T. Sherman on September 1, 1864, Confederate General John B. Hood had been forced to withdraw 30 miles southwest of the city. Short of options, Hood decided to move his army around to the northwest, threaten the Federals' vulnerable rail supply link with Chattanooga in Tennessee, and try to lure the invaders into the north Georgia mountains. There, with a little luck, he might snatch a victory.

Around the same time as this flanking march was in progress, Rebel Major General Nathan Bedford Forrest and his cavalry corps began to raid heavily in middle Tennessee. To deal with Forrest, Sherman sent two divisions back to Tennessee on September 28, and, next day, detached Major General George H. Thomas, to follow them and take charge of the defense of that state. Sherman himself set out with 65,000 men to follow Hood.

However, by October 15, Hood had marched to the mountains at Lafayette, 100 miles north of Atlanta, and was now anxious to bring on a fight. But his three corps commanders—Lieutenant Generals A.P. Stewart, S.D. Lee and B.F. Cheatham—reckoned their troops were not fit enough for a pitched battle. So Hood opted for an invasion of middle Tennessee, with a view to eventually taking Kentucky as well. He would then march through the gaps in the Cumberland Mountains to attack Grant's rear in Virginia, and so relieve pressure on General Robert E. Lee.

With the cautious blessing of General P.G.T. Beauregard (who was now in overall command of Confederate operations in the west) Hood began to execute his ambitious plan. On October 22, he left behind Wheeler's cavalry to harrass Sherman in Georgia and then marched

off through north Alabama. There, he planned to pick up Forrest's horsemen, cross the Tennessee River, and march against Nashville.

By October 26, Sherman realized Hood was making for Tennessee, so he proposed a daring course of action of his own: he would send to Thomas two corps, the IV, under Major General D.S. Stanley, and the XXIII, under Major General John Schofield, plus other reinforcements. Thomas would thus be left to deal with Hood. Sherman himself would go back to Atlanta, and, with a force of 60,000 men, march southeast toward Savannah on the Atlantic coast.

Meanwhile, Hood continued to the Tennessee River, reaching it on October 31, at Tuscumbia, Alabama. After a delay of three weeks while he waited for Forrest's cavalry and supplies to arrive,

Hood initially planned to neutralize the 32,500-strong force under Major General Schofield at Pulaski, about 50 miles south of Nashville. Accordingly, the Confederates came looping in from the west, heading for Columbia, on the Duck River, toward the Federal rear. Schofield, however, spotted the danger and made a dash to Columbia, just ahead of the Rebel infantry.

Thwarted, Hood devised a new plan: he would leave two infantry divisions and his artillery to occupy the Federals at Columbia, while the rest of his army made a flank march on Spring Hill, some 13 miles to the north: Schofield would be caught between the two Rebel forces.

However, the Union cavalry alerted Schofield to the danger he was in, enabling him to get his troops on the turnpike toward Nashville. But only one division had reached Spring Hill when the Rebels began deploying on the afternoon of November 29. The vastly outnumbered Union defenders, however, fought off the piecemeal Rebel attack and held on to Spring Hill until darknesss fell. Throughout that night, Schofield managed to march his men up the pike, past the Rebel camp, to safety.

Hood and the Army of Tennessee had slipped up badly. Hood then chased after Schofield, and caught up with him at Franklin, 19 miles from Nashville, in mid-afternoon on November 30. In a display of impetuousness, Hood committed 20,000 infantry to a grand frontal assault, across exposed ground, on the Union defenses. His casualties were enormous. In five and a half hours of savage fighting, Hood lost 6,250 men, including six generals—20 percent of his total strength. Schofield, whose losses were 2,326, made good his escape to Nashville under cover of darkness.

JAMES HARRISON WILSON (1837–1925)

James Wilson, a gifted young officer who was responsible for breathing new life into the Federal cavalry, played a significant part in the Union victory at Nashville. Born in Illinois, Wilson graduated from the US Military Academy just a year before the Civil War began, and entered the service as a topographical engineer. It was in this capacity that he spent the first two years of hostilities, rising to lieutenant colonel in the process.

In October, 1863, Wilson was commissioned a brigadier general of US Volunteers, and fought at Missionary Ridge and Knoxville in the western theater. In February, 1864, he was in command of the newly created Cavalry Bureau in Washington, despite the fact that he had no training in this arm of the service. His brief from the bureau was to improve the much-maligned Union cavalry. Wilson set about the task and, exhibiting considerable organizational flair, soon raised the arm's standard of efficiency. He also added much to their fighting capacity by arming many of them with the formidable Spencer repeating carbine.

Wilson led the Third Division of the Cavalry Corps in Lieutenant General Ulysses S. Grant's advance from the Wilderness to Petersburg in the spring and summer of 1864. In August and September of that year, he operated with General Philip Sheridan's Army of the Shenandoah.

Grant then sent Wilson to Major General William T. Sherman in the west, telling the latter: "I believe Wilson will add 50 percent to the effectiveness of your cavalry." Commanding the Cavalry Corps of the Military Division of the Mississippi, Wilson, now a major general, helped Major General George Thomas rout General Hood's Confederate army at the Battle of Nashville in December, 1864. In the spring of 1865, he conducted a spectacularly successful raid through Alabama and into Georgia, and ended up capturing Confederate President Jefferson Davis.

Wilson stayed in the US Army until 1870, then left to go into railroad building. When the Spanish-American War broke out in 1898, he was the only major general in civilian life under retirement age, so he volunteered his services, which were accepted. He remained on the active list until 1901, and also took part in quelling the Boxer Rebellion (1898–1900) in China.

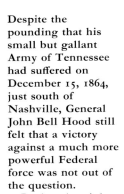

Despite the pounding that his small but gallant Army of Tennessee had suffered on December 15, 1864, just south of Nashville, General John Bell Hood still felt that a victory against a much more powerful Federal force was not out of the question.

During the night of the 15th, therefore, Hood organized a new Rebel line some two miles to the rear of the first, but which covered only two of the all-important turnpikes that could provide him with an escape route to the south. The Rebel left was now anchored on the hill that would be known ever afterward as "Shy's Hill" for the courageous Rebel colonel who fought, and died, there.

Over to the east, the Confederate right was established on Overton's Hill. On and between these two hills, the exhausted Rebels worked throughout the night, constructing breastworks as best they could.

On the Rebel left, now under the command of Lieutenant General B.F. Cheatham, the defenses curved around to the south of Shy's Hill to give some protection against any Federal flank attack.

However, the breastworks on the crown of Shy's Hill itself were wrongly laid out: they were so far back from the brow that the Federal attackers would be able to use the hill's slope for cover until the final dash of 20 yards or so for the enemy works.

When the battle resumed on the 16th, the Rebel right came under attack first, but was able to fight off troops from Major General James Steedman's and Brigadier General T.J. Wood's commands.

Meanwhile, on the Rebel left, dismounted Federal troopers, advancing from the south, had begun to threaten Cheatham's rear. To the north and northwest, a considerable Federal force, under Major Generals John Schofield and Andrew J. Smith, was waiting to be unleashed against the enemy.

Finally, toward the end of a cold, dank afternoon, with only about an hour of daylight left, Federal Brigadier General John McArthur, eager to attack Shy's Hill, informed his commanding officer, A.J. Smith, that unless he heard to the contrary, he would do just this: Smith gave permission with his silence.

The battlefield

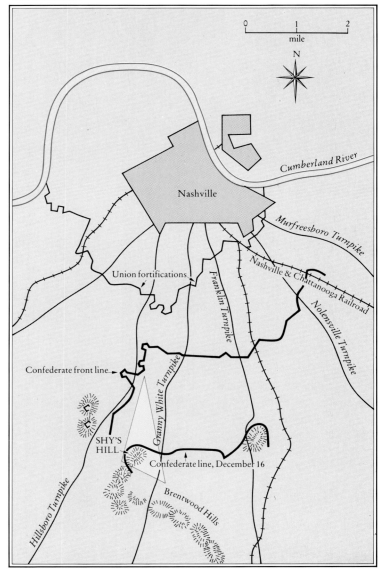

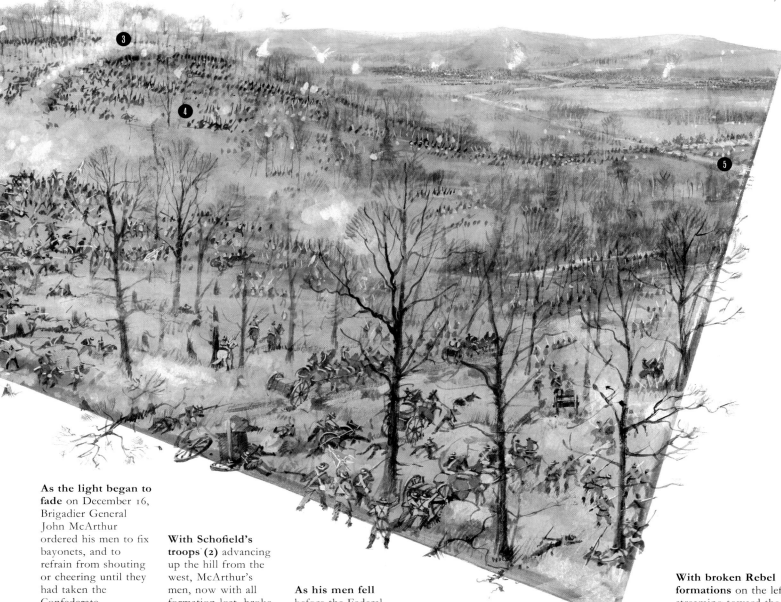

As the light began to fade on December 16, Brigadier General John McArthur ordered his men to fix bayonets, and to refrain from shouting or cheering until they had taken the Confederate breastworks on Shy's Hill **(4)**. Bracing themselves for this Federal assault on the hill were the men of Confederate Major General William B. Bate's division.

As McArthur's Federals advanced, they soon came under fierce Rebel fire. But they continued, unwavering, and quickly fell upon a line of Rebel skirmishers, whom they either put to flight or took prisoner.

With Schofield's troops (2) advancing up the hill from the west, McArthur's men, now with all formation lost, broke the Rebel line **(3)**. Colonel William M. Shy's 37th Tennessee Regiment courageously stood its ground as the Federals burst through—like water through a cracked dam. However, with the Federals fired up by the prospect of victory, and the Confederate rear increasingly under threat from Major General James Wilson's troopers **(1)**, it was only a question of time before the Confederate left would collapse.

As his men fell before the Federal onslaught, Colonel Shy himself was shot in the head and killed. Soon afterward, the flimsy Rebel resistance evaporated and the panic-stricken men took to their heels toward the Granny White Turnpike **(5)**.

A Federal officer, who witnessed this part of the battle from his own lines, later wrote of: "The hillside . . . dotted with the boys in blue swarming up the slope . . . the wonderful outburst of musketry, the ecstatic cheers; the multitude running for life down into the valley below. . . ."

The cheers of their jubilant comrades reached the ears of the Federals over to the east, and inspired them to renew their assault on the Rebel right. This time, Major General Wood's men achieved the breakthrough that had so far eluded them: only an orderly fighting retreat by Lieutenant General Stephen Lee saved the Rebel right from the fate of their fellow countrymen on the left.

With broken Rebel formations on the left streaming toward the Franklin Turnpike— their only remaining escape route—a well-conducted rearguard action by Arkansas troops stalled the advance of the Federals, as darkness began to fall.

The pursuit of the shattered Rebels was now taken up by James Wilson's troopers, who had by this time rejoined their horses. However, they were unable to prevent the remnants of Hood's army reaching the Tennessee River, which the Rebels crossed ten days after the battle.

Hood was now down to only 30,000 effectives, though he was promised reinforcements from Texas by President Davis. With limited options, Hood now decided to move upon Nashville—there was a chance he might snatch a victory against the superior Federal forces there.

On December 2, the little Army of Tennessee appeared before the impressive fortifications of Nashville. Behind the ramparts, General Thomas was frantically organizing his troops. Schofield's veterans and three divisions from the Army of the Tennessee under Major General A.J. Smith formed the core of his 55,000-strong body, which included recruits, convalescents, and blacks. The cavalry had been placed under the command of Brigadier General James H. Wilson, whom Grant had sent west to breathe new life into it.

Thomas wanted to wait until his cavalry had been properly fitted out and drilled before committing them to an offensive. But he was constantly being lobbied by Grant to attack the Confederates before Wilson's troopers were ready to mount an offensive. Thomas stood his ground until December 9, when his cavalry was pronounced fit for action. That day, however, the deteriorating weather prevented any movement. On December 10, Thomas decided against an immediate assault. Grant, meanwhile, was whipping himself up into an uncharacteristic frenzy over the delayed attack at Nashville, and even made plans to relieve Thomas. By the 14th, however, Thomas judged the ground to be firm enough for an attack next day.

The Rebel line formed a four-and-a-half-mile crescent around the southern approaches to the city. The right was held by B.F. Cheatham's corps, commanding the Murfreesboro and Nolensville Turnpikes, and the Nashville & Chattanooga Railroad; the center by S.D. Lee's corps astride the Franklin Turnpike; the left by A.P. Stewart's corps covering the Granny White and Hillsboro Turnpikes. Between the Hillsboro pike and the Cumberland River lay a three-mile stretch of country guarded only by a skirmish line of 1,600 Rebel cavalry and infantry. It was toward this vulnerable area that Thomas addressed his attention.

The Union commander proposed to send Major General James B. Steedman and his division of black and second-grade troops against Hood's right to create a diversion, while Wilson's cavalry, Smith's corps, and the IV Corps, now led by Brigadier General Thomas Wood, would swing around through the gap

The Sanitary and Christian Commissions

As soon as hostilities began, civilians in the North and South—and particularly the womenfolk—clamored to do what they could to ease the lot of their soldiers.

But, after some initial hesitation, it was only the Federal Government which properly organized this support. In June, 1861, the Sanitary Commission was appointed in Washington to harness private fund-raising and volunteer work for the purposes of improving health and hygiene in army camps and generally looking after the care and comfort of the troops.

Over the four years of war the Sanitary Commission grew into a huge relief organization. Apart from its agents at the front, who advised on camp hygiene and handed out "extras" to the soldiers, the Commission provided nursing care, supplementary (and often vital) medical supplies in the field, convalescent homes for the wounded, lodges for troops in transit, an invaluable directory of all wounded in Union hospitals, a free advice service for all military personnel and their dependents, and much more besides.

While the Sanitary Commission looked after the physical well-being of the Union armies, the Christian Commission took care of the soldiers' moral welfare. Formed in November, 1861, by the Young Men's Christian Association, this commission's agents were to be found in every theater, at the front and in reserve, distributing bibles, hymn books and religious tracts, caring for the wounded and ministering to the dying.

The Christian Commission, in addition,

provided hospital supplies, coffee wagons, free writing materials and stamps for soldiers, and well-stocked reading rooms at permanent camps. This organization, which operated on voluntary contributions, estimated that it disbursed over six million dollars in money and goods between 1861 and 1865.

The Confederate States Army never enjoyed such well-organized care as that bestowed on Northern forces by the Sanitary and Christian Commissions. That is not to say that civilians in the South did not share the same enthusiasm for looking after their troops. They did, but their relief efforts were maintained at a local level.

The field headquarters of The US Sanitary and Christian Commissions, at Brandy Station (*below*) and Germantown (*left inset*) respectively, were photographed here by Alexander Gardner in 1863.

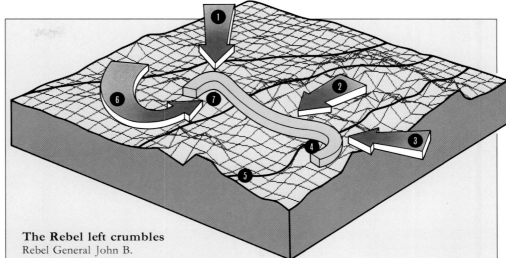

The Rebel left crumbles

Rebel General John B. Hood's Army of Tennessee had nearly been crushed on December 15, just south of Nashville, by Major General George Thomas's Federal force. However, instead of retreating, Hood decided to stay put and slug it out to the end. He therefore formed a new contracted line of battle stretching from the hill which became known afterward as "Shy's Hill" **(7)** eastward to Overton Hill **(4)**.

Lieutenant General B.F. Cheatham now commanded the Rebel left; Lieutenant General A.P. Stewart held the center; and Lieutenant General S.D. Lee commanded the right.

When battle resumed in earnest during the afternoon of the 16th, Major General James Wilson's Federal cavalry **(6)**, which had outflanked the Rebel left, began to push toward the Confederate line from the rear. Meanwhile, Union artillery unleashed a devastating barrage before the massed ranks of Federal infantry advanced.

The right of the Rebel line was assaulted from the east by Major General James Steedman's men **(3)**, and from the north by troops from Brigadier General T.J. Wood's IV Corps **(2)**. The Confederates, however, were able to withstand and repulse these attacks.

But, at about mid-afternoon, Hood decided to siphon off troops from his left to reinforce Lee in the center—despite the fact that Lee seemed capable of holding his own. The weakened left wing, already under a withering fire from Federal artillery, was now attacked in its rear by Wilson's troopers, advancing from the south, and assaulted in front by Brigadier General John McArthur's division **(1)**.

Despite a courageous stand by Tennesseans under Colonel William M. Shy of Bate's division, the Confederates could not resist the Federal onslaught. The Rebels broke, and those who could do so headed toward their only remaining escape route—the Franklin Turnpike **(5)**.

Federals charge a Rebel redoubt on December 15, the first day of the battle.

between the Hillsboro pike and the river, and fall on the Rebel left. Schofield's XXIII Corps was to stay in reserve.

At dawn on December 15, a thick mist prevented the Union troops from moving off at 6 a.m., as Thomas had wanted. By 8 a.m., all was ready, and Steedman's men began their demonstration, keeping Cheatham occupied for the rest of the day. Lee, in the Rebel center, was threatened by the guns of the Nashville garrison and also stayed put. The real action, therefore, was concentrated at Stewart's corps, on Hood's left, just as Thomas had intended.

Wilson's 12,000-strong cavalry corps found the going slow through the mud, but still chased off the scanty Rebel forces

Sherman's epic march

In the fall of 1864, while General John B. Hood and his Confederate army were occupied with their invasion of Tennessee, Major General William T. Sherman decided to proceed with his plan to devastate the Southern heartland. "Sherman's march to the sea," as it became known, was intended to "make Georgia howl." In other words, Sherman meant to destroy as much as possible of anything that could be used for the Southern war effort. He was also intent on breaking civilian morale.

After first destroying much of Atlanta, Sherman set out at the head of 60,000 veterans on November 17. He proceeded on a southeasterly march to the Atlantic coast. Deliberately cutting his communications with the North, Sherman declared that he and his men would live off the rich agricultural land which, so far, had been untouched by war.

For a month, his virtually unopposed army moved through the state on a front 60 miles wide, leaving behind it a trail of wreckage. The general reported to Washington: "I estimate the damage done to Georgia and its military resources at $100,000,000, at least $20,000,000 of which has inured to our advantage and the remainder is simply waste and destruction."

The seaport city of Savannah, Georgia, fell to Sherman on December 22, 1864, and he sent this message to President Lincoln: "I beg to present you as a Christmas gift the city of Savannah, with 150 heavy guns and plenty of ammunition; also about 25,000 bales of cotton." Lincoln was delighted.

Federal foragers raid a Georgia plantation during Major General William T. Sherman's march from Atlanta to Savannah in late 1864.

The foragers, who helped to "make Georgia howl," were, according to one Union soldier, "a picked force from each regiment . . . and were remarkable for intelligence, spirit, and daring."

Union troops (*below*) of Brigadier General John McArthur's command storm the Rebel defenses on Shy's Hill during the last day of the battle on December 16.

in front of them. Smith's corps, with Schofield now in close support, swung in west of the Hillsboro Turnpike. By midday, they had closed with Wood's corps to form a continuous battle line, more than two miles long, fronting and flanking Stewart's position.

Heavy fighting broke out in the afternoon, and parts of Stewart's hard-pressed corps began to give way. Major General Edward Johnston's Rebel division was transferred from Lee's corps to reinforce Stewart in preparation for an anticipated general assault by the Federals. But when the onslaught came in the early evening, Johnston's men ran away. The only Rebel troops remaining west of the Granny White Turnpike were Major General W.B. Bate's division, rushed across from Cheatham's corps, and Brigadier General M.D. Ector's brigade, who were holding out on a hill two miles south of Stewart's original position. With so many fresh Federal units swarming around, Hood's situation was perilous indeed; only darkness saved him from disaster.

The Union troops slept on their weapons that night, ready to take up what they imagined would be the pursuit of a fleeing enemy army on the morning of the 16th. Hood, however, was made of sterner stuff and spent the night pulling back to join Bate and Ector on a shorter and stronger line along the Brentwood Hills, covering his only two remaining lines of retreat, the Granny White and Franklin Turnpikes. In his new dispositions, Cheatham's corps was on the left, Stewart in the center, and Lee on the right.

At daylight, the Federals found themselves faced with a dug-in enemy and no plan of operation. The morning was spent bringing up artillery to pound Hood's new position and moving infantry up for an assault. Meanwhile, Wilson and his cavalry had ridden around the Rebels' left rear and had blocked the Granny White Turnpike.

In mid-afternoon, the Federal infantry launched a strong attack on Hood's right, and he began reinforcing this sector of his front with troops from the left. Then, this weakened left flank came under concerted assault and, despite a valiant stand, was forced to give way. Once this break was made, the whole of what was left of the Army of Tennessee began retreating down the Franklin Turnpike, the only road left open to them. Jubilant Union troops chased them all the way to the Tennessee River, which the Rebels crossed ten days later. Thomas had broken the back of organized Confederate resistance in the west.

The aftermath

The once proud Confederate Army of Tennessee was effectively destroyed at the Battle of Nashville. Major General George Thomas's Union army, about 55,000-strong, suffered minimal casualties of some 3,000 men. The Confederate figures are difficult to calculate, but General John B. Hood probably lost about 9,000 men—almost a third of his estimated 30,000-strong force.

In fact, the Rebels might have been completely annihilated by Brigadier General James H. Wilson's pursuing troops. However, a skillful rearguard action by Rebel infantry and Major General Bedford Forrest's cavalry insured that the remnants of the shattered Confederate army were able to cross the Tennessee River, ten days after the battle.

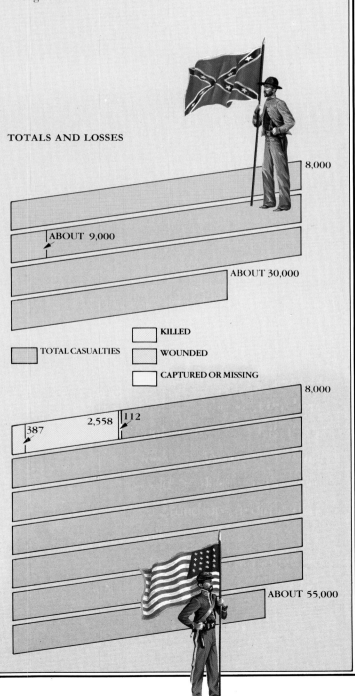

TOTALS AND LOSSES

8,000

ABOUT 9,000

ABOUT 30,000

KILLED

TOTAL CASUALTIES

WOUNDED

CAPTURED OR MISSING

8,000

387   2,558   112

ABOUT 55,000

Five Forks

APRIL 1, 1865

"We at last have drawn the enemy's infantry out of its fortifications, and this is our chance to attack it."

MAJOR GENERAL PHILIP H. SHERIDAN, USA, before the battle

THROUGHOUT THE LATE SPRING of 1864, General Robert E. Lee and the Army of Northern Virginia fought a series of brilliant actions in an attempt to block the Union advance on Richmond, the capital of the Confederacy. They inflicted enormous casualties on an invading force nearly twice their own size, but it seemed that no butcher's bill was too high for Lieutenant General Ulysses S. Grant, the Federal commander in chief, to pay. For, despite heavy losses, Grant kept on advancing, trying to push the Army of the Potomac around Lee's right flank.

By the second week of June, Grant had succeeded in crossing the James River below Richmond, and was now moving on Petersburg. He reasoned that if he could capture that city, through which passed most of Richmond's rail links with the rest of the South, the capital must succumb. But, once again, Lee managed to thwart him. He moved his 40,000 veterans into defenses around Petersburg just in time to reinforce General P.G.T. Beauregard's two divisions and parry the Union lunge for the railroads.

Grant tried to break through with frontal assaults, and was bloodily repulsed; he even tried to blow a gap in the Confederate lines with an enormous mine. Then, he settled for siege tactics. He threw up trenches and redoubts opposite the enemy fortifications and began to extend them, calculating that the Union line would soon become too long for Lee to match with his limited resources.

Eventually, the two opposing earthworks covered an arc 35 miles long, stretching from northeast of Richmond to southwest of Petersburg. Only the onset of winter prevented Grant from putting his plan of action to the test; but, as Lee fully realized, it was a plan that was bound to succeed in the long run.

In March, 1865, nine months after the trench warfare began, Lee was desperately trying to think of a way of extricating his army from the untenable position in which it would find itself when the weather improved. Grant, who was about to be reinforced by Major General Philip H. Sheridan's Cavalry Corps fresh from a victorious campaign in the Shenandoah Valley, resumed his westward movement around Petersburg.

Lee, who just a few weeks earlier had been elevated, belatedly, to overall command of the Confederate land forces, saw only one course of action open to him: he had to break out of the Federal stranglehold and move south to unite with General Joseph E. Johnston's army in North Carolina, which was trying to stand off a Union advance under Major General William T. Sherman. Together, Lee and Johnston might beat Sherman, then turn to take on Grant. The odds in favor of such a plan succeeding were long, but it was the only feasible option open to the Rebel commander.

Lee, therefore, proposed to mount a powerful atack on the Union lines at Fort Steadman, east of Petersburg; the Rebels would breach the lines and sever the military railroad in the rear, along which passed the supplies for the left flank of the Union army. He estimated that Grant would then have no alternative but to pull back his exposed left, leaving the way clear for the Army of Northern Virginia to march south.

Just before dawn on March 25, Major General John B. Gordon's corps took the Federals by surprise and carried Fort Steadman. The assault was badly coordinated, however, and Gordon withdrew with heavy losses in the face of a strong Federal counterattack. Lee's best hope had been dashed.

Meanwhile, over in the Union lines, Grant was putting the finishing touches to his plan to resume his efforts to stretch the Confederate line to breaking point. On March 29, the II Corps under Major General Alexander A. Humphreys, and the V Corps under Major General Gouverneur K. Warren, began to move toward the extreme right of Lee's position. Meanwhile, Major General Sheridan's 12,000-strong Cavalry Corps swung

PHILIP HENRY SHERIDAN (1831–88)

GEORGE EDWARD PICKETT (1825–75)

"Little Phil" Sheridan, who led the Federals to victory at Five Forks, was one of the youngest and most successful of the Union generals. Born in Albany, New York, of Irish parents, Sheridan graduated from West Point in 1853, and served in both the infantry and the cavalry. A lieutenant when the Civil War started, his first field command in May, 1862, was as colonel of the 2nd Michigan Cavalry. From then on, his rise in the ranks was rapid.

By July, 1862, Sheridan was a brigadier general; then in September, 1862, he became infantry commander of a division of the Army of the Ohio (soon to be redesignated the Army of the Cumberland). He fought well at the Battles of Perryville and Stones River, and was promoted to major general for his services. In 1863, Sheridan made a name for himself by storming Missionary Ridge with his IV Corps division during the Chattanooga campaign.

Grant was so impressed with Sheridan that he made him head of the Cavalry Corps of the Army of the Potomac in the eastern theater. After his success against General J.E.B. Stuart's cavalry at Yellow Tavern in May, 1864, Sheridan was elevated to the head of the Army of the Shenandoah, and drove the Rebels from the fertile Shenandoah Valley before laying waste to it. He rejoined Grant's army in March, 1865, and, after Five Forks, he and his cavalry helped to secure the surrender of General Robert E. Lee and his Army of Northern Virginia at Appomattox Court House.

Immortalized by historians for the bloody but futile charge he led at Gettysburg on July 3, 1863, Pickett led the Rebel force routed at Five Forks. A native of Virginia, Pickett graduated from West Point in 1846 at the bottom of his class. He joined the infantry, served in the Mexican War, and was involved in Indian fighting on the frontier.

Pickett did not resign his captaincy in the US Army until the end of June, 1861, more than two months after the outbreak of the Civil War. He became a colonel in the Confederate States Army and his early service was in northern Virginia. In February, 1862, Pickett was promoted to brigadier general, and led the Virginian Gamecock Brigade in operations against McClellan's Union army in the peninsula that spring. He fought at Williamsburg, Seven Pines, and also Gaines's Mill, where he received a severe wound in the shoulder. In October of that year, he rose to major general, and commanded a division at Fredericksburg in December.

In September, 1863, two months after Gettysburg, he became commander of the Department of Virginia and North Carolina, taking his battered division with him to rest and rebuild it. By the end of May, 1864, he and his troops were back with the Army of Northern Virginia and fought with it from North Anna River to Petersburg. On April 1, 1865, Pickett lost the Battle of Five Forks, which precipitated the fall of Richmond and Lee's surrender at Appomattox Court House eight days later.

By the spring of 1865, General Robert E. Lee, besieged by powerful Federal forces at Petersburg, knew that the only hope for the Confederacy lay in his being able to break free of the Union stranglehold and effect a junction with General Joe Johnston's army in North Carolina.

For Lee's hungry and exhausted Army of Northern Virginia, it was a slim hope—especially after a sortie by General John B. Gordon against the Federal lines on March 25 failed.

Lieutenant General Ulysses S. Grant responded to Lee's move by sending Major General Philip Sheridan and his cavalry to turn the Rebels' right flank and capture the vital South Side Railroad, which was supplying Petersburg. Lee, however, anticipated this maneuver and sent Major General George Pickett with five brigades to meet the threat.

After a setback on March 30 at Dinwiddie Court House, Sheridan, now with Major General Gouverneur K. Warren's V Corps in support, moved next day to attack the Rebel line drawn up and around Five Forks crossroads.

Pickett's forces were securely entrenched along the north side of the White Oak Road, which passed through Five Forks, their left flank protected by earthworks thrown up at a right angle to the road. It was Sheridan's aim to breach this bent-back part of the Rebel line, known as the Angle, and then to get in the rear of the Rebels' defenses.

On the day of the attack, Warren's men were slow to form up. But, at about 4 p.m. on April 1, the advance got under way: by 4.30 p.m., the Confederates were crumbling under the fierce Union assault.

The first object of Sheridan's assault was the north-bending, 90°-angle **(1)** formed by Pickett's left flank. Of the three V Corps divisions sent to tackle the Rebel left, only the smallest division **(2)**, under Brigadier General R.B. Ayres, was in the right place to begin with. Those of Brigadier General Samuel Crawford and Brigadier General Charles Griffin (who was to succeed Warren before the

day's end) joined in as soon as they were pointed in the right direction.

Just before the Federal surge into the Angle, Sheridan **(3)** charged back and forth with a red-and-white guidon held high, then leapt his charger over breastworks in a thrilling display of leadership. By contrast, Pickett was relaxing at a shad bake away from the scene of the fighting. However, the sound of gunfire spurred him to rush back to his command.

Pickett's line was strung out along the north side of White Oak Road **(4)**, roughly a mile on either side of the Five Forks junction **(5)**. His center and right were defended by the guns **(6, 8)** of the prodigious 23-year-old artillerist Colonel William Pegram, who was mortally wounded that day.

When Pickett arrived, he found the length of his defenses under attack. The Rebel center was confronted by four divisions of mainly dismounted Federal cavalry, who emerged from the woods armed with Spencer repeating carbines, advancing and firing in open order. This frontal assault complemented the V Corps' flank attack, putting the Confederates under intense pressure.

Meanwhile, on their right, the Rebels came under attack from a mounted charge by Major General George Custer and two brigades of his Third Cavalry Division **(7)**; the Confederates were unable to withstand the spirited Federal assault and were put to flight or captured.

By this time, the ranks of Rebel prisoners had swelled from about 1,500 taken at the Angle to some 5,000. Pickett's force was smashed.

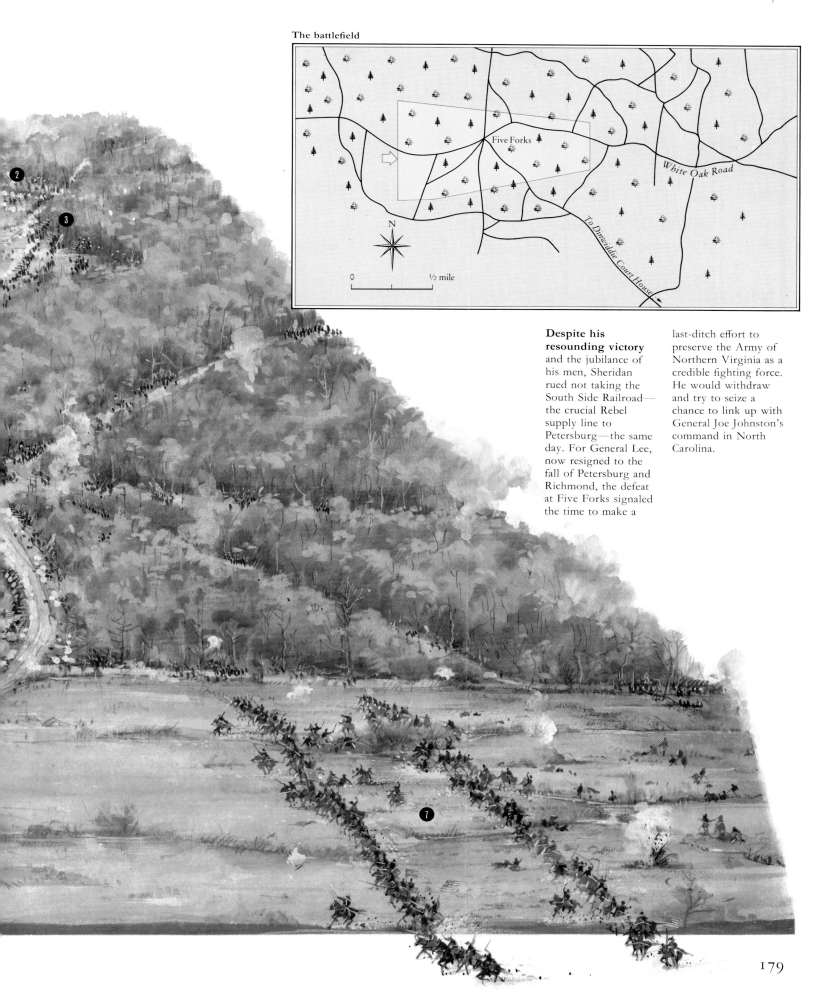

The battlefield

Five Forks

White Oak Road

To Dinwiddie Court House

N

0   ½ mile

Despite his resounding victory and the jubilance of his men, Sheridan rued not taking the South Side Railroad—the crucial Rebel supply line to Petersburg—the same day. For General Lee, now resigned to the fall of Petersburg and Richmond, the defeat at Five Forks signaled the time to make a last-ditch effort to preserve the Army of Northern Virginia as a credible fighting force. He would withdraw and try to seize a chance to link up with General Joe Johnston's command in North Carolina.

farther west with a view to turning the Rebels' flank and capturing the South Side Railroad, their only remaining supply line from the west.

That night, torrential rain fell, turning the countryside into a quagmire and making troop movements extraordinarily difficult. Lee, who had foreseen Grant's flanking attempt, shifted a large part of his infantry and cavalry to his right. On March 31, the Rebels struck Warren on the White Oak Road, near Burgess' Mills, inflicting heavy losses on the Federals before withdrawing to the shelter of entrenchments in the face of superior numbers.

At the same time as this action was taking place, a more serious threat to the Army of Northern Virginia was developing to the west. Sheridan, becoming increasingly impatient because of the delays caused by the rain, was now on the move from his camp at Dinwiddie Court House, some six miles southwest of the nearest Federal infantry. He was heading north toward an important road junction called Five Forks, well beyond the Confederate right wing's fortifications, and on a direct route to the vital South Side Railroad.

Lee, with his usual perspicacity, had hurriedly dispatched to Five Forks a mixed force of cavalry and infantry of an estimated 7,000 to 10,000 men under Major General George E. Pickett, of Gettysburg renown, with the following orders: "Hold Five Forks at all hazards. Protect road to Ford's Depot and prevent Union forces from striking the South Side Railroad." Pickett ran into Sheridan's troopers on their approach to Five Forks and, in a sharp engagement, drove them back to Dinwiddie Court House.

Sheridan, who was waiting for the support of an infantry corps, was not undismayed by the day's events. He was already looking forward to the next day and the prospect of a victory. This diminutive and fiery general told one of Grant's staff officers:

"This [Pickett's] force is more in danger than I am—if I am cut off from the Army of the Potomac, it is cut off from Lee's Army, and not a man in it should ever be allowed to get back to Lee."

Sheridan, who was designated commander of the Army of the Shenandoah serving with the Army of the Potomac, had wanted the assistance of Major General Horatio G. Wright's VI Corps. This corps had fought with him in the Shenandoah Valley and knew his ways; but it was now too far away, and Sheridan had to be

content with Warren's V Corps. In giving the V Corps to Sheridan, Grant added permission for him to relieve Warren summarily should he be dissatisfied with Warren's performance.

April 1—April Fools' Day—dawned to find Sheridan in a somewhat less than jocular mood. Warren had not come up as expected, having started late and encountered numerous obstacles to delay him along the way. Sheridan saw the chance of cutting off Pickett slipping away.

Early that Saturday morning, the Confederates had begun to fall back from Dinwiddie Court House to take up a position in earthworks along the White Oak Road at Five Forks. Pickett's line occupied the north side of the road for about a mile on each side of the junction, with the extreme left flank bent back to protect it from being turned. Cavalry was stationed on each wing. Pickett must have been fairly confident of the strength of his position, for he left the field to enjoy a shad bake with some friends in the rear of his line.

Meanwhile, Warren himself had not

joined Sheridan until 11 a.m. Then, it seemed to the latter that Warren was taking an inordinate length of time to prepare his corps for an attack on the angle formed by the refused section of the Confederate left. As the hours dragged by, and his troopers skirmished with the enemy, Sheridan fumed:

"This battle must be fought and won before the sun goes down. All the conditions may be changed in the morning. We have but a few hours of daylight left us. My cavalry are rapidly exhausting their ammunition, and if the attack is delayed much longer, they may have none left."

Finally, at 4 p.m., the attack went in, but even then it did not go according to plan. Of Warren's three divisions, only that of Brigadier General R.B. Ayres moved in the right direction to make contact with the Rebel left, and staff officers had to be hurried after the other two divisions to correct their line of march. When Ayres' men opened fire, so too did Sheridan's troopers—many of

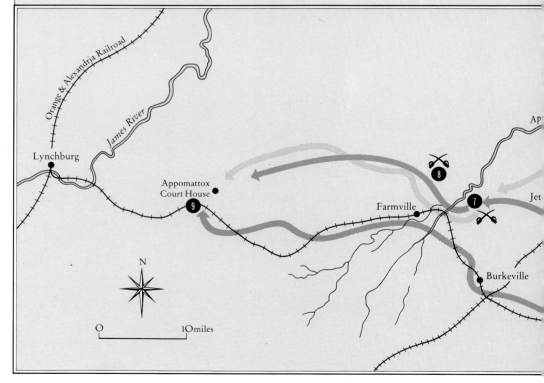

The pursuit of Lee to Appomattox

After the evacuation of the Confederate capital, General Robert E. Lee ordered the Rebel forces (1, 2, 3, 4) covering Richmond and Petersburg to rendezvous at Amelia Court House some 30 miles to the west. Lee had planned to go south and unite with General Joe Johnston's troops in North Carolina, but the Federals already blocked his way, so that the Confederate commander was obliged to move westward.

To head Lee off, Lieutenant General Ulysses S. Grant ordered Major General Philip

Sheridan and his cavalry (5) to give chase and stall the Rebels until the Union infantry could come up to finish the job. Behind Sheridan marched troops under Major General George

Meade. To the south, Grant and two corps (6) under Major General Edward Ord moved westward on a parallel route.

By this time, however, hunger and exhaustion were

crippling the remains of Lee's army. The Rebels' morale sank further on April 3 when they reached Amelia Court House and discovered that their expected rations had not arrived.

Fruitless foraging lost them a precious two days, and allowed large bodies of Union troops to close with them.

Lee continued westward on April 5. Next day, the Rebel army, now reduced to two wings under Lieutenant Generals James Longstreet and R.S. Ewell, suffered a body blow: Ewell's command was cut off at Sayler's Creek (7), and, in the ensuing fight against a powerful Federal force, the majority of the Rebels became prisoners of war. More fighting occurred on April 7 at nearby Cumberland Church (8), costing Lee's men half a day in the race for their supplies, now waiting at Appomattox Station (9). But they had scant hope of reaching their last lifeline ahead of Sheridan's far-ranging cavalry.

That night, Grant wrote to Lee asking him to surrender. Although Longstreet demurred, Lee asked for Grant's terms, while not committing himself to capitulation.

Then, on April 8, Major General George Custer's troopers captured the Rebel food trains at Appomattox Station and went on to attack the enemy camp at Appomattox Court House. Other Union troops came in, virtually surrounding the Confederates. On the night of the 8th, Lee called together his generals to discuss what Major General John Gordon called "the long-dreaded inevitable." It was decided, however, that there would be one last attempt to break through the Union lines.

The next day, Gordon led the last attack made by the Army of Northern

Virginia. When he called for support, Lee knew there was none to give, and a flag of truce was sent into the Union lines with a message requesting a meeting with Grant to arrange terms of surrender.

Later, in his farewell address to his troops, Lee told his men he was "compelled to yield to overwhelming numbers and resources," in order to "avoid useless sacrifice." Grant's war of attrition had finally been won.

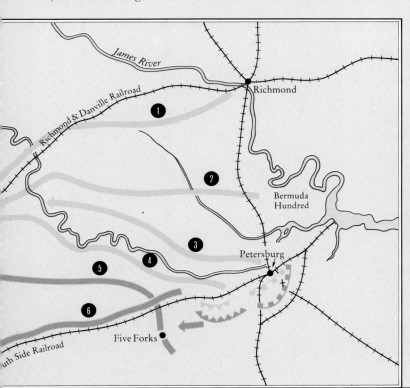

whom were fighting dismounted—as they drove in on Pickett's center and right. As Confederate volleys increased and Ayres' division began to waver, Sheridan galloped up, grabbed his red-and-white headquarters guidon from a sergeant, and rode up and down the line, waving it above his head and doing his utmost to inspire the Union infantrymen to go forward into battle.

The Federals rallied to this hard-swearing and seemingly fearless little general, and followed him in a charge that carried the Rebel breastworks and broke Pickett's left flank. With Union cavalry storming in from the front, and a full corps of infantry pouring into its left and rear, the Confederate defense disintegrated.

Even in the midst of battle, Sheridan had not forgotten, nor forgiven, Warren's slowness. When he met Brigadier General Charles Griffin, the senior divisional commander of the V Corps, Sheridan turned the corps over to him. A shocked Warren was told to report to Grant.

As darkness approached, Sheridan found himself in possession of the important Five Forks crossroads and some 5,000 Confederate prisoners, with the way clear to the South Side Railroad. His only regret was that he had not also captured the track that day. Grant, on hearing the good news, ordered a general assault all along the Rebel line for April 2. Lee, at last, had been overstretched, and the days of the Army of Northern Virginia had to be numbered.

That fateful Sunday, the Petersburg works fell, and Lee told the Confederate government that Richmond would have to be evacuated. He and the remainder of his forces retreated westward, always with the hope of eventually striking south to unite with General Joe Johnston. But it was not to be.

With sabers at the ready, two brigades of Major General George A. Custer's Third Cavalry Division charge the Confederate extreme right at Five Forks on April 1.

During the evacuation of Richmond on the night of April 2, fires that had been started to destroy arsenals, factories, and mills spread to other parts of the city, which became "a blaze of day amid the surrounding darkness." When the Federals arrived the next day, they helped to restore order and put out the fires which had consumed more than 700 buildings, such as those shown (*above* and *right*).

Cannon projectiles are piled up amid the devastation of the Richmond arsenal yard, destroyed during the evacuation of the city. One Rebel soldier noted that on the night of April 2, "hundreds of shells would explode in the air and send their spray down. . . ." In the background are the remains of the Franklin paper mill.

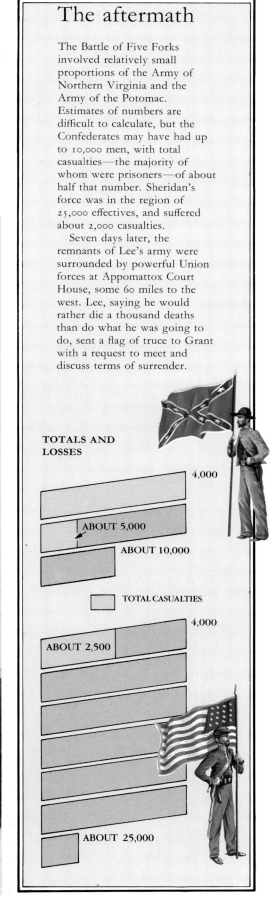

The aftermath

The Battle of Five Forks involved relatively small proportions of the Army of Northern Virginia and the Army of the Potomac. Estimates of numbers are difficult to calculate, but the Confederates may have had up to 10,000 men, with total casualties—the majority of whom were prisoners—of about half that number. Sheridan's force was in the region of 25,000 effectives, and suffered about 2,000 casualties.

Seven days later, the remnants of Lee's army were surrounded by powerful Union forces at Appomattox Court House, some 60 miles to the west. Lee, saying he would rather die a thousand deaths than do what he was going to do, sent a flag of truce to Grant with a request to meet and discuss terms of surrender.

TOTALS AND LOSSES

4,000

ABOUT 5,000

ABOUT 10,000

TOTAL CASUALTIES

4,000

ABOUT 2,500

ABOUT 25,000

The surrender at
Appomattox

"It is with pain that I announce to Your Excellency the surrender of the Army of Northern Virginia."

GENERAL ROBERT E. LEE in a report to PRESIDENT JEFFERSON DAVIS

GENERAL ROBERT E. LEE surrendered the remnants of the Confederate Army of Northern Virginia to Lieutenant General Ulysses S. Grant, on the afternoon of Sunday, April 9, 1865.

Lee explained why he did this in a report to President Jefferson Davis:

"I deemed this course the best under all the circumstances by which we were surrounded. On the morning of the 9th, according to the reports of the ordnance officers, there were 7,892 organized infantry with arms, with an average of 75 rounds of ammunition per man; the artillery, though reduced to 63 pieces with 93 rounds of ammunition, was sufficient. These comprised all the sup-plies of ordnance that could be relied on in the State of Virginia. I have no accurate report of the cavalry, but believe it did not exceed 2,100 effective men. The enemy was more than five times our numbers. If we could have forced our way one day longer it would have been at a great sacrifice of life, and at its end I did not see how a surrender could have been avoided. We had no subsistence for man or horse, and it could not be gathered in the country."

The formalities for the surrender of what friend and foe alike acknowledged to be the best force fielded by the South took place in the parlor of Wilmer McLean's home in the village of Appomattox Court House, Virginia, simply because it was the most commodious room available.

Lee, accompanied only by Colonel Charles Marshall, his military secretary, arrived first. They were both resplendent in full uniform, but not out of any sense of show: when they had to dispense with their baggage on the retreat, they changed into their best clothes, so these were all they had to wear. In contrast, Grant and his officers were in campaign dress.

Raising their inverted muskets high, Confederate soldiers of Lieutenant General Richard S. Ewell's corps surrender after the Battle of Sayler's Creek on April 6, 1865.

In terms of human life, the Civil War is the costliest conflict in which Americans have ever been engaged. The United States and the Confederate States had, between them, a population of 32,300,000. From 1861 to 1865, the North and the South mobilized, respectively, 2,778,304 and 1,400,000 men, of whom the average age was slightly under 26. Of that number more than 600,000 men died—360,222 Federals and an estimated 258,000 Rebels. If these figures are compared with the American dead of World War II (407,316 out of a population of 133,400,000) or Vietnam (about 55,000 out of a population of 208,600,000), then the huge sacrifice of life in this "Brothers' War" is immediately apparent. And the terrible statistics are compounded when 471,000 wounded are added to the more than 600,000 dead.

From the financial point of view, it is calculated that the prosecution of the four-year conflict cost the Confederacy $4 billion and the Union about four times as much.

More than half the North's bill for the war was paid out after hostilities had ceased—in the form of pensions to veterans and their dependents. By 1910, the US government's Civil War expenditure stood at $11.5 billion, and was still rising.

The last Union veteran died in 1956, though more than 3,000 widows of Northern soldiers remained on the government's books. In 1958—just three years before the centennial of the outbreak of the Civil War—a special law was passed enabling the last two surviving Confederate soldiers, and 526 widows of Southern veterans, to draw Federal pensions.

Grant's terms, which Lee accepted, were as follows:

"Rolls of all officers and men to be made in duplicate, one copy to be given to an officer designated by me, the other to be retained by such officer or officers as you may designate. The officers to give their individual paroles not to take up arms against the Government of the United States until properly exchanged, and each company or regimental commander to sign a like parole for the men of their commands.

"The arms, artillery and public property to be parked and stacked and turned over to the officers appointed by me to receive them.

"This will not embrace the side arms of the officers, nor their private horses or baggage. This done, each officer and man will be allowed to return to his home not to be disturbed by the United States authorities so long as they observe their paroles and the law as in force where they may reside."

In addition, Grant, after being told by Lee that his cavalrymen and artillerymen owned their own horses, made a concession to allow them to keep their mounts:

"I take it that most of the men in the ranks are small farmers, and as the country has been so raided by the two armies, it is doubtful whether they will be able to put in a crop to carry themselves and their families through the next winter without the aid of the horses they are now riding. . . ."

Lee replied to him:

"This will have the best possible effect upon the men. It will be very gratifying and will do much toward conciliating our people."

And, in a further gesture of generosity toward the Southerners, Grant arranged for 25,000 rations to be sent immediately into their starving lines. When it came to a headcount, the Army of Northern Virginia returned 27,805 officers and men, compared with Lee's estimate of 10,000 effectives. The difference between the Rebel commander's figure and the actual headcount was commented upon by Brigadier General A.L. Long, CSA:

"It will be noticed that a large seeming discrepancy exists. . . . This difference is easily explainable. Of effective infantry, with arms and in fighting condition, there were less than 8,000, and, about 2,000 cavalry. The remainder of the paroled men

Major General George A. Custer issued this Congratulatory Order to his cavalry division to mark its contribution to the surrender of the Army of Northern Virginia on April 9, 1865.

Robert E. Lee

Head Quarters Army of Northern Va.
10th Apl - 1865 -

General Order
No. 9

After four years of arduous service marked by unsurpassed courage and fortitude, the Army of Northern Virginia has been compelled to yield to overwhelming numbers and resources.

I need not tell the brave survivors of so many hard fought battles who have remained steadfast to the last, that I have consented to this result from no distrust of them.

But feeling that valor and devotion could accomplish nothing that would compensate for the loss that would have attended the continuance of the contest, I determined to avoid the useless sacrifice of those whose past services have endeared them to their countrymen.

By the terms of the agreement officers and men can return to their homes and remain until exchanged. You will take with you the satisfaction that proceeds from the consciousness of duty faithfully performed, and I earnestly pray that a Merciful God will extend to you his blessing and protection.

With an increasing admiration of your constancy and devotion to your Country and a grateful remembrance of your kind and generous consideration for myself, I bid you all an affectionate farewell.

R E Lee
Genl

General Robert E. Lee, resplendent in his dress uniform and watched by his secretary Colonel Charles Marshall, surrenders his Army of Northern Virginia to Lieutenant General Ulysses S. Grant, seated opposite him.

After the surrender, Lee gave a last address—General Order No.9 (*above*)—to his troops; in this, he expressed his gratitude for their "constancy and devotion" to their country.

were composed of unarmed stragglers who had come up since the halt of the army, and of extra-duty and detailed men of every description, the sum of whom very greatly swelled the aggregate present, while adding nothing to the fighting capacity of the army."

With Lee and the Army of Northern Virginia off the board, the fate of the Confederacy was sealed. General Joseph E. Johnston, vainly opposing Sherman in North Carolina, surrendered on April 26. By the end of May, all of the South's widely scattered military formations had laid down their arms, except for Brigadier General Stand Watie's command in the Indian Territory, which surrendered on June 23. The war was finally over.

The nation reunited

"I think it the duty of every citizen, in the present condition of the country, to do all in his power to aid in the restoration of peace and harmony. . . ."

GENERAL ROBERT E. LEE to the Board of Trustees of Washington College, Lexington, Virginia, on August 24, 1865

A GRAND REVIEW OF Federal forces in Washington D.C. on May 23–4, 1865, celebrated victory after four years of massive and terrible civil strife. The Union, though staggering under an enormous war debt, had been preserved. It was time for thousands upon thousands of volunteers and conscripts to hand in their weapons and go home.

Already on their way back to civilian life were the men of the South's surrendered armies, who, for so long and against such great odds, had fought for the aspirations of the now-defunct Confederacy. Except for the fact that they were alive, they had nothing to rejoice about, and little to look forward to. They had been compelled by force of arms to toe the Union line. In the process, the political, economic, and social structure they had known before the war had been destroyed. And worse was to come.

President Abraham Lincoln's plan for a conciliatory peace in which the seces-

THE RE-UNITED STATES.

COLONEL NORTH (TO COLONEL SOUTH.) "WAL, BROTHER; GUESS WE COULDN'T BOTH WIN: SO LET'S SHAKE HANDS, AND JUST LIQUOR UP."

sionist states would be "let up easy" was buried with him after he had been killed by an assassin's bullet. Radical Republicans, eager for revenge on the South, imposed a harsh, frequently unjust rule on the old Confederacy, which lasted until 1876. Corrupt, disdainful state government, sustained by the newly enfranchised blacks and Northern "carpet baggers" who flocked south, was widespread. Such treatment gave birth to the Ku Klux Klan, whose hooded members regarded themselves as protectors of put-upon Southern whites, and caused bitterness among the defeated population, fueling a defiant pride in the lost cause.

But though the Union could impose its will upon the South, it could not rob the Southern people of the memory of its heroes, of battles boldly won, or of its sacrificed sons. There was a spirit abroad which encouraged the opinion that the Confederacy should never be forgotten. Nor has it been.

The assassination of President Lincoln

Five days after General Robert E. Lee surrendered at Appomattox, President Abraham Lincoln, happy and relieved that the war was virtually over, decided to go to the theater with his wife and two friends. It was April 14, 1865—Good Friday—and it turned out to be a dark and fateful day in American history.

As the presidential party sat in a box at Ford's Theater in Washington, enjoying the English comedy "Our American Cousin," John Wilkes Booth (*right*), a 26-year-old actor and fanatical Southern sympathizer, crept in, pointed a derringer at the back of Lincoln's head and shot him. Booth then jumped 11 feet onto the stage, shouted "*Sic Semper Tyrannis*" (Ever Thus

To Tyrants)—the motto of Virginia's coat of arms—at the stunned audience, and made good his escape.

Mortally wounded, President Lincoln was carried from the theater to the Petersen House across the street, where he lingered until 7.22 the following morning. When Lincoln expired, Edwin M. Stanton, the Secretary of War, was heard to murmur, "Now he belongs to the ages."

Booth, meanwhile, headed for what remained of the Confederacy in the mistaken belief that he would be received as a hero. Ten days after the attack, Booth was discovered by a patrol from the 16th New York Cavalry in a barn in Virginia. He refused to surrender and was shot dead.

Booth's homicidal plotting was not confined to Lincoln. With the help of a motley band of conspirators, he had intended to take the lives of Vice President Andrew Johnson, Secretary of State William H. Seward, and Lieutenant General Ulysses S. Grant. Nothing came of his plans to kill Johnson and Grant, but one of his accomplices, Lewis Payne, almost succeeded in stabbing Seward to death as he lay in bed recovering from a carriage accident.

The eight remaining conspirators, who had not been very discreet, were quickly rounded up and tried by a military tribunal. Four, including one woman, Mrs Mary Surratt, who owned the boarding house

where Booth had plotted to attack Lincoln, were judged to be the principal plotters and were hanged; the others were imprisoned.

With Lincoln's death the defeated Confederacy's prospect of a magnanimous reconciliation with the Union also passed away. The man who had wanted to "Let 'em up easy" was gone, replaced by Vice President Johnson, who could not control vengeful radical Republicans. A harsh and bitter period of reconstruction followed.

Columns of blue-clad Federal soldiers march down Pennsylvania Avenue from the Capitol in a Grand Review on May 23 and 24, 1865.

The parade was the most splendid spectacle ever seen in Washington. It gave the thousands of people who turned up to watch a fitting means of celebrating the Union triumph over the Confederacy after four long years of hard fighting.

Although the flags were at half mast in deference to the death of President Lincoln on April 15, the streets resounded to the beat of drums and the cheering of the crowds.

A cartoon (*opposite page*) from an October 1865 issue of the English satirical magazine *Punch* depicts a symbolic reconciliation of the North and South.

Indeed, the valiant exertions of *both* sides in the first of the great modern wars have reverberated down the years. In the immediate aftermath of the conflict, the people of the North and the South separately instituted a Decoration Day as an annual tribute to their dead. On these solemn occasions, soldiers' graves were decked with flowers, glowing memorial

A poignant testament to the 600,000 and more soldiers who lost their lives for both the North and the South is this photograph (*opposite page*) of the Union cemetery at City Point, Virginia.

speeches were delivered, and veterans paraded in honor of their fallen comrades. As the decades passed, however, the ranks of these marchers thinned and their gait grew more halting until, finally, not one man was left to bear personal testament to the bloody events of 1861–5. Yet memories of these veterans' war did not disappear with them.

This program was issued for the ceremony of the re-raising of the Stars and Stripes over Fort Sumter in Charleston harbor, South Carolina, on April 14, 1865. The event took place four years to the day after a Confederate bombardment—the first shots of the war—obliged Major

Robert Anderson and his Federal garrison to lower the national flag and depart to the North. Anderson, now a major general, was fittingly invited to the ceremony to re-hoist the Union banner amid prolonged cheering and a 21-gun salute.

The principal speaker was Henry Ward Beecher, a

Congregational preacher famed for his oratory. In his address he remarked: "We offer to the President of these United States our solemn congratulations that God has sustained his life and health under the unparalleled burdens and sufferings of four bloody years, and permitted him to behold this auspicious

consummation of that national unity for which he has waited with so much patience and fortitude, and for which he has labored with such disinterested wisdom." A few hours later in Washington, however, Abraham Lincoln was fatally wounded by an assassin, and Northern rejoicing turned to mourning.

The participants left a vast legacy of graphic recollections and telling photographs and sketches of those divided years—items which retain the capacity to move all who encounter them. In addition, the great novels of the war, such as *Gone With the Wind* and *The Red Badge of Courage*, remain popular, and film makers and television companies are still making features about heroic or romantic episodes of the period. Partisan societies have been formed to reenact scenes from the campaigns of Lee and Grant, for example, and visitors flock to museums overflowing with an astonishingly wide variety of relics of the confrontation.

But, for many people today, the Civil War comes alive most vividly on a tour of one of the major battlefield sites maintained so respectfully by the National Park Service. These protected strips of "hallowed ground" arguably compose the most fitting and lasting memorials to the men of the United States of America and the short-lived Confederate States of America who contested their principles on them more than a century ago.

"Let us have peace."

General Ulysses S. Grant wrote these words in a letter accepting nomination for the presidency of the United States. Divisions and ill-feeling lingered on after the war, and this simple quote was seized upon as a rallying point for unity. It became Grant's election slogan and was so identified with him that it served as the epitaph on his tomb on Riverside Drive in New York.

Gazetteer

Details on how to get to the sites of the battles described in this book and what to see there are listed below. Those sites which have no outstanding points of interest have been omitted.

First Bull Run

Situated 26 miles southwest of Washington, D.C., near the intersection of US Interstate 66 and Va. 234, Manassas National Battlefield Park preserves the sites of the Battles of First and Second Bull Run (First and Second Manassas).

The park is open daily, except Christmas. The Visitor Center contains a museum, slide program, battle maps, and other literature. Uniformed Park Service personnel provide details of how the various battle sites can be reached both by car and on foot. Points of interest relating to First Bull Run include Stone Bridge, Stone House, and Henry House Hill, scene of the climax of the battle.

Shiloh

Situated 15 miles southeast of Selmer and 10 miles southwest of Savannah, Tennessee, Shiloh National Military Park is open every day except December 25. A self-guided auto tour begins at the Visitor Center.

The park includes the sites of some of the fiercest fighting during the battle—in particular Bloody Pond, the Peach Orchard, and the Hornet's Nest, where outnumbered Federals withstood for several hours nearly a dozen Confederate assaults.

Seven Pines

The Battle of Seven Pines (Fair Oaks) was fought about five miles east of Richmond. Although the battle site is not part of the Richmond National Battlefield Park (see *The Seven Days* for park details), there are historical markers outlining the fighting that occurred around the Seven Pines crossroads and Fair Oaks Station, and which can be conveniently viewed as part of a tour of the park.

The Seven Days

The principal battlefields of the fighting that took place around Richmond between June 25 and July 1, 1862, and which became known as The Seven Days, can be found in the Richmond National Battlefield Park.

To cover the entire park involves a tour of more than 100 miles. Of particular interest is the sector of the Union front that the Confederates unsuccessfully attacked at Ellerson's Mill, the Gaines's Mill battlefield, and Malvern Hill, where the Federals successfully fought off Confederate assaults before retreating to Harrison's Landing.

Each of the nine park units is identified by signs and markers. Audio facilities are available at Chimborazo Visitor Center, 3215 East Broad Street, which also has many interesting exhibits. Park interpreters provide historical information as well as reports on local road conditions. The park is open daily.

Second Bull Run

The battlefield of Second Bull Run (Second Manassas) is part of Manassas National Battlefield Park (see *First Bull Run* for park details).

Of particular interest to Second Bull Run are the Unfinished Railroad Grade, where Stonewall Jackson's troops stoutly defended themselves against numerous Union attacks; the Dogan House, the last surviving building of the wartime village of Groveton; and Chinn Ridge, along which the Union left flank held off Confederate assaults long enough on August 30, 1862, for the Union army to escape destruction.

Antietam

One mile north of Sharpsburg on Md. 65 lies Antietam National Battlefield, the scene of the Battle of Antietam (Sharpsburg).

Before touring the site, spend some time in the Visitor Center, where exhibits and a slide program provide an introduction to the tour. The park is open daily, except Thanksgiving, Christmas Day, and New Year's Day.

The tour includes Miller's Cornfield, between West and East Woods, where particularly savage fighting took place; the Sunken Road (known afterward as Bloody Lane), where more than 5,000 casualties occurred in under four hours, and Burnside Bridge, named after Union Major General Ambrose E. Burnside, whose troops spent most of the morning trying to get across it.

The tour also includes the Antietam National Cemetery, which contains the remains of 4,776 Federal soldiers, 1,836 of whom are unknown.

Fredericksburg

Within the 5,644 acres of the Fredericksburg and Spotsylvania National Military Park are the sites of four battlefields: Fredericksburg, Chancellorsville, the Wilderness, and Spotsylvania. The park is open daily.

A self-guided tour of the Fredericksburg battlefield begins at the Visitor Center on US 1, Lafayette Blvd. The center has a 14-minute slide program and several exhibits. Another Visitor Center is at Chancellorsville, ten miles west of Fredericksburg on Va. 3. Park Rangers are on duty daily at both Centers and at Chatham, a large Georgian mansion on Stafford Heights across the Rappahannock River.

Especially worth seeing are Marye's Heights, the heart of Lee's defenses, and the Sunken Road at the foot of the heights, where Confederate defenders inflicted heavy casualties on their opponents. Also of interest is the Pontoon Crossing Site, one of three locations on the Rappahannock River where the Union army crossed before the battle.

Stones River

The site of the Battle of Stones River is preserved at Stones River National Battlefield 27 miles southeast of Nashville on Route 2, Old Nashville Highway, outside Murfreesboro, Tennessee. The park is open daily and major points of interest can be reached by using a self-guided auto tour.

Chancellorsville

The battlefield of Chancellorsville is part of the Fredericksburg and Spotsylvania National Military Park (see *Fredericksburg* for details).

The Chancellorsville tour begins at the Visitor Center on the north side of Va. 3, about ten miles west of Fredericksburg. The center has various battle-associated exhibits and a 12-minute-film program.

Places of interest on the tour include the remains of the Chancellorsville Tavern, where Union Major General Joseph Hooker made his headquarters; the Lee-Jackson Bivouac, where the two great Confederates planned their battle strategy; and the strategically crucial high ground of Hazel Grove.

Gettysburg

This National Military Park has a host of interesting attractions connected with the historic events of this Civil War battle. Tours of the park can be made either by car, bicycle, or on foot. Tape recordings can be hired describing the events that took place. Auto tours by battlefield guides are also available for a fee.

The park is open daily. The Visitor Center on Taneytown Road features an electric map showing troop movements during the battle. The nearby Cyclorama Center has a spectacular painting of "Pickett's Charge," displayed in a large circular auditorium. Within the National Cemetery, the Soldiers' National Monument, honoring the Union dead who fell in the battle, stands near the site where Lincoln delivered his Gettysburg Address on November 19, 1863.

Many of the landmarks of the war's bloodiest battle are included in the park's auto tour, among them: Little Round Top, Devil's Den, the Wheatfield, and the Confederate High Water Mark, where Pickett's charge momentarily broke through the Union line.

Chickamauga

The battlefield of Chickamauga is seven miles south of Chattanooga and is part of Chickamauga & Chattanooga National Military Park.

The seven-mile self-guided auto tour includes key points on the battlefield and dozens of monuments. The Visitor Center contains an extensive display of military weapons. The park is open daily. The visitor can see the reconstructed Brotherton Cabin, where the Confederates broke through the right of the Union line on the second day of the battle. A log cabin also marks the site of the wartime Snodgrass House on Snodgrass Hill, the focus for the gallant Union resistance which earned Major General George Thomas the sobriquet "The Rock of Chickamauga."

Chattanooga

The battlefield of Chattanooga is part of the Chickamauga & Chattanooga National Military Park (see *Chickamauga* for park details). Places of interest include Orchard Knob, where Ulysses S. Grant watched his troops storm Missionary Ridge and whose headquarters are indicated with a marker. There are also viewpoints from Lookout Mountain and Missionary Ridge.

At the foot of Lookout Mountain on Tennessee Avenue, Chattanooga (off Tenn. 75), is a building that houses "Confederama," the world's largest model Civil War battlefield display. A reproduction of the terrain, together with model soldiers and flashing guns, and an intricate, electronic system that activates battle scenes, produces an exciting exhibition. Confederama is

open daily from 9 a.m. to 8 p.m. in the summer, and from 9 a.m. to 5 p.m. in the winter.

The Wilderness

The battlefield of the Wilderness is part of the 5,644-acre Fredericksburg and Spotsylvania National Military Park (see *Fredericksburg* for park details).

The best place to start a tour of the Wilderness battlefield is from the Exhibit Shelter on Va. 20, about 16 miles west of Fredericksburg. Here, informative displays highlight the fighting that took place in this area on May 5–6, 1864.

Other places of interest are the Tapp Farm, where Robert E. Lee's veterans demanded that their beloved commander go to the rear for safety's sake; and the strategically important Brock–Plank Road Junction.

Spotsylvania

The battlefield of Spotsylvania is part of the Fredericksburg and Spotsylvania National Military Park (see *Fredericksburg* for park details).

The Spotsylvania Exhibit Shelter lies about 13 miles southeast of the Brock–Plank Road Junction, along the route taken by many Union troops in the race for the crossroads at Spotsylvania Court House. The shelter features a number of interesting displays, including one on the death of Union general "Uncle John" Sedgwick, commander of the VI Corps.

Also worth visiting is the Bloody Angle, scene of fierce fighting in the Confederate "Mule Shoe" salient, and the site of the McCoull House, which stood at the center of the salient.

Atlanta

Although there is no national military park at Atlanta itself, there is the Kennesaw Mountain National Battlefield Park, Georgia, three miles north of Marietta, off US 41—the scene of heavy fighting during the Atlanta campaign.

The Visitor Center here has a slide display of several Civil War exhibits. Within the park are 11 miles of Confederate defensive earthworks. An observation overlook provides excellent views of Atlanta.

Appomattox

The Appomattox Court House National Historical Park, which has a Visitor Center, is located on Va. 24, three miles northeast of the town of Appomattox. The park is open daily, except Christmas Day, and uniformed park rangers or interpreters in period dress provide information and direction.

Thanks to a reconstruction program that began after World War II, the major part of the town of Appomattox looks like it did in April, 1865, when General Robert E. Lee surrendered his Army of Northern Virginia to Lieutenant General Ulysses S. Grant. The surrender took place in the house of Wilmer McLean, now reconstructed. About 300 yards east of the McLean House is the Surrender Triangle, where Lee's men laid down their arms and furled their battle flags.

Civil War Parks

The National Park System administers most of the important Civil War sites, offering visitor services and interpretive programs. Further information can be obtained from the addresses below.

Pea Ridge National Military Park
Pea Ridge, Arkansas 72751

Andersonville National Historic Site
Andersonville, Georgia 31711

Chickamauga and Chattanooga
National Military Park
P.O. Box 2128
Fort Oglethorpe, Georgia 30742

Fort Pulaski National Monument
P.O. Box 98
Tybee Island, Georgia 31328

Kennesaw Mountain National
Battlefield Park
P.O. Box 1167
Marietta, Georgia 30061

Antietam National Battlefield
P.O. Box 158
Sharpsburg, Maryland 21782

Brices Cross Roads National Battlefield
Site
c/o Natchez Trace Parkway
Rural Route 1, NT-143
Tupelo, Mississippi 38801

Tupelo National Battlefield
c/o Natchez Trace Parkway
Rural Route 1, NT-143
Tupelo, Mississippi 38801

Vicksburg National Military Park
3201 Clay Street
Vicksburg, Mississippi 39180

Wilson's Creek National Battlefield
Postal Drawer C
Republic, Missouri 65738

Gettysburg National Military Park
Gettysburg, Pennsylvania 17325

Fort Sumter National Monument
1214 Middle Street
Sullivans Island, South Carolina 29482

Fort Donelson National Military Park
P.O. Box F
Dover, Tennessee 37058

Shiloh National Military Park
Shiloh, Tennessee 38376

Stones River National Battlefield
Route 10, Box 495
Old Nashville Highway
Murfreesboro, Tennessee 37130

Appomattox Court House National
Historical Park
P.O. Box 218
Appomattox, Virginia 24522

Arlington House, The Robert E. Lee
Memorial
c/o George Washington Memorial
Parkway
Turkey Run Park
McLean, Virginia 22101

Fredericksburg & Spotsylvania County
Battlefields Memorial National Military
Park
P.O. Box 679
Fredericksburg, Virginia 22404

Manassas National Battlefield Park
P.O. Box 1830
Manassas, Virginia 22110

Petersburg National Battlefield
P.O. Box 549
Petersburg, Virginia 23803

Richmond National Battlefield Park
3215 East Broad Street
Richmond, Virginia 23223

Harpers Ferry National Historical Park
P.O. Box 65
Harpers Ferry, West Virginia 25425

Bibliography

This list includes books which the author and publishers have consulted in preparation for this volume, and also some suggestions for further reading.

Alexander, General E.P. *The American Civil War: A Critical narrative* Siegle, Hill & Co, London, 1908
The American Heritage Picture History of the Civil War The Editors of American Heritage, American Heritage Publishing Co, Inc, New York, 1960
Boatner, Mark Mayo *The Civil War Dictionary* David MacKay Co, Inc, New York, 1959; *Cassell's Biographical Dictionary of the American Civil War 1801–65* Cassell & Co Ltd, London, 1973
Burne, Lieut-Col Alfred H. *Lee, Grant and Sherman: A study in Leadership in the 1864–5 Campaign* Gale & Polden Ltd, Aldershot, UK, 1938
Campaigns of the Civil War Charles Scribner's Sons, New York, 1881–3
Catton, Bruce *Mr Lincoln's Army* 1951; *Glory Road* 1962; *A Stillness at Appomattox* 1953; *Gettysburg* 1974, Doubleday & Co, Inc, New York; *The Civil War* American Heritage Press, New York, 1971; *Grant Moves South* Little, Brown & Co, New York, 1960
Commager, Henry Steele (Ed) *The Blue and the Gray: The Story of the Civil War as told by the Participants* The Bobbs-Merrill Co Inc, New York, 1950; *Illustrated History of the Civil War* Orbis Publishing, London, 1982
Davis, William C. (Ed) *The Image of War: 1861–1865* (6 vols) Doubleday & Company, Inc, New York, 1984
Dowdey, Clifford *The Seven Days: The Emergence of Robert E. Lee* The Fairfax Press, New York, 1964
Earle, Peter *Robert E. Lee* Purnell Book Services, London, 1973; Weidenfeld & Nicolson, London, 1973
Edwards, William B. *Civil War Guns* Castle Books, New York, 1978
Frassanito, William A. *America's Bloodiest Day* Charles Scribner's Sons, New York; Mills & Boon, London 1979
Freeman, Douglas Southall *Lee's Lieutenants: A Study in Command* (2 vols), Charles Scribner's Sons, New York, 1942 and 1943
Fuller, Col. J.F.C. *The Generalship of Ulysses S. Grant* Krauss Reprint Co, New York, 1977
Gardner, Alexander *Gardner's Photographic Sketch Book of the War* (facsimile edition), Dover Publications Inc, New York, 1959
Grant, Ulysses S. *Personal Memoirs of U.S. Grant* L. Webster & Co, New York, 1894
Hood, J.B. *Advance and Retreat: Personal Experiences in the United States and Confederate State Armies* Hood Orphan Memorial Fund, New Orleans, 1880
Humble, Richard *The Illustrated History of the American Civil War* Multimedia Publications (UK) Ltd, London, 1986
Johnson, Robert Underwood and Buell, Clarence Clough (Eds) *Battles & Leaders of the Civil War* (4 vols), The Century Co, New York, 1884–1888
Johnson, Curt and McLaughlin, Mark *Battles of the American Civil War* Sampson Low, Maidenhead, UK, 1977
Long, A.L. *Memoirs of Robert E. Lee* (Ed), The Blue & Gray Press, Secaucus, New Jersey, 1983
Longacre, Edward G. *The Man Behind the Guns* A.S. Barnes & Co, Inc, Cranbury, New Jersey, 1977
Longstreet, James *From Manassas to Appomattox: Memoirs of the Civil War in America* J.B. Lippincott Co, Philadelphia, 1896

Lord, Francis A. *Civil War Collector's Encyclopedia* Castle Books, New York, 1982; *Uniforms of the Civil War* Thomas Yoseloff, New York & London, 1970
Marshall Cornwall, General Sir James *Grant as Military Commander* B.T. Batsford, London; Van Nostrand, New York, 1970
McLaughlin, Jack *The Long Encampment* Bonanza Books, New York, 1963
McWhinney, Grady *Braxton Bragg and Confederate Defeat Vol 1: Field Command* Columbia University Press, New York & London, 1969.
Meredith, Roy *Mr Lincoln's Camera Man* Charles Scribner's Sons, New York, 1945; *Mr Lincoln's Contemporaries: An Album of Portraits by Mathew B. Brady* Charles Scribner's Sons, New York, 1951
Miller, Francis Trevelyan (Ed) *The Photographic History of the Civil War* (10 vols), first printed 1911; reproduction 1957, Castle Books, New York
O'Connor, Richard *Sheridan the Inevitable* The Bobbs Merrill Co, Inc, New York, 1953
Paris, The Comte de *History of the Civil War in America* (Vols 1–4), Jos. H. Coates & Co, Philadelphia; Michel Levy Freres, Paris; Sampson Low, Marston Low & Searle, London, 1875
Rossiter, Johnson *Campfires & Battlefields* The Civil War Press, New York, 1967
Schaff, Morris *The Battle of the Wilderness* Houghton Mifflin Co, Boston & New York, 1910
Selby, John *Stonewall Jackson as Military Commander* B.T. Batsford Ltd, London; Van Nostrand Inc, Princeton, New Jersey, 1968
Sherman, William Tecumseh *Memoirs* D. Appleton & Co, New York, 1875
Taylor, Walter H. *Four Years with General Lee* D. Appleton & Co, New York, 1878
Thompson Jnr, W. Fletcher *The Image of War: The Pictorial Reporting of the American Civil War* Thomas Yoseloff, New York & London, 1960
Time Life Books *The Civil War* (27 vols), Amsterdam BV; Alexandria, Virginia, 1988
The War of the Rebellion: A Compilation of the Official Records of the Union and Confederate Armies Government Printing Office, Washington, 1880–1889
Wheeler, Richard *Voices of the Civil War* Thomas Y. Crowell Co, New York, 1976
Wiley, Bell Irvin *Embattled Confederates: An Illustrated History of Southerners at War* Bonanza Books, New York, 1964
Williams, T.H. *Lincoln and His Generals* Knopf, New York, 1958

Index

Page numbers in **bold** print indicate major references to the battles and the commanders; supplementary text and captions to illustrations are shown in *italic*.

Picture Credits

l = left; *r* = right; *t* = top; *c* = center; *b* = bottom

4/6 Chris Linton; 9*l* BBC Hulton Picture Library; 9*r* Topham Picture Library; 10*t* Department of the Interior, National Park Service; 10*bl* The Museum of the Confederacy, Richmond; 10*br* Virginia Historical Society; 13 Library of Congress; 16 Topham Picture Library; 17 Battles and Leaders of the Civil War; 20*t* James Enos/United States Military Academy History Institute; 20*b* BBC Hulton Picture Library; 21 Library of Congress; 22 Peter Newark's Western Americana; 22/23 from "The Civil War"/First Blood photograph by Lon Mattoon © 1983 Time-Life Books Inc.; 23 Robert Hunt Library; 25 Popperfoto; 28*t* BBC Hulton Picture Library; 28*b* John Frost/Historical Picture Service; 29 American Heritage Picture Collection; 30/31 Chicago Historical Society; 31 Beverley R. Robinson Collection, United States Naval Academy Museum; 33 National Archives/Brady Collection; 36 Battles and Leaders of the Civil War; 37 American Heritage Picture Collection; 38 US Signal Corps/Brady Collection; 39*t* Peter Newark's Western Americana; 39*bl* Chicago Historical Society; 39*br* Picturepoint; 41 The Bettmann Archive/BBC Hulton Picture Library; 44*l* National Library of Medicine, Bethesda, Maryland; 44*r* The Bettmann Archive/BBC Hulton Picture Library; 45/49 Library of Congress; 52 Weidenfeld & Nicolson Ltd; 52/53 Topham Picture Library; 54/55 Eileen Tweedy/by courtesy of The Board of Trustees of the Royal Armouries; 57 Library of Congress; 58 Maryland Historical Society, Baltimore; 58/59 in the collection of the Corcoran Gallery of Art, gift of Genevieve Plummer, 1954; 60 Library of Congress; 60/61 American Heritage Picture Collection; 64*t* James Enos/United States Military Academy History Institute; 64*b* Topham Picture Library; 65*t&c* John Frost/Historical Picture Service; 65*b* Virginia State Library; 66 Library of Congress; 67*t* Historical Pictures Service, Chicago; 67*b* M & M Karolik Collection, courtesy of Museum of Fine Arts, Boston; 69 The Bettmann Archive/BBC Hulton Picture Library; 70 Topham Picture Library; 70/71 Civil War Times Illustrated; 72/73 Department of Special Collections, University Research Library, UCLA; 73*t* American Heritage Picture Collection; 73*b* Topham Picture Library; 76*l* Battles and Leaders of the Civil War; 76*r* Topham Picture Library; 76/77 Department of Special Collections, University Research Library, UCLA; 77 Frank & Marie-T Wood Print Collections; 78/79 West Point Museum Collections, United States Military Academy; 81*l* Library of Congress; 81*r* The Valentine Museum, Richmond; 84 Historical Pictures Service, Chicago; 86*t* Picturepoint; 86*c* Battles and Leaders of the Civil War; 86*b* Peter Newark's Western Americana; 87*t* The Bettmann Archive/BBC Hulton Picture Library; 87*b* Richard Kendzierski/James C. Frasca Collection; 89*l* Topham Picture Library; 89*r* The Valentine Museum, Richmond; 90 Historical Pictures Service, Chicago; 91 Picturepoint; 92 American Heritage Picture Collection; 92/93 Topham Picture Library; 96 Library of Congress; 97*t* American Heritage Picture Collection; 97*b* Library of Congress; 98*l* Aldus Archive; 98*t&br* The Museum of the Confederacy, Richmond; 99 The Corcoran Gallery of Art, Washington; 101 Topham Picture Library; 103 Battles and Leaders of the Civil War; 104 Robert Hunt Library; 105 US National Archives; 108*t* Library of Congress; 108*b* "Civil War in Pictures"; 108/109 Department of Special Collections, University Research Library, UCLA; 110/111 Photo by H.K. Barnett, © 1985 Time-Life Books Inc., from "The Civil War"; 111 John MacDonald; 113*l* Library of Congress; 113*r* The Valentine Museum, Richmond; 114/115 Library of Congress; 115 Old State House, Arkansas Commemorative Commission; 116*t* Robert Hunt Library; 116*b* John Frost/Historical Picture Service; 117 Library of Congress; 120 James Enos/United States Military Academy History Institute; 121*t* American Heritage Picture Collection; 121*b* Topham Picture Library; 122*t* Print collection, Miriam and Ira D. Wallach Division of Art, Prints and Photographs/The New York Public Library, Astor, Lenox and Tilden Foundations; 122*c* James Enos/United States Military Academy History Institute; 122*b* courtesy of the Tennessee State Museum, Nashville; 122/123 Library of Congress; 125 Library of Congress; 128 Battles and Leaders of the Civil War; 129 Topham Picture Library; 130 Chris Linton; 131*t* Anne S.K. Brown Military Collection, Brown University Library; 131*b* Richard Kendzierski/James C. Frasca Collection; 133 Peter Newark's Western Americana; 134 E. Irving Blomstrann/The New Britain Museum of American Art, Harriet Russell Stanley Fund; 135*t* New York Public Library; 135*c* Kean Archives; 135*b* Chris Linton; 136/137 Library of Congress; 140*t* Department of Special Collections, University Research Library, UCLA; 140*b* American Heritage Picture Collection; 141*r* Library of Congress; 142*t* BBC Hulton Picture Library; 142*b* Library of Congress; 142/143 Library of Congress; 145*l* James Enos/United States Military Academy History Institute; 145*r* The Valentine Museum, Richmond; 146/147 Topham Picture Library; 147 Library of Congress; 148/149 James Enos/United States Military Academy History Institute; 152/153 ZEFA; 153 American Heritage Picture Collection; 154/155 Virginia Historical Society; 155 Topham Picture Library; 157*l* Robert Hunt Library; 157*r* The Valentine Museum, Richmond; 158/159 Eileen Tweedy/by courtesy of the Board of Trustees of the Royal Armouries; 159*t* Civil War Times Illustrated; 159*b* Peter Newark's Western Americana; 160/161 Library of Congress, 164/165 Robert Hunt Library; 165 Library of Congress; 166*t* Historical Pictures Service Inc., Chicago; 166*b* M & M Karolik Collection, courtesy of Museum of Fine Arts, Boston; 167*t* Library of Congress; 167*b* Department of Special Collections, University Research Library, UCLA; 169 Brian C. Pohanka; 172 Department of Special Collections, University Research Library, UCLA; 173 Frank & Marie-T Wood Print Collections; 174 Battles and Leaders of the Civil War; 174/175 Minnesota Historical Society; 177 Library of Congress; 181 Topham Picture Library; 182/183 Library of Congress; 184 Battles and Leaders of the Civil War; 185 Chris Linton; 186 The Bettmann Archive/BBC Hulton Picture Library; 186/187 Painting by Tom Lovell, © National Geographic Society; 188 The Mansell Collection; 189*t* Aldus Archive; 189*b* Library of Congress; 190 Chris Linton; 191 Topham Picture Library.

Acknowledgments

The publishers would like to thank Michael Hammerson for allowing items from his Civil War collection to be photographed and also the following people and organizations from whom they received invaluable help:

Anne-Marie Ehrlich
Fred Gill
Candy Lee
The Museum of the Confederacy, Richmond, Va.
Professor Peter Parish
Royal Geographical Society, London
Zilda Tandy
The Valentine Museum, Richmond, Va.

Additional four-color artwork: Richard Hook/Linden Artists
Maps: Richard Prideaux, Technical Art Services, Brian Mayor, Ed Stuart
Retouching: Roy Flooks
Line artwork: Gram Corbett
Computer map grids: Chapman, Bounford & Associates
Index: Don Binney